2014

THE BEST OF
COUNTRY COOKING

Taste of Home

For other *Taste of Home* books and products,
visit www.ShopTasteofHome.com.

COME AND GET IT!

Gather 'round for down-home comfort food, just like Mom used to make. Choose from more than 300 recipes in *The Best of Country Cooking* to create the perfect country-inspired feast. All the dishes come from home cooks just like you, so you already know these are well-loved options. Filling main dishes, satisfying sides, fresh salads, savory soups, decadent desserts and much more—it's all here.

It's time to dig in! These hearty dishes provide everything you're looking for to feed the family, so gather everyone around the dinner table.

Here's more of what you'll find inside:

Award-Winning Recipes
Look for this blue ribbon icon throughout the book. The ribbon indicates recipes that won a *Taste of Home* contest. They'll get a big thumbs-up award from your crowd.

Slow Cooker Favorites
Sometimes you just need to take shortcuts. Set the slow cooker in the morning and come home to a meal that's ready to go, just like that.

Meals in Minutes
When you're running tight on time but want to eat great, these dishes provide ease without sacrificing taste. Not that anyone will guess how simple they are to make!

With so many delicious choices, you're sure to find new favorite recipes in no time. Enjoy the home-cooked goodness!

■ **EDITORIAL**
Editor-in-Chief **Catherine Cassidy**
Creative Director **Howard Greenberg**
Editorial Operations Director **Kerri Balliet**

Managing Editor/Print & Digital Books **Mark Hagen**
Associate Creative Director **Edwin Robles Jr.**
Editor **Molly Jasinski**
Art Director **Catherine Fletcher**
Contributing Layout Designer **Siya Motamedi**
Editorial Production Manager **Dena Ahlers**
Copy Chief **Deb Warlaumont Mulvey**
Copy Editors **Mary C. Hanson, Mary-Liz Shaw**
Chief Food Editor **Karen Berner**
Food Editors **James Schend; Peggy Woodward, RD**
Associate Food Editor **Krista Lanphier**
Recipe Editors **Mary King; Annie Rundle; Jenni Sharp, RD; Irene Yeh**
Content Operations Manager **Colleen King**
Content Operations Assistant **Shannon Stroud**
Executive Assistant **Marie Brannon**

Test Kitchen and Food Styling Manager **Sarah Thompson**
Test Cooks **Nicholas Iverson (lead), Matthew Hass, Lauren Knoelke**
Food Stylists **Kathryn Conrad (senior), Shannon Roum, Leah Rekau**
Prep Cooks **Megumi Garcia, Melissa Hansen, Bethany Van Jacobson**

Photography Director **Stephanie Marchese**
Photographers **Dan Roberts, Jim Wieland**
Photographer/Set Stylist **Grace Natoli Sheldon**
Set Stylists **Stacey Genaw, Melissa Haberman, Dee Dee Jacq**
Business Analyst **Kristy Martin**
Billing Specialist **Mary Ann Koebernik**

■ **BUSINESS**
Vice President, Chief Sales Officer **Mark S. Josephson**
Vice President, Business Development & Marketing **Alain Begun**
General Manager, Taste of Home Cooking School **Erin Puariea**

Vice President, Digital Experience & E-Commerce **Jennifer Smith**
Vice President, Direct to Consumer Marketing **Dave Fiegel**

■ **THE READER'S DIGEST ASSOCIATION, INC.**
President and Chief Executive Officer **Robert E. Guth**
Vice President, Chief Operating Officer, North America **Howard Halligan**
President & Publisher, Books **Harold Clarke**
Vice President, North American Operations **Philippe Cloutier**
Vice President, Chief Marketing Officer **Leslie Doty**
Vice President, North American Human Resources **Phyllis E. Gebhardt, SPHR**
Vice President, Chief Technology Officer **Rob Hilliard**
Vice President, Consumer Marketing Planning **Jim Woods**

PICTURED ON THE FRONT COVER Balsamic Green Bean Salad (p. 47), Sun-Dried Tomato Garlic Bread (p. 112), Baked Potato Cheddar Soup (p. 49) and Chili Hash (p. 121).

PICTURED ON THE BACK COVER Salmon Mousse Tartlets (p. 6), Golden Roasted Turkey (p. 74) and Apricot Pinwheel Cookies (p. 150).

CONTENTS

SNACKS & BEVERAGES

Kick back and relax with these bite-sized treats! Whether you're hosting a get-together, snacking while watching TV or simply craving a nibble, these no-fuss appetizers and beverages are sure to satisfy!

PEANUT CHICKEN WINGS

Here, creamy peanut butter and chili powder become an ideal match for chicken wings. Round out the appetizer menu with cut veggies and ranch or blue cheese salad dressing.

—JANET VAUPEL ROCKWELL HOLLIS, NH

PREP: 15 MIN. + MARINATING • **BAKE:** 35 MIN. • **MAKES:** 9 SERVINGS

- 2 **pounds chicken wings**
- 2 **tablespoons creamy peanut butter**
- 1 **tablespoon lemon juice**
- 1 **tablespoon canola oil**
- 1 **tablespoon reduced-sodium soy sauce**
- ½ **teaspoon salt**
- ½ **teaspoon chili powder**
- ½ **teaspoon browning sauce, optional**
  Dash garlic powder

1. Cut chicken wings into three sections; discard wing tip sections. In a large resealable plastic bag, combine the peanut butter, lemon juice, oil, soy sauce, salt, chili powder, browning sauce if desired and garlic powder. Add wings; seal bag and turn to coat. Refrigerate overnight.

2. Drain and discard marinade. Transfer wings to a greased 13-in. x 9-in. baking dish. Bake, uncovered, at 375° for 35-40 minutes or until chicken juices run clear, turning every 10 minutes.

NOTE *Uncooked chicken wing sections (wingettes) may be substituted for whole chicken wings.*

SALMON MOUSSE TARTLETS

You can also bake these tartlets in the oven at 350 degrees for 10 minutes. Try the baked version for entertaining at home, and take the no-bake version to potlucks.

—DIANA DORAN PITTSBURGH, PA

PREP: 15 MIN. + CHILLING • **MAKES:** 15 APPETIZERS

- 1 **package (8 ounces) cream cheese, softened**
- 1½ **teaspoons seafood seasoning**
- 1 **teaspoon lemon juice**
- 1 **pouch (6 ounces) boneless skinless pink salmon**
- 1 **package (1.9 ounces) frozen miniature phyllo tart shells**
  Fresh dill sprigs, optional

In a large bowl, beat the cream cheese, seafood seasoning and lemon juice until smooth. Beat in salmon. Spoon or pipe into tart shells and garnish with dill if desired. Refrigerate for at least 20 minutes before serving.

PLANNING APPETIZERS

If you decide to serve an appetizer buffet as a meal, offer your guests five or six different appetizers (including some substantial selections) and plan on eight to nine pieces per guest. If the appetizers are served as snacks, then two to three pieces per person is sufficient.

LEMON MINT SPRITZER

Cool down with this refreshing sipper. It's wonderful after a long day or during a backyard barbecue.

—LAURA NIX ELLIJAY, GA

START TO FINISH: 10 MIN. • **MAKES:** 12 SERVINGS (1 CUP EACH)

- 2 medium lemons
- 2 cans (12 ounces each) frozen lemonade concentrate, thawed
- ¼ cup confectioners' sugar
- ¼ cup fresh mint leaves, chopped
- 2 bottles (1 liter each) carbonated water, chilled
  Ice cubes

1. Cut lemons into wedges and squeeze the juice into a large pitcher. Stir in the lemonade concentrate, confectioners' sugar and mint; add lemon wedges. Chill until serving.

2. Just before serving, stir in carbonated water. Serve over ice.

SWEET & SALTY MARSHMALLOW POPCORN TREATS

Popcorn balls are sweet, salty and crunchy when you add a little chocolate and then go nuts!

—NINA VILHAUER MINA, SD

PREP: 20 MIN. + COOLING • **MAKES:** ABOUT 5 DOZEN

- 4 quarts popped popcorn
- 3 cups salted peanuts
- 1 package (12.6 ounces) milk chocolate M&M's
- 1 package (16 ounces) large marshmallows
- 1 cup butter, cubed

1. In a large bowl, combine the popcorn, peanuts and M&M's. In a large saucepan, combine marshmallows and butter. Cook and stir over medium-low heat until melted. Add to popcorn mixture; mix well.

2. When cool enough to handle, shape into 2-in. popcorn balls. Let stand until firm before wrapping in plastic.

MEDITERRANEAN LAYERED DIP

This Greek-style layered dip has purchased hummus as the base. Open a bag of pita chips and enjoy!

—**PATTERSON WATKINS** PHILADELPHIA, PA

START TO FINISH: 15 MIN. • **MAKES:** 20 SERVINGS

- 2½ cups roasted garlic hummus
- ¾ cup chopped roasted sweet red peppers
- 1 cup fresh baby spinach, coarsely chopped
- 3 tablespoons lemon juice
- 2 tablespoons olive oil
- 2 tablespoons coarsely chopped fresh basil
- 1 tablespoon coarsely chopped fresh mint
- ½ cup crumbled feta cheese
- ½ cup Greek olives, sliced
- ¼ cup chopped red onion
  Assorted fresh vegetables or baked pita chips

1. Spread hummus onto a 12-in. round serving platter; top with roasted peppers.

2. In a small bowl, combine the spinach, lemon juice, oil, basil and mint. Using a slotted spoon, spread spinach mixture over peppers. Top with cheese, olives and onion. Serve with vegetables or pita chips.

RASPBERRY-SWIRLED LEMON MILK SHAKES

A basic combination of vanilla ice cream, lemon sorbet and raspberry puree creates a standout shake in minutes. Pour it into a few glasses and get ready to enjoy its cool comfort.

—**LISA SPEER** PALM BEACH, FL

START TO FINISH: 15 MIN. • **MAKES:** 4 SERVINGS

- 2 cups fresh or frozen raspberries, thawed
- ¼ cup confectioners' sugar
- 1 tablespoon raspberry liqueur, optional
- ½ cup 2% milk
- 2 cups vanilla ice cream, softened
- 1 cup lemon sorbet, softened
- ¾ cup crushed ice
  Optional garnishes: whipped cream, fresh raspberries and mint sprigs

1. Place the raspberries, confectioners' sugar and liqueur if desired in a blender; cover and process until blended. Strain and discard seeds.

2. In a clean blender, combine the milk, ice cream, sorbet and ice; cover and process for 30 seconds or until smooth. Layer raspberry puree and ice cream mixture into four serving glasses. Garnish as desired.

STRAWBERRIES WITH CHOCOLATE CREAM FILLING

These party-pretty bites are as easy to make as they are delicious. Try them as a lovely fruit appetizer.
—**LISA HUFF** WILTON, CT

START TO FINISH: 30 MIN. • **MAKES:** 3 DOZEN

- 1½ ounces semisweet chocolate, grated, divided
- 1 package (8 ounces) cream cheese, softened
- 1 teaspoon vanilla extract
- 1 cup whipped topping
- 18 large fresh strawberries, halved

1. Set aside 2 tablespoons chocolate. In a microwave, melt remaining chocolate; stir until smooth. Cool to room temperature.

2. In a small bowl, beat cream cheese and vanilla until smooth. Beat in melted chocolate. Fold in the whipped topping and 1 tablespoon reserved chocolate. Cut a small hole in the corner of pastry or plastic bag; insert #21 star pastry tip. Fill the bag with cream cheese mixture.

3. Place strawberries cut side up on a serving platter. Pipe cream cheese mixture onto strawberries. Sprinkle with remaining chocolate. Refrigerate leftovers.

CHEESE-TRIO ARTICHOKE & SPINACH DIP

No appetizer spread is complete without at least one amazing dip, and this is it!
—**DIANE SPEARE** KISSIMMEE, FL

PREP: 20 MIN. • **COOK:** 2 HOURS • **MAKES:** 4 CUPS

- 1 cup chopped fresh mushrooms
- 1 tablespoon butter
- 2 garlic cloves, minced
- 1½ cups mayonnaise
- 1 package (8 ounces) cream cheese, softened
- 1 cup plus 2 tablespoons grated Parmesan cheese, divided
- 1 cup (4 ounces) shredded part-skim mozzarella cheese, divided
- 1 can (14 ounces) water-packed artichoke hearts, rinsed, drained and chopped
- 1 package (10 ounces) frozen chopped spinach, thawed and squeezed dry
- ¼ cup chopped sweet red pepper
  Toasted French bread baguette slices

1. In a large skillet, saute mushrooms in butter until tender. Add garlic; cook 1 minute longer.

2. In a large bowl, combine the mayonnaise, cream cheese, 1 cup Parmesan cheese and ¾ cup mozzarella cheese. Add the mushroom mixture, artichokes, spinach and red pepper.

3. Transfer to a 3-qt. slow cooker. Sprinkle with remaining cheeses. Cover and cook on low for 2-3 hours or until heated through. Serve with baguette slices.

PEACH BAKED BRIE

The most difficult part about this elegant appetizer? Waiting for it to cool! Apple slices work wonderfully for scooping.
—**CAROLYN CALLAHAN** PLAINFIELD, IL

START TO FINISH: 30 MIN. • **MAKES:** 8 SERVINGS

- 1 sheet frozen puff pastry, thawed
- ½ cup peach or mango preserves
- ½ cup chopped pecans, toasted
- 1 round (8 ounces) Brie cheese
    Toasted cinnamon-raisin bread and assorted crackers

1. On a lightly floured surface, roll out pastry into a 12-in. square. Cut off corners to make a circle. Spread preserves to within 1 in. of pastry edge; sprinkle with pecans. Place Brie on top; fold pastry over the cheese and pinch edges to seal.
2. Place seam side down on an ungreased baking sheet. Bake at 400° for 20-25 minutes or until golden brown. Serve warm with toast and crackers.

ROSEMARY WALNUTS

This recipe comes from my Aunt Mary—she would always have a batch ready for us when we came to visit. Cayenne adds some unexpected zing. When you need a housewarming or hostess gift, double the batch and save one for yourself. Be sure to include a copy of the recipe when you give it as a gift.
—**RENEE CIANCIO** NEW BERN, NC

START TO FINISH: 20 MIN • **MAKES:** 2 CUPS

- 2 cups walnut halves
    Cooking spray
- 2 teaspoons dried rosemary, crushed
- ½ teaspoon kosher salt
- ¼ to ½ teaspoon cayenne pepper

1. Place walnuts in a small bowl. Spritz with cooking spray. Add the seasonings; toss to coat. Place in a single layer on a baking sheet.
2. Bake at 350° for 10 minutes. Serve warm.

HOT COLLARDS AND ARTICHOKE DIP

You've probably had spinach and artichoke dip before, but now it's time to try it with collard greens for a Southern twist. Serve this dish with warm garlic naan or tortilla chips.

—BILLIE WILLIAMS-HENDERSON CROFTON, MD

PREP: 20 MIN. • **BAKE:** 25 MIN.
MAKES: 24 SERVINGS (¼ CUP EACH)

- 12 ounces frozen chopped collard greens (about 4 cups), thawed and squeezed dry
- 2 jars (7½ ounces each) marinated quartered artichoke hearts, drained and chopped
- 1 cup (8 ounces) sour cream
- 1 package (6½ ounces) garlic-herb spreadable cheese
- 1 cup grated Parmesan cheese
- 10 thick-sliced peppered bacon strips, cooked and crumbled
- ¾ cup mayonnaise
- 1½ cups (6 ounces) shredded part-skim mozzarella cheese, divided
  Garlic naan flatbreads, warmed and cut into wedges

1. In a large bowl, mix the first seven ingredients and 1 cup mozzarella cheese until blended. Transfer to a greased 11-in. x 7-in. baking dish. Sprinkle with remaining mozzarella cheese.
2. Bake, uncovered, at 350° for 20-25 minutes or until heated through and cheese is melted. Serve with naan.

BRIE CHERRY PASTRY CUPS

Golden brown and flaky, these tiny puff pastries with creamy Brie and sweet cherry preserves could double as a dessert.

—MARILYN MCSWEEN MENTOR, OH

START TO FINISH: 30 MIN. • **MAKES:** 3 DOZEN

- 1 sheet frozen puff pastry, thawed
- ½ cup cherry preserves
- 4 ounces Brie cheese, cut into ½-inch cubes
- ¼ cup chopped pecans or walnuts
- 2 tablespoons minced chives

1. Unfold puff pastry; cut into 36 squares. Gently press squares onto the bottoms of 36 greased miniature muffin cups.
2. Bake at 375° for 10 minutes. Using the end of a wooden spoon handle, make a ½-in.-deep indentation in the center of each. Bake 6-8 minutes longer or until golden brown. With spoon handle, press squares down again.
3. Spoon a rounded ½ teaspoonful of preserves into each cup. Top with cheese; sprinkle with nuts and chives. Bake for 3-5 minutes or until cheese is melted.

KEEP CHIVES IN THE FREEZER

Chives don't keep very long in the refrigerator, so I mince and store them in a plastic container in the freezer. This way, every time I need chives for a recipe, I just take a few out and add them to my dish as needed.

—JENNIFER W. PEARLAND, TX

Sweet Teas

You'll declare these tea-based beverages the best you've ever tried. When it's time to whet your whistle, grab a pitcher (or a few mugs) and share the goodness with others.

WINTER HERB TEA MIX

This caffeine-free option is a blend of mint, sage, rosemary, thyme and honey that promises to melt away any day's troubles.
—**SUE GRONHOLZ** BEAVER DAM, WI

START TO FINISH: 10 MIN.
MAKES: 18 SERVINGS (9 TABLESPOONS TEA MIX)

- 6 tablespoons dried mint
- 1 tablespoon dried sage leaves
- 1 tablespoon dried rosemary, crushed
- 1 tablespoon dried thyme

ADDITIONAL INGREDIENTS (FOR EACH SERVING)
- 1 cup boiling water
- 1 teaspoon honey
- 1 lemon wedge

In a small airtight container, combine the herbs. Store in a cool, dry place for up to 6 months.

TO PREPARE TEA *Place 1½ teaspoons tea mix in a glass measuring cup. With the end of a wooden spoon handle, crush mixture until aromas are released. Add boiling water. Cover and steep for 10 minutes. Strain tea into a mug, discarding herbs. Stir in honey; serve with lemon.*

APPLE SPICED TEA

Take a moment to enjoy a cup of afternoon tea. Once you sample this sweetly spiced drink, you'll make it a regular event.
—**SUSAN WESTERFIELD** ALBUQUERQUE, NM

START TO FINISH: 10 MIN. • **MAKES:** 1 SERVING

- ½ cup apple cider or juice
- ¼ teaspoon minced fresh gingerroot
- 2 whole allspice
- 2 whole cloves
- 1 black tea bag
- ½ cup boiling water
- 1 tablespoon brown sugar

In a small bowl, combine the first five ingredients. Add boiling water. Cover and steep for 5 minutes. Strain, discarding tea bag and spices. Stir in sugar. Serve immediately.

BELLA BASIL RASPBERRY TEA

Put a grown-up spin on iced tea. Beautiful basil and fresh raspberries lend bright color, and you'll love the fun fizz and make-ahead convenience for parties.
—**LAURIE BOCK** LYNDEN, WA

PREP: 45 MIN. + CHILLING • **MAKES:** 6 SERVINGS

- 3 cups fresh raspberries
- 1 cup sugar
- 1 cup packed fresh basil leaves, coarsely chopped
- ¼ cup lime juice
- 2 individual black tea bags
- 1 bottle (1 liter) carbonated water or 1 bottle (750 milliliters) sparkling rose wine
  Ice cubes
  Fresh basil sprigs, optional

1. In a large saucepan, combine the raspberries, sugar, basil and lime juice. Mash berries. Cook over medium heat for 7 minutes or until juices are released from berries.
2. Remove from the heat; add the tea bags. Cover and steep for 20 minutes. Strain, discarding tea bags and raspberry seeds. Transfer the tea to a 2-qt. pitcher. Cover and refrigerate until serving.
3. Just before serving, slowly add carbonated water to tea. Serve over ice and garnish with basil sprigs if desired.

MOM'S TANGERINE ICED TEA

Enjoy this sweet tea with a citrus twist. It's very refreshing.
—**MARY MILLER** POPLARVILLE, MS

PREP: 10 MIN. • **COOK:** 5 MIN. + CHILLING • **MAKES:** 4 SERVINGS

- 2¾ cups water, divided
- 4 individual black tea bags
- ⅔ cup sugar
- 2 cups fresh tangerine juice (about 12 tangerines)
  Ice cubes
  Tangerine slices and mint sprigs, optional

1. In a small saucepan, bring 2 cups water to a boil. Remove from the heat; add tea bags. Steep for 3-5 minutes. Discard tea bags; cool tea slightly.
2. In another saucepan, combine remaining water and sugar; bring to a boil. Cook and stir until sugar is dissolved. Remove from the heat; cool slightly.
3. Transfer tea and sugar syrup to a large pitcher; stir in the tangerine juice. Refrigerate until chilled.
4. Serve over ice; add tangerine slices and mint if desired.

ROAST BEEF AIOLI BUNDLES

Don't let these dainty bundles fool you—they're a snap to prepare. Everyone will gobble them up!
—TASTE OF HOME TEST KITCHEN

START TO FINISH: 30 MIN. • **MAKES:** 16 APPETIZERS

- 16 fresh asparagus spears, trimmed
- ⅓ cup mayonnaise
- 1 garlic clove, minced
- 1 teaspoon Dijon mustard
- 1 teaspoon lemon juice
- ⅛ teaspoon ground cumin
- 8 thin slices deli roast beef, cut in half lengthwise
- 1 medium sweet yellow pepper, thinly sliced
- 1 medium sweet orange pepper, thinly sliced
- 1 medium sweet red pepper, thinly sliced
- 16 whole chives

1. In a large skillet, bring 1 in. of water to a boil. Add asparagus; cover and cook for 3 minutes. Drain and immediately place in ice water. Drain and pat dry.

2. In a small bowl, combine the mayonnaise, garlic, mustard, lemon juice and cumin. Place the roast beef slices on a work surface; spread each slice with 1 teaspoon aioli. Top each with an asparagus spear and pepper strips. Roll up tightly; tie bundles with chives. Serve immediately.

MAPLE JALAPENOS

Craving something sweet with a little bit of heat? Try these hot, creamy snacks. One bite, and you won't be able to stop!
—NICOLE LARSON AMERICAN FORK, UT

PREP: 45 MIN. • **BAKE:** 20 MIN. • **MAKES:** 50 APPETIZERS

- 25 jalapeno peppers
- 1 package (8 ounces) cream cheese, softened
- 1 cup (4 ounces) crumbled feta cheese
- ½ cup maple syrup
- ½ pound bacon strips, cooked and crumbled
- ¼ cup packed brown sugar

1. Cut jalapenos in half lengthwise and remove seeds. Set aside. In a small bowl, beat the cream cheese, feta cheese and syrup until smooth. Spoon into pepper halves.

2. Place in two greased 15-in. x 10-in. x 1-in. baking pans. Top with bacon and sprinkle with brown sugar. Bake at 350° for 20 minutes for spicy flavor, 30 minutes for medium and 40 minutes for mild.

NOTE *Wear disposable gloves when cutting hot peppers; the oils can burn skin. Avoid touching your face.*

ALL ABOUT FETA
Feta is a white, salty, semi-firm cheese. After feta is formed in a special mold, it is sliced into large pieces, salted and soaked in brine. Although feta cheese is mostly associated with Greek cuisine, the word "feta" comes from the Italian word *fette*, meaning "slice of food."

PIMIENTO & CHEESE DEVILED EGGS

Put leftover hard-cooked eggs to good use when you make these satisfying appetizers. They're perfect for a picnic or potluck.
—**LINDA FOREMAN** LOCUST GROVE, OK

START TO FINISH: 20 MIN. • **MAKES:** 1 DOZEN

- 6 hard-cooked eggs
- ¼ cup finely shredded sharp cheddar cheese
- 2 tablespoons mayonnaise
- 4 teaspoons diced pimientos, divided
- 2 teaspoons Dijon mustard
- 2 teaspoons finely chopped sweet onion
- 1 small garlic clove, minced
  Dash each salt and pepper

Cut eggs in half lengthwise. Remove yolks; set whites aside. In a small bowl, mash yolks. Add the cheese, mayonnaise, 3 teaspoons pimientos, mustard, onion, garlic, salt and pepper; mix well. Stuff or pipe into egg whites. Garnish with remaining pimientos. Refrigerate until serving.

SEAFOOD CAKES WITH HERB SAUCE

This recipe uses salmon and scallops, but shrimp, crab, lobster or any firm white fish, such as halibut or even cod, would work.
—**ELIZABETH TRUESDELL** PETALUMA, CA

PREP: 65 MIN. • **BAKE:** 5 MIN./BATCH
MAKES: 40 APPETIZERS (½ CUP SAUCE)

- ¾ cup mayonnaise
- 4½ teaspoons dill pickle relish
- 1 tablespoon minced chives
- 1 tablespoon minced fresh parsley
- 2 teaspoons tomato paste
- 1 teaspoon grated lemon peel
- ⅛ teaspoon salt
- ⅛ teaspoon pepper

SEAFOOD CAKES
- 1¼ cups panko (Japanese) bread crumbs
- 1 medium sweet red pepper, finely chopped
- 1 medium sweet yellow pepper, finely chopped
- ⅓ cup finely chopped onion
- 1 egg, lightly beaten
- 2 tablespoons minced fresh parsley
- 2 teaspoons minced chives
- 1 pound bay scallops, coarsely chopped
- ½ pound salmon fillet, skin removed and coarsely chopped
- ⅔ cup butter, cubed
  Additional finely chopped sweet red and yellow peppers
    and minced chives

1. In a small bowl, combine the first eight ingredients; set aside ¼ cup. Chill remaining sauce until serving.
2. Combine the bread crumbs, peppers, onion, egg, parsley, chives and reserved sauce. Gently fold in scallops and salmon.
3. With floured hands, shape mixture by 2 tablespoonfuls into ½-in.-thick patties. In a large skillet over medium heat, cook seafood cakes in butter in batches for 2-3 minutes on each side or until golden brown. Transfer to ungreased baking sheets.
4. Bake at 400° for 5-6 minutes or until golden brown. Serve with sauce. Garnish with additional peppers and chives.

RUSTIC ANTIPASTO TART

Ready-made ingredients make this gorgeous tart a hassle-free treat. It's almost like an appetizer pizza.
—**CHERYL LAMA** ROYAL OAK, MI

PREP: 15 MIN. • **BAKE:** 25 MIN. • **MAKES:** 12 SERVINGS

- 1 sheet refrigerated pie pastry
- 2 tablespoons prepared pesto
- 1 cup shredded part-skim mozzarella cheese, divided
- 4 ounces sliced turkey pepperoni
- 1 jar (7 ounces) roasted sweet red peppers, drained and thinly sliced
- 1 jar (7½ ounces) marinated quartered artichoke hearts, drained
- 1 tablespoon water

1. Unroll pastry onto a parchment paper-lined baking sheet. Spread pesto to within 2 in. of edges; sprinkle with ½ cup cheese. Layer with pepperoni and ¼ cup cheese. Top with red peppers and artichokes; sprinkle with remaining cheese.
2. Fold up edges of pastry over the filling, leaving center uncovered. Brush folded pastry with water. Bake at 425° for 25-30 minutes or until crust is golden and cheese is melted. Serve warm.

SPICED MULLED WINE

You'll want to heat this traditional beverage before company arrives—it'll be gone in a flash!
—**LANA GRYGA** GLEN FLORA, WI

PREP: 5 MIN. • **COOK:** 30 MIN. • **MAKES:** 6 SERVINGS

- 1 bottle (750 milliliters) ruby port
- 1 bottle (750 milliliters) merlot
- ½ cup sugar
- 4 orange peel strips (1 to 3 inches)
- 2 cinnamon sticks (3 inches)
- 8 whole allspice
- 6 whole cloves

In a large saucepan, combine all ingredients; bring just to a simmer (do not boil). Reduce heat; simmer gently, uncovered, 30 minutes or until flavors are blended, stirring to dissolve sugar. Strain. Serve warm.

REUBEN DIP

Here's a rich dip that comes together so easily, you can make it just before guests arrive. I often serve it with rye bread wedges.
—**MARY JO HAGEY** GLADWIN, MI

START TO FINISH: 15 MIN. • **MAKES:** 2½ CUPS

- 1 tablespoon butter
- 2 green onions, chopped
- 1½ cups (6 ounces) shredded Muenster cheese
- 4 ounces cream cheese, cubed
- 2 tablespoons ketchup
- 2 teaspoons Dijon mustard
- ¼ teaspoon pepper
- ½ pound cooked corned beef, chopped
- 1 cup sauerkraut, rinsed and well drained
  Assorted crackers

1. Place butter in a small microwave-safe bowl and microwave on high for 20 seconds or until melted. Add onions; cover and cook 1 minute longer.
2. Stir in the cheeses, ketchup, mustard and pepper. Cover and cook on high for 1 minute; stir. Cook 45 seconds longer. Stir in the beef.
3. Place sauerkraut in a microwave-safe 1-qt. dish; top with beef mixture. Cover and microwave on high for 2-3 minutes or until heated through. Serve with crackers.
NOTE *This recipe was tested in a 1,100-watt microwave.*

WHITE GRAPE PUNCH

My mix-ahead punch never sticks around long once I set it out. The refill requests come quickly.
—**DEBRA FRAAKEN** FORT COLLINS, CO

START TO FINISH: 15 MIN. • **MAKES:** 6 QUARTS

- 2 cans (12 ounces each) frozen apple juice concentrate, thawed
- 2 cans (11½ ounces each) frozen white grape juice concentrate
- 6 cups cold water
- 12 cups lemon-lime soda (about 3 liters), chilled
  Lemon and lime slices

1. In a large pitcher, combine the apple juice concentrate, white grape concentrate and water. Refrigerate until serving.
2. Just before serving, pour into two pitchers or a punch bowl. Stir in soda and top with lemon and lime slices.

BEEF & ONION CHEESE BALL

You've seen cheese balls in the cheese and deli department at the supermarket, but did you know they were this easy to make?
—**CHRISSY LESZCZYNSKI** MADISON, WI

PREP: 10 MIN. + CHILLING • **MAKES:** 1⅔ CUPS

- 1 package (8 ounces) cream cheese, softened
- 1 package (2 ounces) thinly sliced deli beef, chopped
- 1 bunch green onions, chopped
- 1 tablespoon prepared horseradish
- 1 cup chopped walnuts
  Assorted crackers and vegetables

1. In a small bowl, combine the cream cheese, beef, onions and horseradish. Cover and refrigerate for 15 minutes. Shape into a ball, then roll in walnuts. Wrap tightly in plastic wrap.
2. Cover and refrigerate until serving. Serve with crackers and vegetables.

SAUSAGE STUFFED MUSHROOMS

I've been making this recipe for years. Use Italian sausage if you'd prefer a little more zip.
—**METTIE BONE** ASHLAND, OH

PREP: 35 MIN. • **BAKE:** 20 MIN. • **MAKES:** 2 DOZEN

- ¾ cup water
- 2 tablespoons butter
- 1 cup pork-flavored stuffing mix
- 24 large fresh mushrooms
- ¾ pound bulk pork sausage
- 1 small onion, finely chopped
- 2¼ teaspoons dried parsley flakes
- 2¼ teaspoons ground mustard
- 1½ cups (6 ounces) shredded part-skim mozzarella cheese

1. In a small saucepan, bring water and butter just to a boil. Remove from the heat; stir in stuffing mix. Cover and let stand for 5 minutes.
2. Meanwhile, remove stems from mushrooms and finely chop stems; set caps aside. In a large skillet, cook the sausage, onion and chopped mushrooms over medium heat until meat is no longer pink; drain.
3. Fluff stuffing with a fork; add to sausage mixture. Stir in parsley and mustard. Stuff into mushroom caps.
4. Place on a foil-lined baking sheet. Bake at 350° for 15 minutes. Sprinkle with cheese; bake 5-10 minutes longer or until mushrooms are tender.

CINNAMON APPLE SHAKES

Shake things up with these change-of-pace milkshakes.
—**NATALIE CARTER** AUSTIN, TX

START TO FINISH: 10 MIN. • **MAKES:** 4 SERVINGS

- 3 cups vanilla ice cream
- ¾ cup 2% milk
- ½ cup cinnamon applesauce
- ¼ cup caramel ice cream topping
- ½ teaspoon rum extract

In a blender, combine all ingredients; cover and process until smooth. Pour into chilled glasses and garnish as desired. Serve immediately.

PINWHEEL PIZZA SNACKS

These pretty bites are a simple party solution, but you could also serve them with a salad for an extra special lunch. They look beautiful and taste fantastic—talk about a winning combination! I'm sure they'll disappear in a flash once you set them out.

—BONNIE HAWKINS ELKHORN, WI

START TO FINISH: 30 MIN. • **MAKES:** 16 APPETIZERS

  1 tube (8 ounces) refrigerated crescent rolls
  ⅓ cup pizza sauce
  ¼ cup grated Parmesan cheese
  ½ cup chopped seeded tomatoes
  ⅓ cup shredded part-skim mozzarella cheese
     Fresh basil leaves, thinly sliced

1. Unroll crescent dough into one long rectangle; seal seams and perforations. Spread pizza sauce to within 1 in. of edges; sprinkle with Parmesan cheese. Roll up jelly-roll style, starting with a short side; pinch seams to seal. Cut into 16 slices.
2. Place pinwheels, cut side down, on a greased baking sheet. Top each with tomatoes and mozzarella cheese. Bake at 375° for 11-13 minutes or until golden brown and cheese is melted. Sprinkle with basil.

ALMOND COFFEE WALNUTS

Semisweet chocolate adds a luscious touch to the coffee and nuts here. You just need a microwave to make it. Even if you normally avoid nuts when you're snacking, I predict this recipe will change your mind. Yum!

—JAMES KORZENOWSKI FENNVILLE, MI

PREP: 40 MIN. + STANDING • **MAKES:** 3 DOZEN

  ⅔ cup almond paste
  2 tablespoons coffee liqueur
  1 teaspoon instant espresso powder
 72 walnut halves
  6 ounces semisweet chocolate, chopped
  1 teaspoon shortening

1. In a small bowl, combine the almond paste, liqueur and espresso powder. Spread about ½ teaspoon mixture on the flat side of half of the walnuts. Top with remaining walnuts, forming a sandwich.
2. In a microwave, melt chocolate and shortening; stir until smooth. Dip one end of sandwiches in chocolate; allow excess to drip off. Place on waxed paper; let stand until set. Store in an airtight container in the refrigerator.

SIDE DISHES & CONDIMENTS

Searching for a side to spice up your next meal? Maybe you need a quick, complementary dressing to jazz up a salad? Well, you've come to the right place. These recipes offer menus a country twist that can't be beat!

SWEET AND SOUR CARROTS

I've rounded out many dinners with my special carrots. I've found that I like them best with a main dish of roast turkey, brisket or braised short ribs.

—HELEN ORESTAD POWDERVILLE, MT

START TO FINISH: 30 MIN. • **MAKES:** 8 SERVINGS

- ¼ cup sugar
- ¼ cup orange juice
- ⅔ cup dried cranberries
- 2 tablespoons grated orange peel
- 3 tablespoons butter
- 2 pounds fresh carrots, sliced
- ⅓ cup water
- ¼ cup pine nuts, toasted
- 4 teaspoons sherry vinegar
- ½ teaspoon salt

1. In a small saucepan, combine the sugar and orange juice. Cook and stir over low heat for 2 minutes or until sugar is dissolved. Remove from the heat. Stir in cranberries and orange peel; set aside.

2. In a large saucepan, melt butter. Add carrots and water; stir until well coated. Bring to a boil. Reduce heat; cover and simmer for 5-7 minutes or until carrots are crisp-tender.

3. Stir in the pine nuts, vinegar, salt and cranberry mixture. Simmer, uncovered, for 5-7 minutes or until carrots are tender.

BLACK BEAN & CORN SALSA

Who knew adding a few ingredients to store-bought salsa could give it so much extra flavor? This one's perfect as a chip dipper or on top of tacos, burritos or eggs.

—PATRICIA SWART GALLOWAY, NJ

START TO FINISH: 5 MIN. • **MAKES:** 4 SERVINGS

- 1 cup chunky salsa
- ½ cup canned black beans, rinsed and drained
- ½ cup canned whole kernel corn, drained
  Tortilla chips

In a small bowl, combine the salsa, beans and corn. Refrigerate until serving. Serve with tortilla chips.

PUT LEFTOVERS TO USE

When I have leftover corn, I make my son's favorite dish. I beat an egg, then add corn and flour to create a thick batter. Drop the batter by spoonfuls into hot oil in a skillet. Fry until the "balls" are crisp.

—LINDA K. PERRY, KS

GARLIC BRUSSELS SPROUTS

For a special side dish, I combine Brussels sprouts with sauteed garlic and cook them in butter and chicken broth. If you can't find fresh sprouts, you can use frozen ones instead.
—**MYRA INNES** AUBURN, KS

START TO FINISH: 30 MIN. • **MAKES:** 6 SERVINGS

1½ pounds fresh Brussels sprouts
4 garlic cloves, chopped
2 teaspoons olive oil
3 teaspoons butter, divided
½ cup reduced-sodium chicken broth
¼ teaspoon salt
⅛ teaspoon pepper

1. Trim the Brussels sprouts and cut an "X" in the core of each; set aside.
2. In a large saucepan, saute garlic in oil and 1 teaspoon butter for 2-3 minutes or until golden brown. Add reserved sprouts; toss to coat.
3. Stir in the broth, salt and pepper. Bring to a boil. Reduce heat; cover and simmer for 8-10 minutes or until tender. Drain; add remaining butter and toss until melted.

WARM PECAN CABBAGE SLAW

Slaw gets a hot new look in this colorful side I usually serve warm. The mild mustard flavor, crisp-tender vegetables and toasted pecans together create a one-of-a-kind recipe.
—**MARIE HATTRUP** SPARKS, NV

START TO FINISH: 20 MIN. • **MAKES:** 6 SERVINGS

4 cups coarsely shredded cabbage
½ cup shredded carrot
¼ cup sliced green onions
2 tablespoons water
½ teaspoon salt
¼ teaspoon pepper
1 tablespoon butter, melted
1 teaspoon Dijon mustard
¼ cup chopped pecans, toasted

1. In a large saucepan, combine the cabbage, carrot, green onions, water, salt and pepper. Cover and cook over medium heat for 5-7 minutes or until cabbage is crisp-tender. Drain, if necessary.
2. Combine butter and mustard; pour over cabbage mixture and toss to coat. Stir in pecans.

GARLIC-CHIVE BAKED FRIES

Yes, you do want fries with that! No one can resist crispy, golden-brown fries seasoned with garlic and fresh chives. They're especially great with juicy steaks, fish fillets or hamburgers, but they're easy enough to make anytime to dress up a meal. As an added bonus, these fries are better for you than traditional French fries.

—STEVE WESTPHAL WIND LAKE, WI

PREP: 15 MIN. • **BAKE:** 20 MIN. • **MAKES:** 4 SERVINGS

- 4 **medium russet potatoes**
- 1 **tablespoon olive oil**
- 4 **teaspoons dried minced chives**
- ½ **teaspoon salt**
- ½ **teaspoon garlic powder**
- ¼ **teaspoon pepper**

1. Cut the potatoes into ¼-in. julienne strips. Rinse well and pat dry.

2. Transfer potatoes to a large bowl. Drizzle with oil; sprinkle with the remaining ingredients. Toss to coat. Arrange in a single layer on two 15-in. x 10-in. x 1-in. baking pans coated with cooking spray.

3. Bake at 450° for 20-25 minutes or until lightly browned, turning once.

LEMON DATE COUSCOUS

Couscous is a perfect way to highlight bold flavors, and it goes with many main dishes. It also cooks up quickly, making it a breezy side dish option when you've got a lot going on. If you've never tried couscous before, it's a commercially produced grain usually made from semolina. You can usually find it in the rice or pasta section of your local grocery store.

—ROXANNE CHAN ALBANY, CA

START TO FINISH: 10 MIN. • **MAKES:** 4 SERVINGS

- ¾ **cup uncooked couscous**
- ½ **cup fresh baby spinach**
- ½ **cup shredded carrots**
- ¼ **cup chopped dates**
- 2 **tablespoons sliced almonds**
- 1 **teaspoon lemon juice**
- ¼ **teaspoon grated lemon peel**
- ⅛ **teaspoon salt**
- ⅛ **teaspoon lemon-pepper seasoning**
  Thinly sliced green onions

1. Cook couscous according to package directions.

2. Meanwhile, in a small bowl, combine the spinach, carrots, dates, almonds, lemon juice, peel, salt and lemon-pepper. Stir in couscous. Garnish with green onions.

MASHED POTATOES WITH GARLIC-OLIVE OIL

Garlic mashed potatoes are high on our "love it" list. To intensify my recipe's taste, I combine garlic and olive oil in the food processor and drizzle it on top of the potatoes.

—**EMORY DOTY** JASPER, GA

START TO FINISH: 30 MIN. • **MAKES:** 12 SERVINGS (¾ CUP EACH)

- 4 pounds red potatoes, quartered
- ½ cup olive oil
- 2 garlic cloves
- ⅔ cup heavy whipping cream
- ¼ cup butter, softened
- 2 teaspoons salt
- ½ teaspoon pepper
- ⅔ to ¾ cup whole milk
- 3 green onions, chopped
- ¾ cup grated Parmesan cheese, optional

1. Place potatoes in a Dutch oven; add water to cover. Bring to a boil. Reduce heat; cook, uncovered, for 15-20 minutes or until tender. Meanwhile, place oil and garlic in a small food processor; process until blended.

2. Drain potatoes; return to pan. Mash potatoes, gradually adding cream, butter, salt, pepper and enough milk to reach desired consistency. Stir in green onions. Serve with garlic olive oil and, if desired, cheese.

NOTE *For food safety purposes, prepare garlic olive oil just before serving; do not store leftover oil mixture.*

CLASSIC PESTO SAUCE

Homemade pesto just can't be beat, and it's a cinch to prepare.

—**SUE JURACK** MEQUON, WI

START TO FINISH: 15 MIN. • **MAKES:** ½ CUP

- ¾ cup loosely packed basil leaves
- 2 tablespoons pine nuts or sunflower kernels
- 1 garlic clove, peeled
- ½ teaspoon salt
- ⅛ teaspoon pepper
- ⅓ cup olive oil
- ⅓ cup grated Parmesan cheese

Place the first five ingredients in a small food processor; pulse until chopped. Continue processing while gradually adding oil in a steady stream. Add cheese; pulse just until blended. Cover and freeze for up to 3 months.

NOTE *When freezing the pesto, leave about ¾ inch in the top of the container, then cover the top with a thin layer of olive oil, so the pesto doesn't brown during freezing.*

BROCCOLI WITH ORANGE BROWNED BUTTER

This no-fuss butter sauce with orange peel, salt and nutmeg will turn everyone into broccoli lovers!

—**CHRISTINE BERGMAN** SUWANEE, GA

START TO FINISH: 15 MIN. • **MAKES:** 4 SERVINGS

- 1 package (12 ounces) frozen Steamfresh broccoli cuts
- 2 tablespoons butter
- 1 teaspoon grated orange peel
- ¼ teaspoon salt
  Dash ground nutmeg

1. Cook broccoli according to package directions. Meanwhile, in a small heavy saucepan, cook butter over medium heat for 3-4 minutes or until golden brown. Stir in the orange peel, salt and nutmeg.

2. Drain broccoli. Add to the saucepan and toss to coat.

LEMON BEANS WITH PROSCIUTTO

Take green beans to a fancy new level with prosciutto and white wine. You'll love this!

—LORI WIESE HUMBOLDT, MN

START TO FINISH: 25 MIN. • **MAKES:** 6 SERVINGS

- 8 thin slices prosciutto or deli ham, julienned
- 2 teaspoons olive oil
- ½ cup white wine or reduced-sodium chicken broth
- ¼ cup lemon juice
- 2 tablespoons butter
- 1½ pounds fresh green beans, trimmed

1. In a large nonstick skillet coated with cooking spray, cook prosciutto in oil over medium heat until crisp. Remove to paper towels with a slotted spoon; drain.

2. In the same skillet, combine the wine, lemon juice and butter. Bring to a boil. Reduce heat; simmer, uncovered, for 5-6 minutes or until sauce is reduced by half.

3. Meanwhile, place beans in a large saucepan and cover with water. Bring to a boil. Cover and cook for 4-7 minutes or until crisp-tender; drain. Add beans to skillet; toss to coat. Sprinkle with prosciutto just before serving.

CITRUS-MARMALADE VINAIGRETTE

Add a fresh-tasting splash of citrus to a wide variety of salad mixings. It's a real pick-me-up for any salad.

—SARAH VASQUES MILFORD, NH

START TO FINISH: 10 MIN. • **MAKES:** ¾ CUP

- ⅓ cup olive oil
- 3 tablespoons lemon juice
- 2 tablespoons orange marmalade
- 4 teaspoons minced fresh thyme
- 1 tablespoon Dijon mustard
- 2 teaspoons grated lemon peel
- ⅛ teaspoon salt

In a small bowl, whisk all ingredients. Chill until serving.

HARVEST CHUTNEY

Seal the best of autumn flavors into a condiment that's delicious all year. The gem-colored chutney is sweet and slightly spicy, and it'll be gone in a flash.

—WENDY BALL BATTLE CREEK, MI

PREP: 30 MIN. • **COOK:** 20 MIN. • **MAKES:** 3½ CUPS

- ⅓ cup sugar
- ¼ cup water
- 4 medium apples, peeled and chopped
- 2 cups fresh or frozen cranberries
- 5 shallots, chopped
- ⅓ cup packed brown sugar
- ¼ cup cider vinegar
- ¼ cup cranberry juice
- ¼ cup orange juice
- 4 teaspoons grated orange peel
- ½ teaspoon salt
- ½ teaspoon white pepper
- ½ teaspoon ground cinnamon
- ¼ teaspoon ground ginger
- ⅛ teaspoon ground cloves
- ½ cup chopped pecans, toasted

1. In a large saucepan, bring sugar and water to a boil over medium heat. Stir in the apples, cranberries, shallots, brown sugar, vinegar, cranberry juice, orange juice, peel and seasonings.

2. Return to a boil. Reduce heat; simmer, uncovered, for 15-20 minutes or until desired thickness, stirring occasionally. Stir in pecans. Cool. Spoon into jars. Cover and store in the refrigerator for up to 3 weeks.

GINGER & SPICE BUTTERNUT SQUASH

I came up with this side dish one year while cooking Christmas dinner with my mom. The spiced-up squash is just as sweet as it is comforting.

—AMY BURTON CARY, NC

PREP: 15 MIN. • **BAKE:** 20 MIN. • **MAKES:** 4 SERVINGS

- 1 medium butternut squash (about 3 pounds), cut into ¾-inch cubes
- 2 tablespoons canola oil
- ⅓ cup packed brown sugar
- 3 tablespoons butter, melted
- 4½ teaspoons minced fresh gingerroot
- 1 teaspoon ground cinnamon
- 1 teaspoon vanilla extract
- ½ teaspoon ground cardamom
- ½ teaspoon ground allspice
- ¼ teaspoon salt

1. In a large bowl, combine squash and oil. Transfer to a greased 15-in. x 10-in. x 1-in. baking pan. Bake, uncovered, at 400° for 20-25 minutes or until squash is tender.

2. In a small bowl, combine the remaining ingredients. Pour over squash; toss to coat.

HERB-ROASTED MUSHROOMS

My husband grows herbs, and we use whatever's in season for this dish. Our favorite blend is oregano, rosemary and basil, but we also suggest trying parsley, dill and mint.
—**JENNIFER NIEMI** TUCSON, AZ

START TO FINISH: 30 MIN. • **MAKES:** 4 SERVINGS

- ½ pound medium fresh mushrooms
- ½ pound baby portobello mushrooms
- 5 ounces fresh shiitake mushrooms, stems removed
- 2 tablespoons olive oil
- 2 tablespoons minced fresh basil
- 1 tablespoon minced fresh oregano
- 1 tablespoon minced fresh rosemary
- ¼ teaspoon salt
- ¼ teaspoon pepper
- 2 tablespoons balsamic vinegar

1. Cut mushrooms into quarters; place in a large bowl. Add oil, herbs, salt and pepper; toss to combine. Place on two 15-in. x 10-in. x 1-in. baking pans coated with cooking spray.
2. Bake, uncovered, at 425° for 9-11 minutes or until tender. Transfer to a bowl. Drizzle with vinegar; toss to coat.

SOUTHERN BLACK-EYED PEAS

The secret to a good black-eyed pea recipe? Pork!
—**EMORY DOTY** JASPER, GA

PREP: 20 MIN. + STANDING • **COOK:** 45 MIN. • **MAKES:** 6 SERVINGS

- 1 pound dried black-eyed peas, sorted and rinsed
- 1 large onion, chopped
- 2 tablespoons olive oil
- 2 ounces sliced salt pork belly, chopped
- 6 garlic cloves, minced
- 2 bay leaves
- 1 tablespoon minced fresh thyme or 1 teaspoon dried thyme
- ¼ teaspoon crushed red pepper flakes
- ¼ teaspoon pepper
- 1 carton (32 ounces) reduced-sodium chicken broth
- 2 smoked ham hocks

1. Place the peas in a Dutch oven; add water to cover by 2 in. Bring to a boil; boil for 2 minutes. Remove from the heat; cover and let stand for 1 hour. Drain and rinse peas, discarding liquid; set aside.
2. In the same pan, saute onion in oil until tender. Add the pork belly, garlic, bay leaves, thyme, pepper flakes and pepper; cook 1 minute longer.
3. Add the broth, ham hocks and peas; bring to a boil. Reduce heat; simmer, uncovered, for 35-40 minutes or until the peas are tender, stirring occasionally and adding additional water if desired.
4. Discard bay leaves. Remove ham hocks; cool slightly. Remove meat from bones if desired; finely chop and return to pan. Discard bones.

MOZZARELLA MASHED POTATO REMIX

Wondering what to do with leftover mashed potatoes? Gooey cheese, creamy potatoes and a golden crust blend perfectly for a match made in taste bud heaven!

—ROSEMARIE WELESKI NATRONA HEIGHTS, PA

PREP: 20 MIN. • **BAKE:** 25 MIN. • **MAKES:** 6 SERVINGS

- 2 tablespoons dry bread crumbs
- 2 medium onions, chopped
- 1 celery rib, chopped
- 2 tablespoons chopped green pepper
- 3 tablespoons canola oil
- 1 garlic clove, minced
- 3 cups mashed potatoes (with added milk and butter)
- 1¼ cups cubed part-skim mozzarella cheese
- ½ cup shredded part-skim mozzarella cheese

1. Grease a 1½-qt. baking dish and sprinkle with bread crumbs; set aside.

2. In a large skillet, saute the onions, celery and pepper in oil until tender. Add garlic; cook 1 minute longer. Remove from the heat; stir in mashed potatoes and cheese cubes. Transfer to prepared baking dish and sprinkle with shredded cheese.

3. Bake, uncovered, at 375° for 25-30 minutes or until golden brown.

CLASSIC TARTAR SAUCE

Love dunking your fish in tarter sauce? You may never buy another bottle of it again once you've tried this super-easy recipe!
—**MICHELLE STROMKO** DARLINGTON, MD

START TO FINISH: 10 MIN. • **MAKES:** 1 CUP

- ⅔ cup chopped dill pickles
- ½ cup mayonnaise
- 3 tablespoons finely chopped onion
  Dash pepper

In a small bowl, combine all ingredients. Cover and refrigerate until serving.

PASTA WITH GARLIC OIL

My family is Italian, and they can't get enough of this garlic-, mushrooms- and herbs-loaded dish. Don't rinse the pasta in water after you drain it, otherwise the sauce won't stick.
—**PAM VITTORI** CHICAGO HEIGHTS, IL

START TO FINISH: 20 MIN. • **MAKES:** 5 SERVINGS

- 8 ounces uncooked spaghetti
- 2 garlic cloves, minced
- ⅓ cup olive oil
- ½ cup jarred sliced mushrooms
- ¼ cup sliced ripe olives
- 2 to 3 teaspoons minced fresh basil
- 2 to 3 teaspoons minced fresh parsley
- ⅛ teaspoon garlic salt
- ⅛ to ¼ teaspoon pepper
  Shredded Parmesan cheese, optional

1. Cook spaghetti according to package directions.
2. Meanwhile, in a large skillet, saute garlic in oil. Stir in the mushrooms, olives, basil, parsley, garlic salt and pepper. Cook for 5 minutes. Drain spaghetti; place in a serving bowl. Pour sauce over pasta; toss to coat. Sprinkle with Parmesan cheese if desired.

POMEGRANATE ORANGE SALSA

Pomegranates give this salsa a wonderful sweet-tart taste. You'll need about 4 to 5 medium-sized fruits for this recipe.
—**NANCEE MAYNARD** BOX ELDER, SD

PREP: 10 MIN. + CHILLING • **MAKES:** 4 CUPS

- 1 can (15 ounces) mandarin oranges
- 3⅓ cups pomegranate seeds
- ¼ cup minced fresh cilantro
- 2 jalapeno peppers, seeded and finely chopped
  Tortilla chips

Drain oranges, reserving 2 tablespoons juice. Cut oranges in half; transfer to a large bowl. Add the pomegranate seeds, cilantro, jalapenos and reserved juice. Cover and refrigerate for 2 hours. Serve with tortilla chips.
NOTE *Wear disposable gloves when cutting hot peppers; the oils can burn skin. Avoid touching your face.*

POMEGRANATE POINTERS
Select pomegranates that have a fresh leather-like skin free from cracks and splits. Once pomegranate seeds are taken out, they can be kept in the refrigerator for up to 3 days. To freeze, place them in a single layer on a baking pan. Once the seeds are frozen, transfer them to an airtight container and keep in freezer up to 6 months.

Bring on the Tomatoes

From dressing up pasta to creating a unique side dish, tomatoes are sure to become your new favorite ingredient. These recipes will make your mouth water, so head out to the farmers market!

CLASSIC RATATOUILLE

Hearty and full of veggies, this ratatouille fills the kitchen with the comforting aroma of thyme, onions and garlic.

—DIANE TRESTER SHEBOYGAN, WI

PREP: 1 HOUR • **COOK:** 40 MIN. • **MAKES:** 8 SERVINGS

- 5 medium onions, chopped
- 3 garlic cloves, minced
- 6 tablespoons olive oil, divided
- 1 small eggplant, peeled and cubed
- 3 medium zucchini, chopped
- 2 medium yellow summer squash, chopped
- 3 medium green peppers, chopped
- 2 medium sweet red peppers, chopped
- 2 medium sweet yellow peppers, chopped
- ¾ cup vegetable stock
- 1 bay leaf
- 2 teaspoons minced fresh thyme or ½ teaspoon dried thyme
- 1 teaspoon minced fresh rosemary or ¼ teaspoon dried rosemary, crushed
- ¾ teaspoon salt
- ½ teaspoon pepper
- 2 medium tomatoes

1. In a Dutch oven, saute onions and garlic in 1 tablespoon oil until tender. Reduce heat to low.

2. In a skillet, saute the eggplant, zucchini, squash and green, red and yellow peppers in batches in remaining oil until lightly browned, adding each batch of the sauteed vegetables to the Dutch oven.

3. Stir the stock, bay leaf, thyme, rosemary, salt and pepper into the Dutch oven. Bring to a boil. Reduce heat; simmer, uncovered, for 30 minutes.

4. Meanwhile, fill a large saucepan two-thirds with water; bring to a boil. Score an "X" on the bottom of each tomato. Using a slotted spoon, place tomatoes in boiling water for 30-60 seconds. Remove tomatoes and immediately plunge into ice water. Discard peel and coarsely chop tomatoes.

5. Drain and reserve juices from vegetable mixture. Remove vegetables from the pan and set aside. Return juices to Dutch oven. Bring to a boil; cook until thickened, about 5 minutes. Return vegetables to pan and stir in tomatoes. Discard bay leaf.

FRIED GREEN TOMATOES WITH JALAPENO PESTO

I loved fried green tomatoes when I was a child, so as an adult I was able to combine two more of my favorite culinary delights to complement the classic dish.

—VICKIE BIRKENMEYER WEST PALM BEACH, FL

PREP: 25 MIN. • **COOK:** 5 MIN./BATCH • **MAKES:** 1 DOZEN

- 1½ cups fresh cilantro leaves
- 2 tablespoons olive oil
- 2 tablespoons grated Parmesan cheese
- ½ small onion, halved
- 1 jalapeno pepper, seeded and halved
- 1 tablespoon pine nuts, toasted
- 1 tablespoon lime juice
- 1 garlic clove, peeled

TOMATOES

- 1 cup all-purpose flour
- 2 eggs
- 1¾ cups panko (Japanese) bread crumbs
- ¼ teaspoon salt
- ¼ teaspoon pepper
- 4 medium green tomatoes, cut into ¼-inch slices
- 6 tablespoons olive oil
- ¾ cup crumbled goat cheese

1. For the pesto, place the first eight ingredients in a food processor; cover and process until finely chopped. Set aside.

2. Place flour and eggs in separate shallow bowls. In another shallow bowl, combine the bread crumbs, salt and pepper. Dip tomato slices in flour, eggs, then bread crumb mixture.

3. In a large skillet, fry tomatoes in oil in batches for 2-3 minutes on each side or until golden brown. Drain on paper towels. Layer 12 tomato slices with 1 tablespoon pesto and 1 tablespoon goat cheese; top with remaining tomato slices.

NOTE *Wear disposable gloves when cutting hot peppers; the oils can burn skin. Avoid touching your face.*

STUFFED TOMATOES WITH CHORIZO AND CORN BREAD

Stuff vine-ripe tomatoes with sausage and corn bread for a truly terrific first course. They're great partnered with grilled meat or shrimp, too.

—**MARIE RIZZIO** INTERLOCHEN, MI

PREP: 30 MIN. • **BAKE:** 20 MIN. • **MAKES:** 6 SERVINGS

- 1 **cup yellow cornmeal**
- ¾ **teaspoon kosher salt**
- ¾ **teaspoon baking powder**
- ¼ **teaspoon baking soda**
- 2 **eggs**
- ¾ **cup buttermilk**
- 4 **teaspoons canola oil**

TOMATOES
- 6 **large tomatoes**
- 1½ **teaspoons kosher salt**
- 5 **ounces uncooked chorizo or bulk Italian sausage**
- 1 **medium onion, chopped**
- 1 **medium sweet orange or red pepper, finely chopped**
- ⅓ **cup minced fresh cilantro**
- ¾ **teaspoon ground cumin**
- 3 **eggs, lightly beaten**

1. In a large bowl, combine the cornmeal, salt, baking powder and baking soda. In another bowl, whisk eggs and buttermilk.
2. Place oil in an 8-in. ovenproof skillet; heat skillet in a 450° oven for 3 minutes. Meanwhile, stir egg mixture into dry ingredients just until moistened.
3. Swirl the oil in the skillet to coat the sides and bottom of pan; add batter. Bake at 450° for 12-16 minutes or until a toothpick inserted near the center comes out clean. Cool completely.
4. Place corn bread into a food processor; cover and process until coarse crumbs form. Set aside.
5. Cut a ¼-in. slice off the top of each tomato; with a spoon or melon baller, hollow out each tomato, leaving a ½-in. shell. Discard pulp. Sprinkle salt into each tomato; place upside down on paper towel for 10 minutes to drain.
6. Crumble chorizo into a large skillet; add onion and pepper. Cook over medium heat for 6-8 minutes or until meat is fully cooked; drain. Cool slightly.
7. In a large bowl, combine the corn bread crumbs, chorizo mixture, cilantro and cumin; stir in eggs. Place tomatoes in a greased 13-in. x 9-in. baking dish. Spoon corn bread mixture into each tomato, mounding in the center.
8. Bake, uncovered, at 350° for 20-25 minutes or until a knife inserted near the center comes out clean and the tops are golden brown.

ROASTED RUSSET & SWEET POTATO WEDGES

A cool sour cream sauce tames the heat in these taters, but if you're looking for more kick, add chili powder to the seasonings.
—**THERESA EISCHENS** HUTCHINSON, MN

PREP: 20 MIN. • **BAKE:** 25 MIN. • **MAKES:** 8 SERVINGS

2   **medium russet potatoes, peeled**
2   **medium sweet potatoes, peeled**
2   **tablespoons olive oil**
2   **teaspoons garlic powder**
2   **teaspoons ground cumin**
2   **teaspoons paprika**
1   **teaspoon seasoned salt**
¼ to ½ **teaspoon crushed red pepper flakes**
⅛   **teaspoon pepper**
DIP
½   **cup sour cream**
½   **teaspoon seasoned salt**
½   **teaspoon garlic powder**

1. Cut each russet and sweet potato lengthwise into eight wedges; place in two greased 15-in. x 10-in. x 1-in. baking pans. Drizzle with oil. Combine the seasonings; sprinkle over potatoes and toss to coat.
2. Bake wedges at 400° for 25-30 minutes or until tender, turning once.
3. In a small bowl, combine the dip ingredients. Serve with potato wedges.

TRIPLE BEAN BAKE WITH BACON

Ordinary baked beans become extraordinary when you mix bean varieties and add the zing of horseradish.
—**SHERRI MELOTIK** OAK CREEK, WI

PREP: 15 MIN. • **BAKE:** 30 MIN. • **MAKES:** 8 SERVINGS

½   **pound bacon strips, cut into ½-inch pieces**
⅔   **cup chopped onion (about 1 medium)**
1   **can (15½ ounces) great northern beans, undrained**
1   **can (16 ounces) butter beans, rinsed and drained**
1   **can (16 ounces) kidney beans, rinsed and drained**
¾   **cup packed brown sugar**
1   **tablespoon prepared horseradish**
1   **tablespoon yellow mustard**

1. In a Dutch oven, cook bacon over medium heat until crisp. Remove to paper towels with a slotted spoon; drain, reserving 1 tablespoon drippings. Add onion to drippings; cook and stir over medium heat until tender.
2. Stir in the remaining ingredients; return bacon to pan. Transfer to a greased 2-qt. baking dish. Cover and bake at 325° for 30-35 minutes or until heated through. Uncover and bake until desired consistency.

HARVEST SQUASH MEDLEY

To me, cooking is an art, and I love trying new recipes. You can really dress up baked butternut squash, sweet potatoes and apples with citrus and spices with this recipe.
—**RUTH COWLEY** PIPE CREEK, TX

PREP: 25 MIN. • **BAKE:** 1 HOUR • **MAKES:** 10 SERVINGS

  6 **cups water**
  1 **butternut squash, peeled, seeded and cut into ¾-inch pieces**
  2 **medium sweet potatoes, peeled and cut into ¾-inch pieces**
  ¼ **cup honey**
  ¼ **cup orange juice**
  3 **tablespoons butter**
  1 **tablespoon grated orange peel**
  ½ **teaspoon ground cinnamon**
  ⅛ **teaspoon ground nutmeg**
  2 **small apples, peeled and sliced**
  ½ **cup chopped walnuts, toasted**

1. In a large saucepan, bring water to a boil. Add squash and return to a boil. Reduce heat; cover and simmer for 10 minutes. Drain. Place squash and sweet potatoes in a greased 13-in. x 9-in. baking dish.

2. In a small saucepan, combine the honey, orange juice, butter, orange peel, cinnamon and nutmeg. Bring to a boil, stirring constantly. Pour over squash and potatoes.

3. Cover and bake at 350° for 30 minutes, stirring occasionally. Uncover; stir in apples. Bake 30-35 minutes longer or until tender, stirring occasionally. Sprinkle with walnuts.

SOUTHWEST RICE PILAF

This side dish is especially tasty with tacos and fajitas—two of my family's favorite meals.
—**MARTHA ULFELDER** SOUTHBOROUGH, MA

START TO FINISH: 30 MIN. • **MAKES:** 6 SERVINGS

  2 **cups uncooked instant rice**
  1 **can (11 ounces) Mexicorn, drained**
  ⅓ **cup minced fresh cilantro**
  2 **tablespoons butter**
  ½ **teaspoon salt**

Cook rice according to package directions. Stir in the Mexicorn, cilantro, butter and salt.

CRUNCHY BROCCOLI BAKE

Lima beans combine nicely with broccoli in this veggie casserole. Water chestnuts and a cereal topping add fun crunch.
—**RON SLIVON** SURPRISE, AZ

PREP: 15 MIN. • **BAKE:** 30 MIN. • **MAKES:** 9 SERVINGS

  6 **cups frozen chopped broccoli, thawed**
1½ **cups frozen lima beans, thawed**
  1 **can (10¾ ounces) condensed cream of mushroom soup, undiluted**
  1 **cup (8 ounces) sour cream**
  1 **envelope onion soup mix**
  1 **can (8 ounces) water chestnuts, drained and chopped**
  ¼ **teaspoon garlic powder**
  3 **cups crisp rice cereal, crushed**
  ½ **cup butter, melted**

1. Place the vegetables in a greased 2-qt. baking dish. Combine the soup, sour cream, soup mix, water chestnuts and garlic powder. Spread over vegetables.

2. Combine cereal and butter; sprinkle over top. Bake, uncovered, at 325° for 30-35 minutes or until the edges begin to brown.

MAKING A SOUR CREAM SUBSTITUTE

Out of sour cream? You can substitute plain yogurt in equal amounts for sour cream in baking recipes, along with casseroles, dips and sauces. Be aware that there may be a slightly thinner consistency in the final product if you use yogurt. Don't use nonfat yogurt, as it won't work in baked recipes.

BRUSSELS SPROUT GRATIN

If you don't typically enjoy Brussels sprouts, this recipe will change your mind. It's creamy, savory and delicious. You've probably never tried a gratin quite like this one!

—KEVIN LIEBERMAN OKLAHOMA CITY, OK

PREP: 45 MIN. • **BAKE:** 10 MIN. • **MAKES:** 10 SERVINGS

- 2 **pounds Brussels sprouts, quartered**
- 2 **tablespoons butter, melted**
- ¾ **teaspoon salt**
- ⅛ **teaspoon pepper**

CREAM SAUCE
- 1 **large onion, chopped**
- 3 **tablespoons butter**
- 3 **tablespoons all-purpose flour**
- 1 **cup whole milk**
- 1 **cup heavy whipping cream**
- ⅛ **teaspoon white pepper**
  Dash ground nutmeg

TOPPING
- ½ **cup shredded Gruyere cheese**
- ¼ **cup grated Parmesan cheese**

1. In a large bowl, combine the Brussels sprouts, butter, salt and pepper; toss to coat. Transfer to a greased 13-in. x 9-in. baking dish. Bake, uncovered, at 425° for 25-30 minutes or until Brussels sprouts are tender, stirring occasionally.

2. Meanwhile, in a large skillet, saute onion in butter until tender. Stir in flour until blended; gradually add milk and cream. Bring to a boil; cook and stir for 2 minutes or until thickened. Stir in pepper and nutmeg; pour over Brussels sprouts. Sprinkle with cheeses.

3. Reduce heat to 350°. Bake, uncovered, for 10-15 minutes or until heated through and the cheeses are melted.

GARLIC & CHIVE MASHED RED POTATOES

My husband loved the mashed potatoes at a local restaurant, so I came up with this recipe to replicate them.
—**SHERRY BEVER** AKRON, IN

START TO FINISH: 30 MIN. • **MAKES:** 10 SERVINGS

- 3½ pounds medium red potatoes, cubed
- 2 cups (16 ounces) sour cream
- ½ cup 2% milk
- ⅓ cup minced chives
- 3 garlic cloves, minced
- 1 teaspoon salt
- ½ teaspoon pepper

Place potatoes in a Dutch oven and cover with water. Bring to a boil. Reduce heat; cover and cook for 10-15 minutes or until tender. Drain; mash potatoes with sour cream and milk. Stir in the chives, garlic, salt and pepper.

SAUTEED SPINACH

My dad has grown spinach for years, and we've developed several recipes for it, but this one beats them all!
—**TERRA FONDRIEST** ST. JOE, ARKANSAS

START TO FINISH: 15 MIN. • **MAKES:** 4 SERVINGS

- 3 garlic cloves, minced
- 2 tablespoons olive oil
- 2 tablespoons white wine or chicken broth
- 2 packages (9 ounces each) fresh spinach
- ¾ teaspoon salt

1. In a large skillet, saute the garlic in oil for 1 minute. Add wine. Bring to a boil; cook until liquid is reduced by half.
2. Add spinach and salt; cook and stir for 2 minutes or just until spinach is wilted. Serve with a slotted spoon.

ZUCCHINI & TOMATO SAUTE

Throw this dish together quickly on a busy weeknight. It's fresh and full of tasty ingredients.
—**SANDRA GRIMM** PORT ORANGE, FL

START TO FINISH: 15 MIN. • **MAKES:** 4 SERVINGS

- 3 medium zucchini, sliced
- 1 medium onion, sliced
- 2 tablespoons butter
- 2 medium tomatoes, cut into wedges
- 1 teaspoon garlic salt
- ⅛ teaspoon pepper

In a large skillet, saute zucchini and onion in butter until tender. Add the tomatoes, garlic salt and pepper; saute 1-2 minutes longer or until heated through.

BRANDY-GLAZED CARROTS

Coat carrots in a light brandy sauce for this beautiful side. It'll be a true hit!
—**TAMMY LANDRY** SAUCIER, MS

START TO FINISH: 30 MIN. • **MAKES:** 12 SERVINGS

- 3 pounds fresh baby carrots
- ½ cup butter, cubed
- ½ cup honey
- ¼ cup brandy
- ¼ cup minced fresh parsley
- ½ teaspoon salt
- ¼ teaspoon pepper

In a large skillet, bring ½ in. of water to a boil. Add carrots. Cover and cook for 5-9 minutes or until crisp-tender. Drain; remove carrots and set aside. In the same skillet, cook butter and honey over medium heat until butter is melted. Remove from heat; stir in brandy. Bring to a boil; cook until liquid is reduced to about ½ cup. Add the carrots, parsley, salt and pepper; heat through.

DELI-STYLE POTATO SALAD

I was inspired by my grandmother to cook, and I loved going to her house for Sunday dinner. She passed her cooking skills down, and today my mom and I still make this potato salad.
—**SALLY MINER** EL MIRAGE, AZ

PREP: 25 MIN. • **COOK:** 20 MIN. + CHILLING • **MAKES:** 8 SERVINGS

- 1 **pound potatoes, peeled and cubed**
- 6 **hard-cooked eggs**
- 8 **whole baby dill pickles, sliced**
- 1 **small onion, chopped**
- 4 **radishes, sliced**

DRESSING

- 1 **cup Miracle Whip**
- 1 **tablespoon 2% milk**
- 1 **teaspoon prepared mustard**
- ½ **teaspoon dill pickle juice**
- ¼ **teaspoon sugar**
- ¼ **teaspoon salt**
- ¼ **teaspoon pepper**
-    **Paprika, optional**

1. Place potatoes in a large saucepan and cover with water. Bring to a boil. Reduce heat; cover and cook for 10-15 minutes or until tender. Drain and set aside to cool.

2. Coarsely chop four eggs. In a large bowl, combine the chopped eggs, pickles, onion and radishes; add potatoes. In a small bowl, combine the Miracle Whip, milk, mustard, pickle juice, sugar, salt and pepper. Pour over the potato mixture; stir to combine.

3. Slice the remaining eggs and arrange over the salad; sprinkle with paprika if desired. Cover and refrigerate for 4 hours before serving.

GREEN BEANS WITH SHALLOTS

Start this recipe off with a package of frozen green beans. It's a simple, dill-icious solution to any meal!
—**LINDA RABBITT** CHARLES CITY, IA

START TO FINISH: 15 MIN. • **MAKES:** 4 SERVINGS

- 1 **package (12 ounces) frozen Steamfresh whole green beans**
- 1¾ **cups sliced fresh mushrooms**
- 2 **shallots, chopped**
- 1 **tablespoon olive oil**
- ½ **teaspoon salt**
- ½ **teaspoon dill weed**
- ½ **teaspoon pepper**

1. Cook green beans according to package directions.

2. Meanwhile, in a large skillet, saute mushrooms and shallots in oil until tender. Remove from the heat. Add the green beans, salt, dill and pepper; toss to coat.

VEGETABLE TRIO

Wake up those taste buds! This mix of fresh green beans, carrots and mushrooms will highlight any meal.
—**MARY LOU WAYMAN** SALT LAKE CITY, UT

START TO FINISH: 25 MIN. • **MAKES:** 4 SERVINGS

- 4 **large carrots, julienned**
- ½ **pound fresh green beans, cut into 2-inch pieces**
- 1½ **cups sliced fresh mushrooms**
- 1 **teaspoon salt**
- ½ **teaspoon dried thyme**
- 2 **tablespoons butter**

In a large skillet, cook and stir the carrots, green beans, mushrooms, salt and thyme in butter over medium heat for 15 minutes or until beans are crisp-tender.

PAN GRAVY

Use this basic recipe to prepare gravy from meats and poultry that have been roasted in an uncovered roasting pan.
—**TASTE OF HOME TEST KITCHEN**

START TO FINISH: 15 MIN. • **MAKES:** 2 CUPS

Roasted meat drippings
¼ cup all-purpose flour
Chicken broth or water
Salt, pepper and browning sauce, optional

1. Pour pan drippings into a measuring cup. Loosen the browned bits from the roasting pan and add to drippings. Skim fat.

2. Reserve ¼ cup fat and transfer to a small saucepan; whisk in flour until smooth. Add enough broth or water to pan drippings to measure 2 cups. Gradually stir into flour mixture in saucepan. Bring to a boil; cook and stir for 2 minutes or until thickened. Season with salt, pepper and browning sauce if desired.

CHIVE SMASHED POTATOES

No need to peel the potatoes—in fact, this is the only way we make mashed potatoes anymore. Mixing in the flavored cream cheese is a delightful twist.
—**BEVERLY NORRIS** EVANSTON, WY

START TO FINISH: 30 MIN. • **MAKES:** 12 SERVINGS (⅔ CUP EACH)

4 pounds red potatoes, quartered
2 teaspoons chicken bouillon granules
1 carton (8 ounces) spreadable chive and onion cream cheese
½ cup half-and-half cream
¼ cup butter, cubed
1 teaspoon salt
¼ teaspoon pepper

1. Place potatoes and bouillon in a Dutch oven and cover with 8 cups water. Bring to a boil. Reduce heat; cover and cook for 15-20 minutes or until tender.

2. Drain and return to pan. Mash potatoes with cream cheese, cream, butter, salt and pepper.

GREEN BEAN CASSEROLE STUFFED MUSHROOMS

Green bean casserole is a constant go-to for us, but it needed some updating. This bite-size version gets fun reactions every time.
—**KAYTIE PICKETT** JACKSON, MS

PREP: 20 MIN. • **BAKE:** 20 MIN. • **MAKES:** 2½ DOZEN

3 turkey bacon strips, diced
1½ teaspoons minced garlic
1 can (14½ ounces) French-style green beans, drained
¾ cup grated Parmesan cheese, divided
¼ cup condensed cream of onion soup, undiluted
¼ cup water
⅛ teaspoon ground nutmeg
⅛ teaspoon pepper
1 cup dry bread crumbs
30 whole baby portobello mushrooms
Cooking spray
1 can (2.8 ounces) French-fried onions

1. In a small skillet, cook bacon over medium heat until crisp. Add garlic; cook 1 minute longer. Place the green beans, ½ cup cheese, soup, water, nutmeg, pepper and bacon mixture in a food processor; process until blended. Transfer to a small bowl; fold in bread crumbs.

2. Remove stems from mushrooms; discard stems or save for another use. Spritz mushroom caps with cooking spray; place in an ungreased 15-in. x 10-in. x 1-in. baking pan, stem side down. Bake at 425° for 10 minutes, turning once.

3. Drain liquid from caps; fill with green bean mixture. Top with remaining cheese and fried onions. Bake 8-10 minutes longer or until mushrooms are tender and filling is heated through.

HONEY MUSTARD COLESLAW

I switched up a family coleslaw recipe—using packaged shredded cabbage is a real time-saver. And now there's very little cleanup!
—**REBECCA ANDERSON** MELISSA, TX

START TO FINISH: 10 MIN. • **MAKES:** 5 SERVINGS

- 1 package (14 ounces) coleslaw mix
- ½ cup mayonnaise
- 2 tablespoons honey
- 1 tablespoon cider vinegar
- 1 tablespoon spicy brown mustard
- ½ teaspoon lemon-pepper seasoning
- ⅛ teaspoon celery seed

Place coleslaw mix in a large bowl. Combine the remaining ingredients. Pour over the coleslaw mix and toss to coat. Chill until serving.

GARDEN REFRIGERATOR PICKLES

No need to can here! You can still get crisp-tender, tangy pickles—just keep them in the fridge and eat them up within a month.
—**LINDA CHAPMAN** MERIDEN, IA

PREP: 20 MIN. • **COOK:** 15 MIN. + CHILLING • **MAKES:** 7 PINTS

- 6 cups sugar
- 6 cups white vinegar
- ¼ cup celery seed
- ¼ cup mustard seed
- 2 tablespoons canning salt
- 10 medium carrots, halved and quartered
- 3 medium cucumbers, sliced
- 3 medium sweet red peppers, cut into 1-inch pieces
- 2 large onions, halved and sliced
- 1 bunch green onions, cut into 2-inch pieces

1. In a Dutch oven, combine the first five ingredients; bring to a boil, stirring to dissolve sugar. Meanwhile, place the remaining ingredients in a large bowl.
2. Pour hot liquid over vegetables; cool. Transfer to jars, if desired; cover tightly. Refrigerate for 6-8 hours before serving. Store in the refrigerator for up to 1 month.

BACON-GOUDA STUFFED ONIONS

Serve these tender sweet-savory onions as a side with steak. For an added splash, drizzle everything with any leftover buttery pan juices from baking the onions.
—**BARB TEMPLIN** NORWOOD, MN

PREP: 10 MIN. • **BAKE:** 45 MIN. • **MAKES:** 4 SERVINGS

- 4 large sweet onions
- ¼ teaspoon salt
- ¼ teaspoon pepper
- 5 bacon strips, cooked and crumbled
- ½ cup shredded smoked Gouda cheese
- ¼ cup butter, softened
  Minced chives

1. Cut a ¼-in. slice from the top and bottom of each onion. Peel onions. Carefully cut and remove the center of each onion, leaving a ½-in. shell; discard removed onion or save for another use.
2. Place onions in a greased 8-in. square baking dish. Sprinkle with salt and pepper. Cover and bake at 400° for 40-45 minutes or until onions are tender. Combine the bacon, cheese and butter; spoon into onions. Bake, uncovered, 5-10 minutes longer or until cheese is melted. Sprinkle with chives.

TUSCAN SUN-DRIED TOMATO JAM

Tomato jam? You bet! My simple jam has a robust flavor that complements anything it's served with, so try it on fresh bread, crackers or as a sandwich topping. The taste and texture also make it a yummy substitute for tomato paste.

—**BARB MILLER** OAKDALE, MN

PREP: 15 MIN. • **COOK:** 55 MIN. • **MAKES:** 1½ CUPS

- 1 jar (7 ounces) oil-packed sun-dried tomatoes
- ½ medium onion, thinly sliced
- 1 garlic clove, minced
- 1 cup water
- ½ cup chicken stock
- ¼ cup red wine vinegar
- 1 tablespoon sugar
- 1 teaspoon dried basil
- ½ teaspoon salt
- ½ teaspoon pepper

1. Drain tomatoes, reserving 1 tablespoon of the oil. Finely chop tomatoes. In a large saucepan, saute the tomatoes and onion in reserved oil until onion is tender. Add garlic; cook 1 minute longer.

2. Stir in the water, stock, vinegar, sugar, basil, salt and pepper. Bring to a boil. Reduce heat; cover and simmer for 30 minutes. Uncover; simmer for 15-20 minutes or until liquid has evaporated and mixture is the consistency of jam.

SOUPS, SALADS & SANDWICHES

It's time to get cozy! Spoon up a hot bowl of soup and serve a sandwich on the side for a soothing lunch. Easily round out the meal with a fresh fruit or crisp vegetable salad. It's like bringing your favorite deli eats home!

TUNA CIABATTA MELTS

Use any good crusty bread when putting together this tuna sandwich. Top with slices of crunchy cucumber for an extra touch of freshness.

—BARB TEMPLIN NORWOOD, MN

START TO FINISH: 10 MIN. • **MAKES:** 4 SERVINGS

- 1 pouch (11 ounces) light tuna in water
- ⅓ cup each finely chopped celery, cucumber and red onion
- ¼ cup mayonnaise
- 2 teaspoons dill weed
- 1 teaspoon lemon juice
- ⅛ teaspoon salt
- ⅛ teaspoon pepper
- 4 ciabatta rolls, split
- 2 cups (8 ounces) shredded cheddar cheese

1. In a small bowl, combine the tuna, celery, cucumber, onion, mayonnaise, dill, lemon juice, salt and pepper; mix well.
2. Place rolls on a baking sheet. Spread each half with tuna mixture; sprinkle with cheese. Broil 2-3 in. from the heat for 2-4 minutes or until cheese is melted.

WINTER ENDIVE SALAD

Here's a salad with a bit of panache. The citrus balances the hint of bitterness in the endive, and the sweet-tart pomegranate seeds add stunning ruby color.

—ALYSHA BRAUN ST. CATHARINES, ON

START TO FINISH: 25 MIN. • **MAKES:** 8 SERVINGS

- 5 cups torn curly endive
- 2 cups watercress
- 1 shallot, thinly sliced
- ⅓ cup pecan halves, toasted
- ¼ cup pomegranate seeds
- ¼ cup olive oil
- 1½ tablespoons lemon juice
- 1 teaspoon grated lemon peel
- ⅛ teaspoon salt
- ⅛ teaspoon pepper

1. In a large bowl, combine the endive, watercress and shallot. Sprinkle with pecans and pomegranate seeds.
2. In a small bowl, whisk the oil, lemon juice, lemon peel, salt and pepper. Drizzle over salad; serve immediately.

PEPPERONI-ARTICHOKE PASTA SALAD

Everyone loves a good pasta salad, and this one will make them feel like you went to a lot of trouble. Bottled dressing, artichoke hearts, olives, pepperoni and mozzarella cubes give it outstanding flavor—and make it easy!

—**CLARA COULSON MINNEY** WASHINGTON COURT HOUSE, OH

START TO FINISH: 30 MIN. • **MAKES:** 6 SERVINGS

- 1 cup uncooked bow tie pasta
- 1 cup cubed part-skim mozzarella cheese
- ¾ cup water-packed artichoke hearts, rinsed, drained and chopped
- 1 can (2¼ ounces) sliced ripe olives, drained
- 2 ounces sliced pepperoni
- 1 small red onion, halved and sliced
- ¼ cup shredded Parmesan cheese
- ¼ cup chopped green pepper
- ½ cup Italian salad dressing

1. Cook pasta according to package directions. Meanwhile, in a large bowl, combine the mozzarella cheese, artichokes, olives, pepperoni, onion, Parmesan cheese and green pepper.

2. Drain pasta and rinse in cold water. Add to salad. Drizzle with salad dressing and toss to coat. Chill until serving.

HEARTY CHICKEN & WILD RICE SOUP

Garlic-and-herb cream cheese punches up the flavor of this soup. On a chilly day, it's like having a bowlful of comfort.

—**SHELISA TERRY** HENDERSON, NV

START TO FINISH: 25 MIN. • **MAKES:** 6 SERVINGS (2¼ QUARTS)

- 1 package (6.2 ounces) fast-cooking long grain and wild rice mix
- 2 cans (10¾ ounces each) condensed cream of chicken and mushroom soup, undiluted
- 3 cups 2% milk
- 2 packages (6 ounces each) ready-to-use grilled chicken breast strips
- 2 cups frozen California-blend vegetables, thawed and coarsely chopped
- ¾ cup spreadable garlic-and-herb cream cheese

Prepare rice mix according to package directions using a Dutch oven. Stir in the remaining ingredients; heat through.

WHAT'S A DUTCH OVEN?
A Dutch oven is a multipurpose cooking pot that can range in size from 5 to 8 quarts. Best of all, it can be transferred between a stovetop and an oven depending on your cooking needs.

MAKE-AHEAD HEARTY SIX-LAYER SALAD

I reach for this recipe whenever I need a dish to pass because it's easy to make and can even be assembled ahead of time!

—**NOREEN MEYER** MADISON, WI

PREP: 20 MIN. + CHILLING • **MAKES:** 12 SERVINGS

- 1½ cups uncooked small pasta shells
- 1 tablespoon vegetable oil
- 3 cups shredded lettuce
- 3 hard-cooked eggs, sliced
- ¼ teaspoon salt
- ⅛ teaspoon pepper
- 2 cups shredded cooked chicken breast
- 1 package (10 ounces) frozen peas, thawed

DRESSING

- 1 cup mayonnaise
- ¼ cup sour cream
- 2 green onions, chopped
- 2 teaspoons Dijon mustard

TOPPINGS

- 1 cup (4 ounces) shredded Colby or Monterey Jack cheese
- 2 tablespoons minced fresh parsley

1. Cook pasta according to package directions; drain and rinse with cold water. Drizzle with oil and toss to coat.

2. Place the lettuce in a 2½-qt. glass serving bowl; top with pasta and eggs. Sprinkle with salt and pepper. Layer with chicken and peas. In a small bowl, mix dressing ingredients until blended; spread over top. Refrigerate, covered, for several hours or overnight.

3. Just before serving, sprinkle with cheese and parsley.

SPICY CAJUN SALSA BURGERS

Use a few on-hand seasonings such as Creole, red pepper flakes and garlic powder to create these flavorful, irresistible burgers.

—**DAVID DALTON** ORLEANS, IN

START TO FINISH: 20 MIN. • **MAKES:** 4 SERVINGS

- ½ cup salsa
- 1 teaspoon Creole seasoning
- ½ teaspoon garlic powder
- ½ teaspoon crushed red pepper flakes
- ½ teaspoon pepper
- 1 pound ground beef
- 4 kaiser rolls, split and toasted

1. In a large bowl, combine the first five ingredients. Add beef; mix lightly but thoroughly. Shape into four ½-in.-thick patties.

2. Grill burgers, covered, over medium heat or broil 4 in. from heat 4-5 minutes on each side or until a thermometer reads 160°. Serve on rolls.

NOTE *The following spices may be substituted for 1 teaspoon Creole seasoning: ¼ teaspoon each salt, garlic powder and paprika; and a pinch each of dried thyme, ground cumin and cayenne pepper.*

KALE & BEAN SOUP

Full of veggies, this soup soothes both the body and the spirit. The kale is packed with nutrients, and the beans add protein to this hearty recipe.
—**BETH SOLLARS** DELRAY BEACH, FL

PREP: 20 MIN. • **COOK:** 70 MIN. • **MAKES:** 8 SERVINGS (2½ QUARTS)

- 2 medium onions, chopped
- 2 cups cubed peeled potatoes
- 1 tablespoon olive oil
- 4 garlic cloves, minced
- 1 bunch kale, trimmed and coarsely chopped
- 3½ cups vegetable broth
- 1 can (28 ounces) diced tomatoes, undrained
- 1½ cups water
- 1 teaspoon Italian seasoning
- 1 teaspoon paprika
- ½ teaspoon pepper
- 1 bay leaf
- 1 can (15 ounces) white kidney or cannellini beans, rinsed and drained

1. In a Dutch oven, saute onions and potatoes in oil until tender. Add garlic; cook 1 minute longer. Stir in the kale, broth, tomatoes, water, Italian seasoning, paprika, pepper and bay leaf. Bring to a boil. Reduce heat; cover and simmer for 50-60 minutes or until kale is tender.

2. Cool slightly. Discard bay leaf. In a blender, process 3 cups of soup until smooth. Return to pan; add beans and heat through.

CHICKEN PHILLY SANDWICHES

A Philly cheesesteak sandwich is a wonderful thing, but I wanted to switch it up. So I replaced the steak with chicken and use colorful red and orange sweet peppers.
—**SHELLY EPLEY** THORNTON, CO

START TO FINISH: 30 MIN. • **MAKES:** 4 SERVINGS

- ½ pound boneless skinless chicken breasts, cut into strips
- 2 teaspoons olive oil
- ½ teaspoon salt
- ½ teaspoon freshly ground pepper
- 1 large onion, halved and sliced
- 1 medium sweet red pepper, julienned
- 1 medium sweet orange or yellow pepper, julienned
- 6 slices provolone cheese, cut into strips
- 4 whole wheat hoagie buns, split and warmed

1. In a large skillet, saute chicken in oil until no longer pink; sprinkle with salt and pepper. Remove and set aside. In the same skillet, saute onion and sweet peppers until crisp-tender.

2. Return chicken to the pan. Reduce heat to medium. Add cheese. Cook and stir for 1-2 minutes or until cheese is melted. Serve on buns.

QUICK POTATO CORN CHOWDER

This can be a meal in itself if you want! It works in every season, so enjoy it anytime.

—**LUCIA JOHNSON** MASSENA, NY

START TO FINISH: 30 MIN. • **MAKES:** 8 SERVINGS (2 QUARTS)

- 1 medium onion, chopped
- 1 tablespoon olive oil
- 2 cans (14½ ounces each) chicken broth
- 3 large Yukon Gold potatoes, peeled and cubed
- 1 can (15¼ ounces) whole kernel corn, drained
- 1 cup 2% milk, divided
- ½ teaspoon salt
- ½ teaspoon pepper
- ⅓ cup all-purpose flour
  Minced fresh parsley, optional

1. In a large saucepan, cook and stir onion in oil over medium heat until tender. Add broth and potatoes; bring to a boil. Reduce heat; cover and simmer for 10-15 minutes or until potatoes are tender.

2. Stir in the corn, ½ cup milk, salt and pepper. In a small bowl, whisk flour and remaining milk until smooth. Stir into soup; return to a boil. Cook and stir for 2-3 minutes or until thickened. Sprinkle with parsley if desired.

SUNDAY SUPPER SANDWICHES

Want to free up some time? You can make this recipe in the slow cooker. Put the ingredients in a 4-quart slow cooker, cover and cook on low for 8-10 hours or until meat is tender.

—**LIBBY WALP** CHICAGO, IL

PREP: 25 MIN. • **BAKE:** 2 HOURS 30 MIN. • **MAKES:** 8 SERVINGS

- 1 can (14 ounces) sauerkraut, rinsed and well drained
- 1 boneless pork shoulder butt roast (2½ to 3 pounds)
- ½ teaspoon salt
- ¼ teaspoon pepper
- ¼ cup stone-ground mustard, divided
- 1 cup apple cider or unsweetened apple juice
- ¼ cup sweetened applesauce
- 8 slices rye bread, toasted
- 1 cup (4 ounces) shredded Swiss cheese

1. Place sauerkraut in an ovenproof Dutch oven. Sprinkle pork with salt and pepper; brush with 2 tablespoons mustard. Place over sauerkraut. Add cider and applesauce.

2. Cover and bake at 325° for 2½ to 3 hours or until pork is tender. Remove roast; cool slightly. Drain sauerkraut mixture; set aside. Shred pork with two forks.

3. Place toast on an ungreased baking sheet. Spread with remaining mustard. Top with pork, then sauerkraut mixture; sprinkle with cheese. Broil 4-6 in. from the heat for 2-3 minutes or until cheese is melted.

BALSAMIC GREEN BEAN SALAD

Serve up those green beans in a whole new way! The tanginess and crunch of this recipe will hook you.

—**MEGAN SPENCER** FARMINGTON HILLS, MI

PREP: 30 MIN. + CHILLING • **MAKES:** 16 SERVINGS

- 2 pounds green beans, trimmed and cut into 1½-inch pieces
- ¼ cup olive oil
- 3 tablespoons lemon juice
- 3 tablespoons balsamic vinegar
- ¼ teaspoon salt
- ¼ teaspoon garlic powder
- ¼ teaspoon ground mustard
- ⅛ teaspoon pepper
- 1 large red onion, chopped
- 4 cups cherry tomatoes, halved
- 1 cup (4 ounces) crumbled feta cheese

1. Place beans in a Dutch oven and cover with water. Bring to a boil. Cover and cook for 8-10 minutes or until crisp-tender. Drain and immediately place beans in ice water. Drain and pat dry.

2. In a small bowl, whisk the oil, lemon juice, vinegar, salt, garlic powder, mustard and pepper. Drizzle over beans. Add the onion; toss to coat. Cover and refrigerate for at least 1 hour. Just before serving, stir in tomatoes and cheese.

GREEN CHILI GRILLED CHEESE SANDWICHES

This surprising take on grilled cheese is a meal in itself, but it would be just as great with a side of chicken chili.

—**LESLIE NEELY** ALBUQUERQUE, NM

START TO FINISH: 20 MIN. • **MAKES:** 4 SERVINGS

- ¼ cup mayonnaise
- 8 slices whole wheat bread
- 4 slices process American cheese
- 4 slices Monterey Jack cheese
- 1 can (4 ounces) chopped green chilies
- 8 teaspoons butter

1. Spread mayonnaise over four slices of bread; layer with cheese slices and green chilies. Top with remaining bread.

2. Butter outsides of sandwiches. In a small skillet over medium heat, toast sandwiches for 2-3 minutes on each side or until cheese is melted.

TOSSED SALAD

When you're trying to clean out the fridge and use up the produce you have, this is the recipe you'll want.

—**LAURA ODELL** EDEN, NC

START TO FINISH: 15 MIN. • **MAKES:** 6 SERVINGS

- 5 cups torn mixed greens
- 1 medium tomato, diced
- 1 cup sliced radishes
- 1 cup sliced red onion
- ¼ cup bacon bits
- ⅔ cup canola oil
- ⅓ cup cider vinegar
- 1¼ teaspoons salt
- ½ teaspoon pepper

In a salad bowl, toss the first five ingredients. In a bowl, whisk the remaining ingredients. Pour over salad and toss to coat.

BROCCOLI SALAD WITH CUCUMBER

Cucumber adds freshness and texture to this easy broccoli salad. Sprinkle shredded cheddar and bacon bits on top for a delicious topping combo.

—**LISA CARTER** WARREN, IN

START TO FINISH: 10 MIN. • **MAKES:** 4 SERVINGS

- 2 cups fresh broccoli florets
- ⅔ cup chopped cucumber
- ½ cup shredded cheddar cheese
- ½ cup mayonnaise
- 3 tablespoons chopped onion
- 3 tablespoons bacon bits

Place all ingredients in a large bowl and toss to coat. Cover and refrigerate until serving.

ZUCCHINI APPLE SALAD

Pull out a beautiful glass bowl to show off this colorful salad of red apples and green zucchini. Everyone will enjoy its cool crunch, and you'll like how quickly it comes together.

—**LOIS FRAZEE** FERNLEY, NV

START TO FINISH: 15 MIN. • **MAKES:** 6 SERVINGS

- 2 medium red apples, chopped
- 2 small zucchini, chopped
- ½ cup coarsely chopped walnuts
- ⅔ cup Italian salad dressing

In a large bowl, combine the apples, zucchini and walnuts. Add salad dressing; toss to coat.

FRENCH DIP SUBS WITH BEER AU JUS

Make a family-pleasing meal in no time with these savory subs. The tender roast beef goes great with the hearty beer dipping sauce and a garnish of banana peppers.

—**SUSAN SIMONS** EATONVILLE, WA

START TO FINISH: 15 MIN. • **MAKES:** 6 SERVINGS

- 2 garlic cloves, minced
- 1 tablespoon butter
- 1 pound thinly sliced deli roast beef
- 2 tablespoons spicy ketchup
- 4 teaspoons Worcestershire sauce
- ½ teaspoon dried basil
- ½ teaspoon dried oregano
- ¼ teaspoon pepper
- 1 bottle (12 ounces) dark beer or nonalcoholic beer
- 6 hoagie buns, split

In a large skillet, saute garlic in butter for 1 minute. Add the roast beef, ketchup, Worcestershire sauce, basil, oregano and pepper. Stir in beer. Bring to a boil. Reduce heat; simmer, uncovered, for 2 minutes, stirring frequently. Using a slotted spoon, place beef on buns. Serve with cooking juices.

PASTA & SUN-DRIED TOMATO SALAD

Orzo pasta can be served warm or cold, making it an ideal dish for casual picnics and cookouts.
—**DAWN WILLIAMS** SCOTTSBORO, AL

PREP: 20 MIN. • **COOK:** 15 MIN. • **MAKES:** 8 SERVINGS

- 1 can (49 ounces) reduced-sodium chicken broth
- 1 package (16 ounces) orzo pasta
- ¼ cup chopped oil-packed sun-dried tomatoes plus 2 teaspoons oil from the jar
- 1 garlic clove, minced
- ¾ teaspoon salt
- ¼ teaspoon pepper
- ⅓ cup shredded Parmesan cheese
- 4 fresh basil leaves, thinly sliced
  Optional toppings: crumbled feta cheese and canned garbanzo beans

1. In a large saucepan, bring broth to a boil. Stir in orzo; return to a boil. Cook for 8-10 minutes or until tender, stirring occasionally.
2. Drain orzo; transfer to a large bowl. (Discard broth or save for another use.) Stir in the tomatoes, the oil from sun-dried tomatoes, garlic, salt and pepper; cool completely.
3. Add Parmesan cheese and basil; toss to combine. Cover and refrigerate until serving. Serve with toppings if desired.

BAKED POTATO CHEDDAR SOUP

With just a few simple kitchen staples, you can stir up an impressive soup. Use a good yellow cheddar cheese; it adds greater depth of color and flavor to this dish.
—**KRISTIN REYNOLDS** VAN BUREN, AR

START TO FINISH: 30 MIN. • **MAKES:** 4 SERVINGS

- ⅓ cup all-purpose flour
- 3 cups milk
- 2 large potatoes, baked, peeled and coarsely mashed (1½ pounds)
- ⅓ cup plus 2 tablespoons shredded cheddar cheese, divided
- ½ teaspoon salt
- ¼ teaspoon pepper
- ½ cup sour cream
- ½ cup thinly sliced green onions, divided
  Crumbled cooked bacon, optional

1. In a large saucepan, whisk flour and milk until smooth. Bring to a boil; cook and stir for 2 minutes or until thickened. Stir in the potatoes, ⅓ cup cheese, salt and pepper. Cook over medium heat for 2-3 minutes or until cheese is melted.
2. Remove from the heat. Stir in sour cream and ¼ cup onions until blended. Cover; cook over medium heat for 10-12 minutes or until heated through (do not boil). Garnish with remaining cheese, onions and, if desired, bacon.

Fruit-Filled Favorites

Oranges, watermelon and strawberries are just a few of the fruits to get special treatment here. Give your dishes a tasty punch of color, while celebrating the best nature has to offer.

SUMMER SALADS WITH MANDARIN ORANGES

Fresh and pretty, this arranged salad is a terrific way to fit fruit and veggies into your day. Sweet oranges and the tangy dressing make a delightful match.

—**FRANCIS GARLAND** ANNISTON, AL

START TO FINISH: 25 MIN. • **MAKES:** 6 SERVINGS

- 3 tablespoons red wine vinegar
- 1 tablespoon lemon juice
- 1 garlic clove, minced
- ¾ teaspoon minced chives
- ¾ teaspoon minced fresh parsley
- ⅛ teaspoon salt
- ⅛ teaspoon coarsely ground pepper
- ½ cup olive oil
- 4 cups torn Boston lettuce
- 2 plum tomatoes, chopped
- 1 medium ripe avocado, peeled and cubed
- ½ small cucumber, halved and sliced
- 1 can (11 ounces) mandarin oranges, drained
- ¼ cup sliced ripe olives

1. In a small bowl, whisk the first seven ingredients. Gradually whisk in oil. Set aside.
2. Divide lettuce among six serving plates. Top with tomatoes, avocado, cucumber, oranges and olives. Drizzle with dressing.

REFRESHING TROPICAL FRUIT SALAD

Both kids and adults will love this juicy side salad—and it's such a visually appealing way to serve up fresh fruit.

—**SHARON RICCI** SPOONER, WI

START TO FINISH: 30 MIN. • **MAKES:** 12 SERVINGS (1 CUP EACH)

- 2 large bananas, sliced
- 2 medium pears, cubed
- ⅓ cup fresh orange juice
- ⅓ cup unsweetened pineapple juice
- 3 cups cubed fresh pineapple
- 1½ cups sliced fresh strawberries
- 1 cup seedless red grapes, halved
- 4 medium kiwifruit, peeled and sliced
- 2 medium mangos, peeled and cubed
- 2 star fruit, sliced

In a large bowl, combine the bananas, pears and juices. Add the pineapple, strawberries, grapes, kiwi and mangos; stir gently to combine. Arrange star fruit over top.

MANDARIN WATERMELON SALAD

Fruit tossed with feta? You bet! In fact, there's nothing better! Fresh mint, cilantro and parsley add the perfect pop. I'm always looking for something different to serve to my mom, who is a vegetarian, and she really likes this.
—JADE BAUSELL MIAMI, FL

START TO FINISH: 20 MIN. • **MAKES:** 8 SERVINGS

- 4½ cups cubed seedless watermelon
- 1 can (11 ounces) mandarin oranges, drained
- ½ small red onion, sliced
- ¼ cup crumbled feta cheese
- 2 tablespoons minced fresh mint
- 2 tablespoons minced fresh cilantro
- 2 tablespoons lime juice
- 1 tablespoon minced fresh parsley

Place all ingredients in a large bowl; gently toss to combine. Serve immediately.

CHICKEN & FRUIT SPINACH SALADS

It takes just 10 minutes to prepare this substantial salad. Serve with whole grain rolls to round out your meal.
—JESSE KLAUSMEIER BURBANK, CA

START TO FINISH: 10 MIN. • **MAKES:** 4 SERVINGS

- 1 package (6 ounces) fresh baby spinach
- 1 package (10 ounces) ready-to-use grilled chicken breast strips
- 1 can (11 ounces) mandarin oranges, drained
- 1 cup sliced fresh strawberries
- 2 slices red onion, separated into rings
- ½ cup reduced-fat raspberry vinaigrette
- ¼ cup honey-roasted sliced almonds

Divide spinach among four serving plates. Top with chicken, oranges, strawberries and onion. Drizzle with vinaigrette and sprinkle with almonds.

CAJUN POPCORN SHRIMP SANDWICHES

You can adjust the heat level in these seafood sammies to your liking by tweaking the amount of seasoning and hot sauce. I use even more hot sauce for dipping.

—KENT WHITAKER ROSSVILLE, GA

START TO FINISH: 30 MIN. • **MAKES:** 4 SERVINGS

- 2 tablespoons butter, melted
- 1 teaspoon garlic powder
- ¼ to ½ teaspoon Cajun seasoning
- 3½ cups frozen breaded popcorn shrimp
- ½ cup mayonnaise
- 1 tablespoon hot pepper sauce
- 1 teaspoon sweet pickle relish
- ½ teaspoon prepared mustard
- 8 pita pocket halves, warmed
- 1 cup shredded lettuce
- 8 thin slices tomato

1. In a resealable plastic bag, combine the butter, garlic powder and Cajun seasoning; add shrimp. Seal bag and toss to coat. Prepare shrimp according to package directions for baking.

2. In a small bowl, combine the mayonnaise, pepper sauce, relish and mustard. Spread into warmed pitas. Fill each pita half with shrimp, lettuce and tomato slices.

MUSHROOM SALAD

Here's a fast salad that we often serve when my husband grills steak. It's the ideal partner for almost any entree, and better yet, it's ready in minutes! You don't typically see mushrooms as the star ingredient in salad recipes, but this one will have you convinced. You decide the kind of mushroom you'd like to use.

—ANNA STODOLAK VOLANT, PA

START TO FINISH: 15 MIN. • **MAKES:** 4 SERVINGS

- ½ pound sliced fresh mushrooms
- 2 green onions, thinly sliced
- 1 garlic clove, minced
- 4½ teaspoons canola oil
- 1 tablespoon minced chives
- 1 tablespoon lemon juice
- 1 tablespoon balsamic vinegar
- ¾ teaspoon sugar
- 6 cups torn mixed salad greens
- ¾ cup salad croutons
- ¼ cup shredded Parmesan cheese

1. In a large skillet, saute the mushrooms, onions and garlic in oil for 3-4 minutes or until mushrooms are tender. Stir in the chives, lemon juice, vinegar and sugar.

2. Arrange salad greens on serving plates; top with mushroom mixture. Sprinkle with croutons and cheese.

PAT'S KING OF STEAKS PHILLY CHEESE STEAK

This ultimate cheesesteak, an iconic sandwich in Philly, is a best-seller at Pat's King of Steaks Restaurant. Patrons praise Pat's thinly cut beef and crusty Italian rolls.

—FRANK OLIVIERI PHILADELPHIA, PA

PREP: 15 MIN. • **COOK:** 5 MIN./BATCH • **MAKES:** 4 SERVINGS

- 1 large onion, sliced
- ½ pound sliced fresh mushrooms, optional
- 1 small green pepper, sliced, optional
- 1 small sweet red pepper, sliced, optional
- 6 tablespoons canola oil, divided
- 1½ pounds beef ribeye steaks, thinly sliced
- 4 crusty Italian rolls, split
  Process cheese sauce
  Ketchup, optional

1. In a large skillet, saute the onion and, if desired, mushrooms and peppers in 3 tablespoons oil until tender. Remove and keep warm. In the same pan, saute beef in remaining oil for 45-60 seconds or until meat reaches desired doneness.

2. On each roll bottom, layer the beef, onion mixture, cheese and ketchup if desired. Replace tops.

TASTE-OF-FALL SALAD

The first time I served this salad, people were so impressed that I knew it was a winner.

—KRISTIN KOSSAK BOZEMAN, MT

START TO FINISH: 25 MIN. • **MAKES:** 6 SERVINGS

- ⅔ cup pecan halves
- ¼ cup balsamic vinegar, divided
  Dash cayenne pepper
  Dash ground cinnamon
- 3 tablespoons sugar, divided
- 1 package (5 ounces) spring mix salad greens
- ¼ cup olive oil
- 1 teaspoon Dijon mustard
- ⅛ teaspoon salt
- 1 medium pear, thinly sliced
- ¼ cup shredded Parmesan cheese

1. In a large heavy skillet, cook the pecans, 2 tablespoons vinegar, cayenne and cinnamon over medium heat until nuts are toasted, about 4 minutes. Sprinkle with 1 tablespoon sugar. Cook and stir for 2-4 minutes or until sugar is melted. Spread on foil to cool.

2. Place salad greens in a large bowl. In a small bowl, whisk the oil, mustard, salt and remaining vinegar and sugar; drizzle over greens and toss to coat. Arrange the greens, pear slices and pecans on six salad plates. Sprinkle with cheese.

SPICY PEANUT SOUP

After enjoying a similar soup at a little cafe, I knew I had to try and duplicate it at home. I think my version comes pretty close. It's the best way I know to chase away winter chills.

—LISA MEREDITH EAGAN, MN

PREP: 35 MIN. • **COOK:** 20 MIN. • **MAKES:** 7 SERVINGS

- 2 medium carrots, chopped
- 1 small onion, chopped
- 2 tablespoons olive oil
- 2 garlic cloves, minced
- 1 large sweet potato, peeled and cubed
- ½ cup chunky peanut butter
- 2 tablespoons red curry paste
- 2 cans (14½ ounces each) vegetable broth
- 1 can (14½ ounces) fire-roasted diced tomatoes, undrained
- 1 bay leaf
- 1 fresh thyme sprig
- ½ teaspoon pepper
- ½ cup unsalted peanuts

1. In a large saucepan, cook carrots and onion in oil over medium heat for 2 minutes. Add garlic; cook 1 minute longer.
2. Stir in sweet potato; cook 2 minutes longer. Stir in peanut butter and curry paste until blended. Add the broth, tomatoes, bay leaf, thyme and pepper.
3. Bring to a boil. Reduce heat; cover and simmer for 15-20 minutes or until sweet potatoes and carrots are tender. (Soup will appear curdled.) Discard bay leaf and thyme sprig. Stir soup until blended. Sprinkle with peanuts.

BLT CATFISH SANDWICHES

A classic gets a rockin' new twist with lemon-grilled catfish and tangy chili sauce instead of mayo. I love to serve these sandwiches with sweet red pepper strips and grilled potato wedges. They're always a huge hit!

—MARY ANN DELL PHOENIXVILLE, PA

START TO FINISH: 30 MIN. • **MAKES:** 4 SERVINGS

- 2 tablespoons chili sauce
- 2 tablespoons ketchup
- ¼ teaspoon hot pepper sauce
- 4 tablespoons lemon juice, divided
- 4 catfish fillets (6 ounces each)
- ½ teaspoon lemon-pepper seasoning
- ¼ teaspoon salt
- 8 slices whole wheat bread, toasted
- 8 cooked bacon strips
- 4 lettuce leaves
- 4 thin slices tomato
- 4 slices red onion

1. In a small bowl, combine the chili sauce, ketchup, pepper sauce and 2 tablespoons lemon juice; set aside.
2. Drizzle remaining lemon juice over fillets; sprinkle with lemon-pepper and salt. Using long-handled tongs, moisten a paper towel with cooking oil and lightly coat the grill rack.
3. Grill catfish, covered, over medium-hot heat or broil 4 in. from the heat for 3-5 minutes on each side or until fish flakes easily with a fork.
4. Layer four slices of toast with catfish, bacon, lettuce, tomato and onion. Spread sauce mixture over remaining toast slices; place on top.

BALSAMIC ARUGULA SALAD

With just four ingredients, this arugula salad comes together in a flash and makes a sophisticated side.

—**LISA SPEER** PALM BEACH, FL

START TO FINISH: 5 MIN. • **MAKES:** 4 SERVINGS

- 6 **cups fresh arugula or baby spinach**
- ½ **cup cherry tomatoes, halved**
- ¼ **cup grated Parmesan cheese**
- ¼ **cup balsamic vinaigrette**

In a large bowl, combine the arugula, tomatoes and cheese. Drizzle with vinaigrette; toss to coat. Serve immediately.

CHILI-BASIL TOMATO SOUP

A co-worker shared this recipe with us, and my husband and I both love it. We serve it with a salad and bread.

—**PENNY LUND** FORT COLLINS, CO

START TO FINISH: 20 MIN. • **MAKES:** 6 SERVINGS (2 QUARTS)

- 1 **can (26 ounces) condensed tomato soup, undiluted**
- 3 **cups 2% milk**
- 1 **can (12 ounces) evaporated milk**
- 1 **can (10 ounces) diced tomatoes and green chilies, undrained**
- 1 **tablespoon minced fresh basil or 1 teaspoon dried basil**
- ½ **teaspoon salt**
- ¼ **teaspoon pepper**
  Shredded Parmesan cheese, optional

In a Dutch oven, combine the first seven ingredients. Cook and stir over medium heat until heated through. Garnish servings with cheese if desired.

ASPARAGUS SALAD WITH GRILLED SALMON

This salad's a little sweet, a little savory and very refreshing. Asparagus is fabulous when grilled!

—**JENNE DELKUS** DES PERES, MO

START TO FINISH: 30 MIN. • **MAKES:** 4 SERVINGS

- ⅓ **cup maple syrup**
- 2 **tablespoons Dijon mustard**
- 1 **tablespoon olive oil**
- 1 **teaspoon snipped fresh dill**
- 4 **salmon fillets (4 ounces each)**
- 1 **pound fresh asparagus, trimmed**
- 4 **cups spring mix salad greens**
- 1 **cup shredded carrots**
- 1 **hard-cooked egg, cut into eight wedges**
  Coarsely ground pepper

1. In a small bowl, whisk the syrup, mustard, oil and dill; set mixture aside.

2. Place salmon skin side down on grill rack. Grill, covered, over medium heat for 5 minutes. Meanwhile, in a shallow bowl, drizzle asparagus with 1 tablespoon dressing; toss to coat. Arrange asparagus on a grilling grid; place on the grill rack with salmon. Spoon 1 tablespoon dressing over salmon.

3. Grill salmon and asparagus, covered, for 4-6 minutes or until salmon flakes easily with a fork and asparagus is crisp-tender, turning asparagus once.

4. Divide salad greens among four plates and sprinkle with carrots. Remove skin from salmon. Arrange the egg wedges, asparagus and salmon over salads. Drizzle with remaining dressing; sprinkle with pepper.

NOTE *If you do not have a grilling grid, use a disposable foil pan. Poke holes in the bottom of the pan with a meat fork to allow liquid to drain.*

SPIRAL STROMBOLI

Two types of deli meat and three kinds of cheese make this satisfying sandwich a tasty way to fill up. I frequently fix this on days when I need a fast meal.

—JEAN GRUENERT BURLINGTON, WI

PREP: 10 MIN. • **BAKE:** 25 MIN. • **MAKES:** 4 SERVINGS

- 1 tube (11 ounces) refrigerated crusty French loaf
- ¾ cup shredded part-skim mozzarella cheese
- ¾ cup shredded cheddar cheese
- ¼ pound each thinly sliced deli salami and ham
- ¼ cup chopped roasted red peppers or 1 jar (2 ounces) pimientos, drained
- 1 tablespoon butter, melted
- 2 tablespoons shredded Parmesan cheese

1. Unroll the dough and pat into a 14-in. x 12-in. rectangle. Sprinkle with mozzarella and cheddar cheese to within ½ in. of edges; top with meat and red peppers. Roll up jelly-roll style, starting with a short side; seal seam and tuck ends under.
2. Place seam side down on a greased baking sheet. Brush with butter; sprinkle with Parmesan cheese. Bake at 375° for 25-30 minutes or until golden brown. Slice with a serrated knife.

AVOCADO-TOMATO SALAD

My mother came up with this salad when she had too many ripe avocados and tomatoes on hand. It's a lovely way to use them up.

—JENNIFER REID FARMINGTON, ME

START TO FINISH: 10 MIN. • **MAKES:** 4 SERVINGS

- 2 medium ripe avocados, peeled and cubed
- 2 cups grape tomatoes
- ¼ cup thinly sliced red onion
- ¼ cup reduced-fat Italian salad dressing
- 1 tablespoon lime juice
- 1 teaspoon sugar
- ½ teaspoon chili powder
- ¼ teaspoon salt
- ¼ teaspoon pepper

In a large bowl, combine the avocados, tomatoes and onion. In a small bowl, whisk the remaining ingredients. Pour over avocado mixture; toss gently to coat.

COCONUT FRUIT SALAD

This refreshing fruit salad will be equally delicious at breakfast, lunch or dinner.

—MILDRED SHERRER FORT WORTH, TX

START TO FINISH: 10 MIN. • **MAKES:** 4 SERVINGS

- 1 can (11 ounces) mandarin oranges, drained
- 1 can (8 ounces) pineapple chunks, drained
- 1 large banana, sliced
- 1 large apple, chopped
- ⅓ cup golden raisins
- ¼ cup flaked coconut, toasted

In a large bowl, combine the first five ingredients. Sprinkle with coconut just before serving.

PORK BURGERS WITH SASSY BARBECUE SAUCE

Even friends not crazy about a little heat will eat up these juicy burgers. You can slap the sauce on chops or ribs as well.
—**ALISA FUNK** KANSAS CITY, MO

PREP: 25 MIN. • **GRILL:** 15 MIN. • **MAKES:** 6 SERVINGS

1¼ cups fresh or frozen pitted dark sweet cherries, thawed
½ cup ketchup
½ cup cherry preserves
1 tablespoon Worcestershire sauce
1 tablespoon honey
1¼ teaspoons cayenne pepper
¾ teaspoon fennel seed, crushed
12 center-cut bacon strips
⅓ cup chopped onion
1 garlic clove, minced
2¼ pounds ground pork
2 teaspoons coarsely ground pepper
1½ teaspoons salt
6 ounces Havarti cheese, sliced
6 hamburger buns, split and toasted
3 cups fresh arugula

1. Place the first seven ingredients in a food processor; cover and process until blended. Set aside. In a large skillet, cook bacon over medium heat until crisp. Remove to paper towels; drain, reserving 1 tablespoon drippings.
2. Saute onion in drippings until tender. Add garlic; cook for 1 minute longer. Add sauce mixture; bring to a boil. Reduce heat; simmer, uncovered, 5-7 minutes until slightly thickened.
3. Meanwhile, in a large bowl, combine pork, pepper and salt. Shape into six patties.
4. Moisten a paper towel with cooking oil; using long-handled tongs, lightly coat the grill rack. Grill burgers, covered, over medium heat or broil 4 in. from the heat for 6-8 minutes on each side or until a thermometer reads 160° and juices run clear.
5. Top with cheese; cover and grill 1-2 minutes longer or until cheese is melted. Serve on buns with arugula, bacon and sauce mixture.

LAND OF ENCHANTMENT POSOLE

We usually make this spicy soup for the holidays when we have lots of family over. But be warned—we never have leftovers.

—SUZANNE CALDWELL ARTESIA, NM

PREP: 30 MIN. • **COOK:** 1 HOUR • **MAKES:** 5 SERVINGS

- 1½ pounds pork stew meat, cut into ¾-inch cubes
- 1 large onion, chopped
- 2 tablespoons canola oil
- 2 garlic cloves, minced
- 3 cups beef broth
- 2 cans (15½ ounces each) hominy, rinsed and drained
- 2 cans (4 ounces each) chopped green chilies
- 1 to 2 jalapeno peppers, seeded and chopped, optional
- ½ teaspoon salt
- ½ teaspoon ground cumin
- ½ teaspoon dried oregano
- ¼ teaspoon pepper
- ¼ teaspoon cayenne pepper
- ½ cup minced fresh cilantro
  Tortilla strips, optional

1. In a Dutch oven, cook pork and onion in oil over medium heat until meat is no longer pink. Add garlic; cook 1 minute longer. Drain. Stir in the broth, hominy, chilies, jalapeno if desired, salt, cumin, oregano, pepper and cayenne.

2. Bring to a boil. Reduce heat; cover and simmer for 45-60 minutes or until meat is tender. Stir in cilantro. Serve with tortilla strips if desired.

NOTE *Wear disposable gloves when cutting hot peppers; the oils can burn skin. Avoid touching your face.*

TORTELLINI TOSSED SALAD

Quick and satisfying, this hearty salad with cheese tortellini will surprise and delight the whole family. For a change of pace, drizzle your favorite salad dressing over the top.

—TASTE OF HOME TEST KITCHEN

START TO FINISH: 25 MIN. • **MAKES:** 6 SERVINGS

- 1 package (9 ounces) refrigerated cheese tortellini
- 4 ounces sliced pancetta, chopped
- 1 package (10 ounces) ready-to-serve Italian blend salad greens
- 1 cup (4 ounces) shredded cheddar cheese
- 1 medium red onion, halved and thinly sliced
- ¾ cup poppy seed salad dressing

1. Cook tortellini according to package directions. Meanwhile, in a large skillet, cook pancetta over medium heat until crisp. Remove to paper towels to drain. Drain tortellini and rinse in cold water.

2. In a large bowl, combine the salad greens, cheese, onion, tortellini and pancetta. Drizzle with salad dressing; toss to coat. Serve immediately.

CHEESY FACTS

If you are buying cheese in bulk (instead of shredded), keep in mind that every 4 ounces of cheese will equal 1 cup shredded. If you notice mold on a block of cheese, trim off the mold plus an extra ½ inch of cheese; the rest of the cheese can still be eaten.

PECAN-CRUSTED CHICKEN WAFFLE SANDWICHES

Chicken and waffles is a Southern tradition, so I turned it into a sandwich with a sweet and spicy mustard sauce to give it a kick.
—**ELIZABETH DUMONT** BOULDER, CO

START TO FINISH: 30 MIN. • **MAKES:** 4 SERVINGS

- 4 boneless skinless chicken breast halves (5 ounces each)
- 1 egg
- ½ cup plus ⅓ cup maple syrup, divided
- 1 cup finely chopped pecans
- ⅔ cup dry bread crumbs
- ¾ teaspoon plus ⅛ teaspoon salt, divided
- ½ teaspoon plus ⅛ teaspoon pepper, divided
- ¼ cup canola oil
- ¼ cup spicy brown mustard
- 1 tablespoon white wine vinegar
- 8 frozen waffles, toasted

1. Flatten chicken to ½-in. thickness. In a shallow bowl, whisk egg and ½ cup syrup. In another shallow bowl, combine the pecans, bread crumbs, ¾ teaspoon salt and ½ teaspoon pepper. Dip the chicken in egg mixture, then coat with the pecan mixture.

2. In a large skillet over medium heat, cook chicken in oil in batches for 5-6 minutes on each side or until no longer pink. Meanwhile, combine the mustard, vinegar and remaining syrup, salt and pepper.

3. Drizzle 1 tablespoon sauce mixture over each of four waffles; top with chicken and drizzle with remaining sauce mixture. Top with remaining waffles.

ROASTED TOMATO AND PEPPER SOUP

You'll want to capture everything the roasted tomatoes, pepper, onion and garlic have to offer in this colorful soup. Add cubed bread pieces to soak it up.
—**DEBBY HARDEN** WILLIAMSTON, MI

PREP: 45 MIN. • **COOK:** 45 MIN. • **MAKES:** 4 SERVINGS

- 2 pounds plum tomatoes, halved lengthwise
- 2 medium sweet red peppers, quartered and seeded
- 2 medium onions, finely chopped
- 2 tablespoons olive oil
- 3 garlic cloves, minced
- 2 teaspoons ground cumin
- 1 teaspoon ground coriander
- 1 carton (32 ounces) reduced-sodium chicken broth
- 3 slices day-old French bread (1 inch thick), crusts removed and cubed
- 1 tablespoon balsamic vinegar
- ¼ teaspoon salt
- ¼ teaspoon pepper
  Shaved Parmesan cheese

1. Place tomatoes and peppers, cut side down, in a 15-in. x 10-in. x 1-in. baking pan. Bake at 425° for 20 minutes. Turn tomatoes and peppers; bake 10-15 minutes longer or until skins are blistered and blackened.

2. Immediately place peppers and tomatoes in a large bowl; cover and let stand for 10 minutes. Peel off and discard skins; coarsely chop tomatoes and peppers.

3. In a large saucepan, saute onions in oil until tender. Add the garlic, cumin and coriander; saute 1 minute longer. Add the broth, tomatoes and peppers. Bring to a boil. Reduce heat; simmer, uncovered, for 30 minutes.

4. Stir in the bread, vinegar, salt and pepper; heat through. Sprinkle servings with cheese.

HOMEMADE CREAM OF MUSHROOM SOUP

Wow friends and family with this rich blend featuring both shiitake and portobello mushrooms. Who knew making homemade soup could be so easy?

—**MICHAEL WILLIAMS** MORENO VALLEY, CA

PREP: 40 MIN. • **COOK:** 50 MIN. • **MAKES:** 8 SERVINGS (2 QUARTS)

½ pound fresh shiitake mushrooms
½ pound baby portobello mushrooms
1 medium onion, chopped
1 medium carrot, chopped
1 tablespoon olive oil
1 tablespoon plus ½ cup butter, divided
5 cups water
1 fresh thyme sprig
1¼ teaspoons salt, divided
¾ teaspoon coarsely ground pepper, divided
2 cups chopped leeks (white portion only)
¼ cup all-purpose flour
1 cup white wine or chicken broth
1 teaspoon minced fresh thyme
1 cup heavy whipping cream
1 cup half-and-half cream
½ cup minced fresh parsley

1. Remove mushroom stems and coarsely chop. Slice mushroom caps into ¼-in. slices. Set aside mushrooms.

2. In a large saucepan, cook the onion, carrot and mushroom stems in oil and 1 tablespoon butter over medium heat until tender. Stir in the water, thyme sprig, ½ teaspoon salt and

¼ teaspoon pepper. Bring to a boil. Reduce heat; simmer, uncovered, for 30 minutes. Strain broth, discarding vegetables and seasonings. Set aside 4½ cups broth.

3. In a Dutch oven, cook leeks in remaining butter over low heat for 25-30 minutes or just until leeks begin to brown, stirring occasionally. Stir in mushroom caps; cook 10 minutes longer or until tender.

4. Stir in flour until blended; gradually add wine. Stir in the thyme, remaining salt and pepper and reserved mushroom broth. Bring to a boil; cook and stir for 2 minutes or until thickened. Stir in the creams and parsley; heat through (do not boil).

BBQ PORK SALAD

This meal is hearty enough for my meat-and-potatoes-loving husband. And did I mention it's delicious? It also looks beautiful served in a glass bowl.

—**VICTORIA SKREDSVIG** SNOHOMISH, WA

START TO FINISH: 10 MIN. • **MAKES:** 4 SERVINGS

1 package (10 ounces) ready-to-serve salad greens
1 can (11 ounces) mandarin oranges, drained
1 cup refrigerated fully cooked barbecued shredded pork, warmed
1 cup smoked almonds
1 medium apple, chopped
½ cup fresh snow or sugar snap peas
¼ cup reduced-fat balsamic vinaigrette

In a large bowl, combine the first six ingredients. Drizzle with vinaigrette; serve immediately.

TURKEY-TARRAGON NOODLE SOUP

I think tarragon and turkey are a match made in flavor heaven—and this recipe proves it!

—CAROLYN KETCHUM WAKEFIELD, MA

START TO FINISH: 30 MIN. • **MAKES:** 6 SERVINGS

- 6 cups chicken broth
- 2 medium carrots, thinly sliced
- 1 celery rib, thinly sliced
- 2 tablespoons lemon juice
- 1 bay leaf
- ½ teaspoon salt
- ¼ teaspoon pepper
- 3 cups uncooked medium egg noodles
- 3 cups coarsely chopped cooked turkey
- 2 tablespoons torn fresh tarragon leaves
  Additional fresh tarragon leaves, optional

1. In a large saucepan, combine the first seven ingredients; bring to a boil. Reduce heat; cover and simmer for 8-10 minutes or until vegetables are tender.

2. Return to a boil; add noodles. Cook 5-6 minutes longer or until noodles are tender. Stir in turkey and tarragon; heat through. Discard bay leaf. If desired, top servings with additional tarragon.

CREOLE-SPICED SHRIMP PO' BOYS

My father is Cajun, and I grew up eating Cajun food. This recipe makes me recall happy childhood memories. Sometimes I use oysters or crawfish in addition to—or instead of—the shrimp.

—STACEY JOHNSON BONNEY LAKE, WA

PREP: 30 MIN. • **COOK:** 5 MIN./BATCH
MAKES: 4 SANDWICHES (1 CUP SAUCE)

- ¾ cup mayonnaise
- ½ cup ketchup
- 1 teaspoon prepared horseradish
- 1 teaspoon hot pepper sauce
  Oil for frying
- ¾ cup all-purpose flour
- ¾ cup cornmeal
- 1 tablespoon Creole seasoning
- 1 teaspoon salt
- 1 pound uncooked medium shrimp, peeled and deveined
  (tails removed)
- 4 French rolls, split
- 2 cups shredded lettuce
- 2 medium tomatoes, sliced

1. In a small bowl, mix the mayonnaise, ketchup, horseradish and pepper sauce. Cover and chill until serving.

2. In an electric skillet, heat ½ in. of oil to 375°. In a large resealable plastic bag, combine the flour, cornmeal, Creole seasoning and salt.

3. Add shrimp, a few at a time; seal bag and toss to coat. Fry shrimp in oil for 2-3 minutes on each side or until golden brown. Drain on paper towels.

4. Spread rolls with some of the sauce. Layer bottoms with lettuce, shrimp and tomatoes; replace tops. Serve with remaining sauce.

NOTE *The following spices may be substituted for 1 tablespoon Creole seasoning: ¾ teaspoon each paprika, garlic powder and salt; and a pinch each of cayenne, dried thyme and ground cumin.*

CHEESE & HAM FILLED SANDWICHES

Here's a blue-ribbon version of a classic sandwich. When guests first try the crusty buns filled with ham and melted goat cheese, they quickly reach for seconds. It's bound to become a go-to recipe for you!

—CLARA HEDRICH CHILTON, WI

START TO FINISH: 30 MIN. • **MAKES:** 4 SERVINGS

- 4 hoagie buns
- 1 small red onion, chopped
- 1 teaspoon olive oil
- 1 cup (4 ounces) shredded fontina cheese
- 1 cup (4 ounces) shredded aged goat cheese
- 1 cup cubed fully cooked ham
- ⅓ cup roasted sweet red peppers, drained and cut into strips
- 2 teaspoons minced fresh parsley
- ½ teaspoon minced fresh thyme or ¼ teaspoon dried thyme
- ⅛ teaspoon salt
- ⅛ teaspoon pepper

1. Cut a thin slice off the top of each bun. Hollow out bottoms of buns, leaving a ¼-in. shell (discard removed bread or save for another use).

2. In a small skillet, saute onion in oil until tender. Remove from the heat; stir in the cheeses, ham, red peppers, parsley, thyme, salt and pepper.

3. Spoon into shells; replace tops. Wrap each sandwich in foil, leaving top open. Place on a baking sheet. Bake at 375° for 10-14 minutes or until cheese is melted.

MAIN DISHES

There's nothing like welcoming folks to your table for a home-cooked meal. It's a snap to prepare those tried-and-true favorites with this chapter. Simply turn here for all of the comfort foods your family and friends crave!

NUTTY OVEN-FRIED CHICKEN

Pecans are plentiful in the South, and so is fried chicken! I love to prepare and serve this easy dish because the chicken comes out moist and crispy.

—DIANE HIXON NICEVILLE, FL

PREP: 10 MIN. • **BAKE:** 1 HOUR • **MAKES:** 6 SERVINGS

- ½ cup evaporated milk
- 1 cup biscuit/baking mix
- ⅓ cup finely chopped pecans
- 2 teaspoons paprika
- ½ teaspoon salt
- ½ teaspoon poultry seasoning
- ½ teaspoon rubbed sage
- 1 broiler/fryer chicken (3 to 4 pounds), cut up
- ⅓ cup butter, melted

1. Place milk in a shallow bowl. In another shallow bowl, combine the baking mix, pecans and seasonings. Dip chicken pieces in milk, then coat generously with pecan mixture.

2. Place in a lightly greased 13-in. x 9-in. baking dish. Drizzle with butter. Bake, uncovered, at 350° for 1 hour or until chicken is golden brown and crispy and juices run clear.

PORK CHOPS WITH CREAMY MUSTARD NOODLES

Here's an entree you'll turn to time and again. Try it with chicken! Poultry works well with the zesty mix of mustards.

—MARGARET BRACHER ROBERTSDALE, AL

START TO FINISH: 30 MIN. • **MAKES:** 4 SERVINGS

- 6 cups uncooked egg noodles
- ½ teaspoon salt
- ½ teaspoon pepper
- ¼ teaspoon garlic powder
- ¼ teaspoon dried thyme
- ¼ teaspoon dried oregano
- 4 boneless pork loin chops (6 ounces each)
- 1 tablespoon olive oil
- 1 can (10½ ounces) condensed beef broth, undiluted
- ½ cup water
- ⅔ cup whipped cream cheese
- 2 tablespoons butter
- 1 tablespoon spicy brown mustard
- 1 tablespoon yellow mustard
  Minced fresh parsley

1. Cook noodles according to package directions.

2. Meanwhile, combine the salt, pepper, garlic powder, thyme and oregano; rub over pork chops. In a large skillet, brown chops in oil. Add broth and water. Bring to a boil. Reduce heat; cover and simmer for 8-10 minutes or until a thermometer reads 160°, turning once. Remove chops and keep warm.

3. Stir the cream cheese, butter and mustards into the skillet. Cook and stir over medium heat until thickened. Drain noodles; add to skillet and toss to coat. Serve with pork chops. Garnish with parsley.

CHIPOTLE MAC & CHEESE

Beefy and bubbly, this Southwestern pasta bake heats up dinner with a chipotle-pepper bite.

—**CYNDY GERKEN** NAPLES, FL

PREP: 35 MIN. • **BAKE:** 30 MIN. • **MAKES:** 2 PANS (4 SERVINGS EACH)

- 1 package (16 ounces) spiral pasta
- 2 pounds ground beef
- 2 large onions, chopped
- 2 large green peppers, chopped
- 3 garlic cloves, minced
- 1 can (28 ounces) crushed tomatoes
- 1 can (10¾ ounces) condensed cheddar cheese soup, undiluted
- ½ cup 2% milk
- 1 chipotle pepper in adobo sauce, chopped
- 2 tablespoons chili powder
- 1 tablespoon ground cumin
- 1 teaspoon cayenne pepper
- 1 teaspoon dried oregano
- ½ teaspoon salt
- ¼ teaspoon pepper
- 2 cups (8 ounces) shredded Monterey Jack cheese
- 2 tablespoons minced fresh cilantro, optional

1. Cook pasta according to package directions to al dente. Meanwhile, in a Dutch oven, cook the beef, onions, green peppers and garlic over medium heat until meat is no longer pink. Drain.

2. Stir in the tomatoes, soup, milk, chipotle pepper and seasonings. Bring to a boil. Reduce heat; cover and simmer for 15 minutes or until thickened.

3. Drain pasta; stir into meat mixture. Divide between two greased 8-in. square baking dishes; sprinkle with cheese and cilantro if desired.

4. Cover and freeze one casserole for up to 3 months. Cover and bake the remaining casserole at 350° for 20 minutes. Uncover; bake 8-10 minutes longer or until bubbly and cheese is melted.

SOUTHERN SHRIMP AND GRITS

We sometimes call this dish breakfast shrimp. Serve it for brunch, dinner or when company's coming. It's down-home comfort food at its finest.

—**MANDY RIVERS** LEXINGTON, SC

PREP: 15 MIN. • **COOK:** 20 MIN. • **MAKES:** 4 SERVINGS

- 2 cups reduced-sodium chicken broth
- 2 cups 2% milk
- ⅓ cup butter, cubed
- ¾ teaspoon salt
- ½ teaspoon pepper
- ¾ cup uncooked old-fashioned grits
- 1 cup (4 ounces) shredded cheddar cheese

SHRIMP

- 8 thick-sliced bacon strips, chopped
- 1 pound uncooked medium shrimp, peeled and deveined
- 3 garlic cloves, minced
- 1 teaspoon Cajun or blackened seasoning
- 4 green onions, chopped

1. In a large saucepan, bring the broth, milk, butter, salt and pepper to a boil. Slowly stir in grits. Reduce heat. Cover and cook for 12-14 minutes or until thickened, stirring occasionally. Stir in cheese until melted. Set aside and keep warm.

2. In a large skillet, cook bacon over medium heat until crisp. Remove to paper towels with a slotted spoon; drain, reserving 4 teaspoons drippings. Saute the shrimp, garlic and seasoning in drippings until shrimp turn pink. Serve with grits and sprinkle with onions.

SLOPPY JOE VEGGIE CASSEROLE

Sloppy joe flavor meets veggie lasagna wholesomeness in this recipe. My family really goes for the dynamic duo.
—**SUE SCHMIDTKE** ORO VALLEY, AZ

PREP: 25 MIN. • **BAKE:** 30 MIN. • **MAKES:** 8 SERVINGS

- 2½ cups uncooked penne pasta
- 1 pound ground beef
- 1 small onion, chopped
- 1 package (16 ounces) frozen mixed vegetables
- 1½ cups water
- 1 can (15 ounces) tomato sauce
- 1 can (6 ounces) tomato paste
- 1 envelope sloppy joe mix
- 1 tablespoon dried parsley flakes
- ½ teaspoon dried oregano
- 2 cups (16 ounces) 2% cottage cheese
- 1½ cups (6 ounces) shredded Colby-Monterey Jack cheese

1. Cook pasta according to package directions.
2. Meanwhile, cook beef and onion in a large skillet over medium heat until meat is no longer pink; drain. Add the vegetables, water, tomato sauce, tomato paste, sloppy joe mix, parsley and oregano. Bring to a boil. Reduce heat; simmer, uncovered, for 7-9 minutes or until vegetables are crisp-tender. Drain pasta; stir into beef mixture. Spoon half of the mixture into a greased 13-in. x 9-in. baking dish. Top with cottage cheese, ¾ cup Colby-Monterey Jack and the remaining pasta mixture. Cover and bake at 350° for 25 minutes. Uncover; sprinkle with remaining Colby-Monterey Jack cheese. Bake 5-10 minutes longer or until bubbly and cheese is melted.

DESERT OASIS CHICKEN

Boneless, skinless chicken breasts cook quickly and pair nicely with sweet and spicy ingredients found in this fast main course.
—**ROXANNE CHAN** ALBANY, CA

START TO FINISH: 20 MIN. • **MAKES:** 4 SERVINGS

- 4 boneless skinless chicken breast halves (5 ounces each)
- 1 tablespoon olive oil
- ¼ teaspoon salt
- ¼ teaspoon crushed red pepper flakes
- ¼ teaspoon ground cumin
- ¼ teaspoon ground cinnamon
- 1 cup canned apricot halves, sliced
- ⅓ cup dried tropical fruit
- ¼ cup water
- 1 tablespoon honey
  Minced fresh parsley

1. Flatten chicken slightly; rub with oil. Combine the salt, pepper flakes, cumin and cinnamon. Sprinkle over chicken.
2. In a large skillet, brown chicken on both sides. Add the apricots, tropical fruit, water and honey; bring to a boil. Reduce heat; cover and simmer for 5-6 minutes or until a thermometer reads 170°. Garnish with parsley.

OLD-WORLD PIZZA MEAT LOAF

Good food and memories are made in the kitchen. A recipe like this one, that's been passed down through generations, is worth its weight in gold. In fact, this recipe comes from my grandma; we all love it!

—**NICHOLAS KING** DULUTH, MN

PREP: 20 MIN. • **BAKE:** 55 MIN. + STANDING
MAKES: 8 SERVINGS

- 1 egg, lightly beaten
- 1½ cups seasoned bread crumbs
- 1 can (4¼ ounces) chopped ripe olives, drained
- 1 can (4 ounces) mushroom stems and pieces, drained
- 1 cup (4 ounces) shredded part-skim mozzarella cheese
- 1 small green pepper, chopped
- 1 small onion, chopped
- 2 tablespoons onion soup mix
- 1 cup pizza sauce, divided
- 2 pounds ground beef
- ¼ cup grated Parmesan cheese

1. In a large bowl, combine the egg, bread crumbs, olives, mushrooms, mozzarella cheese, pepper, onion, soup mix and ½ cup pizza sauce. Crumble beef over mixture and mix well. Shape into a 10-in. x 6-in. rectangle and place in a greased 15-in. x 10-in. x 1-in. baking pan; Spoon remaining pizza sauce over top.
2. Bake, uncovered, at 350° for 45 minutes. Sprinkle with Parmesan cheese. Bake 10-15 minutes longer or until no pink remains and a thermometer reads 160°. Let stand 10 minutes before slicing.

EASY TEXAS BBQ BRISKET

My mom tried my brisket and said it was even better than the version she used to prepare. What a compliment! Jazz up your sandwiches and tacos with the leftovers.

—**AUDRA RORICK** SOUTH FORK, CO

PREP: 15 MIN. + MARINATING • **BAKE:** 4 HOURS
MAKES: 10 SERVINGS

- 2 tablespoons packed brown sugar
- 1 tablespoon salt
- 1 tablespoon onion powder
- 1 tablespoon garlic powder
- 1 tablespoon ground mustard
- 1 tablespoon smoked paprika
- 1 tablespoon pepper
- 2 fresh beef briskets (3½ pounds each)
- 1 bottle (10 ounces) Heinz 57 steak sauce
- ½ cup liquid smoke
- ¼ cup Worcestershire sauce

1. In a small bowl, combine the first seven ingredients. With a fork or sharp knife, prick holes in briskets. Rub meat with seasoning mixture. Cover and refrigerate overnight.
2. Place briskets, fat sides up, in a roasting pan. In a small bowl, combine the steak sauce, liquid smoke and Worcestershire sauce; pour over meat.
3. Cover tightly with foil; bake at 325° for 4 to 5 hours or until tender. Let stand in juices for 15 minutes. To serve, thinly slice across the grain. Skim fat from pan juices; spoon over meat.
NOTE *This is a fresh beef brisket, not corned beef.*

BASIL POLENTA WITH RATATOUILLE

We served this during our wedding reception...and our guests loved it! We heard raves about the polenta topped with colorful ratatouille, our version of the classic French classic.
—**KIMBERLY HAMMOND** KINGWOOD, TX

PREP: 25 MIN. + CHILLING • **COOK:** 40 MIN. • **MAKES:** 4 SERVINGS

- 4 cups water
- ½ teaspoon salt, divided
- 1 cup cornmeal
- ½ cup minced fresh basil
- 1 medium eggplant, peeled and cut into ½-inch cubes
- 1 medium onion, halved and sliced
- 1 medium green pepper, julienned
- 5 tablespoons olive oil, divided
- 4 garlic cloves, minced
- 1 can (14½ ounces) diced tomatoes, drained
- ½ cup pitted Greek olives, sliced
- 1 teaspoon dried oregano
- ¼ teaspoon pepper
  Fresh basil leaves

1. In a large heavy saucepan, bring water and ¼ teaspoon salt to a boil. Reduce heat to a gentle boil; slowly whisk in cornmeal. Cook and stir with a wooden spoon for 15-20 minutes or until polenta is thickened and pulls away cleanly from the sides of the pan. Stir in basil.

2. Spread into an 8-in. square baking dish coated with cooking spray. Refrigerate for 30 minutes.

3. Meanwhile, in a large skillet, saute the eggplant, onion and green pepper in 2 tablespoons oil until crisp-tender. Add garlic; cook 1 minute longer. Stir in the tomatoes, olives, oregano, pepper and remaining salt. Cook and stir over medium heat for 10-12 minutes or until vegetables are tender.

4. Cut polenta into four squares. In another large skillet, cook polenta in remaining oil in batches for 7-8 minutes on each side or until golden brown. Serve with ratatouille; garnish with basil.

TACO SHEPHERD'S PIE

When lean ground beef is on sale, you'll want to stock up so you can whip up this family-pleasing entree any time. The recipe makes two hearty meat pies, so you can enjoy one for dinner and pop the other one in the freezer for busy nights.
—**SANDRA PARKER** GLEN BURNIE, MD

PREP: 30 MIN. • **BAKE:** 40 MIN. • **MAKES:** 2 PIES (6 SERVINGS EACH)

- 1 package (14.1 ounces) refrigerated pie pastry
- 6 large potatoes, peeled and cut into chunks
- 2 pounds lean ground beef (90% lean)
- 14 green onions, chopped (white portion only)
- 1¼ cups water
- 2 envelopes taco seasoning
- 1 cup 2% milk
- ¼ cup butter
- 2 teaspoons garlic powder
- ¼ teaspoon salt
- ¼ teaspoon pepper
- 2 cups (8 ounces) shredded sharp cheddar cheese
- 2 cups (8 ounces) shredded pepper jack cheese

1. Roll out pastry to fit two 9-in. deep-dish pie plates. Transfer pastry to pie plates; flute edges. Line unpricked pastry with a double thickness of heavy-duty foil. Fill with dried beans, uncooked rice or pie weights.

2. Bake at 450° for 8 minutes. Remove foil and weights; bake 5 minutes longer. Cool on a wire rack.

3. Place the potatoes in a Dutch oven and cover with water. Bring to a boil. Reduce heat; cover and cook for 15-20 minutes or until tender.

4. Meanwhile, in a large skillet, cook beef and onions over medium heat until meat is no longer pink; drain. Stir in water and taco seasoning. Bring to a boil; cook until liquid is evaporated. Spoon into pastry shells.

5. Drain potatoes and place in a large bowl. Add the milk, butter, garlic powder, salt and pepper; mash until smooth. Spread over meat mixture.

6. Sprinkle one pie with half of the cheeses. Cover and freeze for up to 3 months. Bake remaining pie, uncovered, at 350° for 35 minutes. Sprinkle with remaining cheeses. Bake 5-10 minutes longer or until heated through and cheese is melted.
NOTE *Let pie weights cool before storing. Beans and rice may be reused for pie weights, but not for cooking.*

GET CHOPPIN'!

To chop veggies, hold the handle of a chef's knife with one hand, and rest the fingers of your other hand on the top of the blade near the tip. Using the handle to guide and apply pressure, move the knife in an arc across the food with a rocking motion until the pieces are the desired size. Chopping should produce ¼-in. to ½-in. pieces.

SPEEDY STOVETOP SPAGHETTI

Here's a new take on an old favorite that you're sure to make often. The pasta cooks in the skillet, and because it simmers for 20 minutes, you'll have plenty of time to fix the rest of the meal.
—**KRISTIN NANNEY** MARBLE HILL, MO

PREP: 10 MIN. • **COOK:** 30 MIN. • **MAKES:** 4 SERVINGS

- 1 **pound bulk Italian sausage**
- ½ **cup finely chopped onion**
- 1 **garlic clove, minced**
- 3 **ounces uncooked spaghetti, broken into 1-inch pieces**
- 1 **tablespoon minced fresh parsley or 1 teaspoon dried parsley flakes**
- 1 **teaspoon dried basil**
- 1 **can (28 ounces) diced tomatoes, undrained**
- 1 **can (15 ounces) tomato sauce**
- 3 **tablespoons dry red wine or beef broth**
- ½ **teaspoon sugar**
- 3 **tablespoons shredded Parmesan cheese**

1. Saute the sausage, onion and garlic in a large skillet for 5-7 minutes or until sausage is no longer pink; drain. Stir in the spaghetti, parsley, basil, tomatoes, tomato sauce, wine and sugar.
2. Bring to a boil. Reduce heat; cover and simmer for 20 minutes or until spaghetti is tender. Sprinkle with cheese. Cover and cook 2-3 minutes longer or until cheese is melted.

STACKED CHICKEN CORDON BLEU

Sliced deli ham and Swiss cheese come together in a restaurant-quality entree that cooks in moments. It's wonderful for company or a special weeknight meal.
—**ANGELA SPENGLER** CLOVIS, NM

PREP: 25 MIN. • **COOK:** 15 MIN. • **MAKES:** 4 SERVINGS

- 4 **boneless skinless chicken breast halves (5 ounces each)**
- ¼ **cup all-purpose flour**
- ¼ **teaspoon salt**
- ¼ **teaspoon pepper**
- 1 **egg**
- 1 **tablespoon water**
- ½ **cup dry bread crumbs**
- ½ **cup ground almonds**
- ¼ **cup olive oil**
- 4 **thin slices deli ham**
- 2 **slices Swiss cheese, halved**

SAUCE
- ⅔ **cup condensed cream of chicken and mushroom soup, undiluted**
- 2 **tablespoons sour cream**
- 2 **tablespoons 2% milk**
- ¼ **teaspoon pepper**
- ⅛ **teaspoon salt**
  Minced fresh parsley

1. Flatten chicken to ½-in. thickness; set aside. In a shallow bowl, combine the flour, salt and pepper. In another shallow bowl, whisk egg and water. In a third bowl, combine bread crumbs and almonds. Coat chicken with flour mixture, then dip in egg mixture and coat with bread crumb mixture.
2. In a large skillet, cook chicken in oil over medium heat for 5-6 minutes on each side or until a thermometer reads 170°. Top with ham and cheese; cover and cook 1-2 minutes longer or until cheese is melted.
3. Meanwhile, in a small saucepan, combine the soup, sour cream, milk, pepper and salt. Cook and stir over medium heat until heated through. Serve with chicken; sprinkle with parsley.

Catch of the Day

Whether you reel in the fish fresh or buy it locally, serve it up with these enticing recipes ready in no time at all. You won't need to go "fishing" for compliments with any of them!

SPINACH SALMON BUNDLES

Rich salmon encased in flaky golden-brown pastry will delight family and guests—and no one has to know how easy it is.

—**LARISSA GEDNEY** MYRTLE BEACH, SC

START TO FINISH: 30 MIN. • **MAKES:** 4 SERVINGS

- 2 tubes (8 ounces each) refrigerated crescent rolls
- 4 salmon fillets (6 ounces each)
- ¼ teaspoon salt
- ¼ teaspoon pepper
- ⅓ cup garlic-herb spreadable cheese
- 1 package (10 ounces) frozen chopped spinach, thawed and squeezed dry

1. Unroll crescent dough and separate into four rectangles; seal perforations. Place a salmon fillet in the center of each rectangle; sprinkle with salt and pepper. Spoon spreadable cheese over each; top with spinach. Fold dough over filling and pinch edges to seal.
2. Place on an ungreased baking sheet. Bake at 400° for 20-25 minutes or until golden brown.
NOTE *This recipe was tested with Alouette spreadable cheese.*

BATTER-UP WALLEYE

Nothing is more rewarding than celebrating the day's catch with this fresh dish. Don't have walleye? Go ahead and switch up the recipe with a different fish.

—**ALESHA OSTER** WILLISTON, ND

START TO FINISH: 30 MIN. • **MAKES:** 4 SERVINGS

- 1 cup biscuit/baking mix
- 1 tablespoon garlic powder
- 1 tablespoon onion powder
- 1 tablespoon Cajun seasoning
- 1½ teaspoons pepper
- 1 teaspoon salt
- ½ cup 2% milk
  Oil for frying
- 1 pound walleye fillets, skin removed
  Lemon wedges

1. In a shallow bowl, mix the first six ingredients. Place milk in a separate shallow bowl. In an electric skillet, heat ¼ in. of oil to 375°.
2. In batches, dip fish in milk, then coat with baking mix mixture; fry for 5 minutes on each side or until golden brown and fish flakes easily with a fork. Serve immediately with lemon wedges.

SOUTHERN PECAN CATFISH

I coat the catfish in pecans, then top it with a thick, rich cream sauce. It looks like I spent all day on it, but it's actually very speedy to prepare. Garnish it with lemon wedges, parsley or more chopped pecans if desired. It's loaded with the sort of goodness everyone craves.

—**MARY ANN GRIFFIN** BOWLING GREEN, KY

START TO FINISH: 30 MIN. • **MAKES:** 4 SERVINGS

- 1 **cup finely chopped pecans, divided**
- ½ **cup cornmeal**
- 1 **teaspoon salt, divided**
- 1 **teaspoon pepper, divided**
- 4 **catfish fillets (6 ounces each)**
- ½ **cup butter, divided**
- ½ **cup heavy whipping cream**
- 2 **tablespoons lemon juice**
- 1 **to 2 tablespoons minced fresh parsley**

1. In a shallow bowl, combine ½ cup pecans, cornmeal, ½ teaspoon salt and ½ teaspoon pepper. Coat catfish with pecan mixture.

2. In a large skillet, melt ¼ cup butter over medium-high heat; fry fillets for 6-7 minutes on each side or until fish flakes easily with a fork. Remove and keep warm.

3. In the same skillet, melt remaining butter over medium heat. Add remaining pecans; cook and stir for 1 minute. Add the cream, lemon juice and remaining salt and pepper; cook and stir for 1 minute. Stir in parsley. Serve with catfish.

TILAPIA & LEMON SAUCE

Enjoy a fish and citrus combo when it's chilly out! It's sure to evoke thoughts of warm summer days.

—**SUSAN TAUL** BIRMINGHAM, AL

START TO FINISH: 30 MIN. • **MAKES:** 4 SERVINGS

- ¼ **cup plus 1 tablespoon all-purpose flour, divided**
- 1 **teaspoon salt**
- 4 **tilapia fillets (4 ounces each)**
- 2 **tablespoons plus 2 teaspoons butter, divided**
- ⅓ **cup reduced-sodium chicken broth**
- 2 **tablespoons white wine or additional reduced-sodium chicken broth**
- 1½ **teaspoons lemon juice**
- 1½ **teaspoons minced fresh parsley**
- 2 **cups hot cooked rice**
- ¼ **cup sliced almonds, toasted**

1. In a shallow bowl, combine ¼ cup flour and salt. Dip fillets in flour mixture.

2. In a large nonstick skillet coated with cooking spray, cook fillets in 2 tablespoons butter over medium-high heat for 4-5 minutes on each side or until fish flakes easily with a fork. Remove and keep warm.

3. In the same skillet, melt remaining butter. Stir in remaining flour until smooth; gradually add the broth, wine and lemon juice. Bring to a boil; cook and stir for 2 minutes or until thickened. Stir in parsley. Serve fish and sauce with rice; garnish with almonds.

HERBED BLUE CHEESE STEAKS

Fresh herbs and tangy cheese top my tenderloin steaks. I've also made this recipe with pork tenderloin, replacing the basil and tarragon with sage.

—BRENDA PROSSER PULASKI, VA

PREP: 25 MIN. • **BAKE:** 15 MIN. • **MAKES:** 4 SERVINGS

- ¼ cup crumbled blue cheese
- ¼ cup soft bread crumbs
- 4 teaspoons olive oil, divided
- 1 teaspoon pepper, divided
- ¾ teaspoon minced fresh basil or ¼ teaspoon dried basil
- ¾ teaspoon minced fresh oregano or ¼ teaspoon dried oregano
- ¾ teaspoon snipped fresh dill or ¼ teaspoon dill weed
- ¾ teaspoon minced chives
- ½ teaspoon minced fresh tarragon or ¼ teaspoon dried tarragon
- 4 beef tenderloin steaks (6 ounces each)
- ½ teaspoon salt
- ¼ cup chopped onion
- 2 garlic cloves, minced
- 1 cup reduced-sodium beef broth
- ¾ cup Cognac or additional reduced-sodium beef broth

1. In a small bowl, combine the blue cheese, bread crumbs, 1 teaspoon oil, ½ teaspoon pepper, basil, oregano, dill, chives and tarragon; set aside.

2. Sprinkle steaks with salt and remaining pepper. In a large skillet over medium-high heat, cook steaks in remaining oil for 2 minutes on each side. Transfer to a greased 15-in. x 10-in. x 1-in. baking pan; top with blue cheese mixture.

3. Bake at 350° for 12-18 minutes or until meat reaches desired doneness (for medium-rare, a thermometer should read 145°; medium, 160°; well-done, 170°).

4. Meanwhile, in the same skillet, saute onion until tender. Add garlic; cook 1 minute longer. Gradually stir in broth and Cognac, scraping up any browned bits from bottom of pan. Cook until liquid is reduced by half. Serve with steaks.

MOM'S TURKEY TETRAZZINI

This hearty dish is just the kind of stick-to-your-ribs comfort food you're looking for.

—JUDY BATSON TAMPA, FL

PREP: 25 MIN. • **BAKE:** 25 MIN. + STANDING • **MAKES:** 6 SERVINGS

- 1 package (12 ounces) fettuccine
- ½ pound sliced fresh mushrooms
- 1 medium onion, chopped
- ¼ cup butter, cubed
- 3 tablespoons all-purpose flour
- 3 cups 2% milk
- 1 cup white wine or chicken broth
- 3 cups cubed cooked turkey
- ¾ teaspoon salt
- ½ teaspoon pepper
- ½ teaspoon hot pepper sauce
- ½ cup shredded Parmesan cheese
  Paprika, optional

1. Cook fettuccine according to package directions.

2. Meanwhile, in a large skillet, saute the mushrooms and onion in butter until tender. Stir in flour until blended; gradually add milk and wine. Bring to a boil; cook and stir for 2 minutes or until thickened. Stir in the turkey, salt, pepper and pepper sauce.

3. Drain fettuccine. Layer half of the fettuccine, turkey mixture and cheese in a greased 13-in. x 9-in. baking dish. Repeat layers. Sprinkle with paprika if desired.

4. Cover and bake at 375° for 25-30 minutes or until heated through. Let stand for 10 minutes before serving.

SAUSAGE BROCCOLI CALZONE

Impress guests with just a few easy ingredients, such as packaged French bread dough, sausage, cheese and veggies.

—**ANGIE COLOMBO** OLDSMAR, FL

PREP: 20 MIN. • **BAKE:** 20 MIN. • **MAKES:** 6 SERVINGS

- 12 ounces bulk pork sausage
- 1½ teaspoons minced fresh sage
- 1 tube (11 ounces) refrigerated crusty French loaf
- 2 cups frozen chopped broccoli, thawed and drained
- 1 cup (4 ounces) shredded part-skim mozzarella cheese
- 1 cup (4 ounces) shredded cheddar cheese

1. In a small skillet, cook sausage over medium heat until no longer pink; drain. Stir in sage.

2. On an ungreased baking sheet, unroll dough starting at the seam; pat into a 14-in. x 12-in. rectangle. Spoon sausage lengthwise across center of dough. Sprinkle with broccoli and cheeses. Bring long sides of dough to the center over filling; pinch seams to seal. Turn calzone seam side down.

3. Bake at 350° for 20-25 minutes or until golden brown. Serve warm.

MACARONI AND CHEESE WITH GARLIC BREAD CUBES

Creamy and ooey-gooey, my homemade macaroni and cheese is over-the-top good. Garlicky croutons add a delicious crunch.

—**AMY WARREN** MAINEVILLE, OH

PREP: 50 MIN. • **BAKE:** 30 MIN. • **MAKES:** 12 SERVINGS

- 1 pound uncooked spiral pasta
- 2 tablespoons butter, melted

BREAD CUBES

- 1 garlic clove, minced
- 3 tablespoons butter
- 4 cups cubed French bread (½-inch cubes)
- ¼ teaspoon seasoned salt

SAUCE

- 1 small onion, finely chopped
- 3 tablespoons butter
- 1 garlic clove, minced
- 3 tablespoons all-purpose flour
- 3 cups half-and-half cream
- 1 package (8 ounces) process cheese (Velveeta), cubed
- ½ teaspoon sugar
- ½ teaspoon seasoned salt
- ½ teaspoon ground mustard
- ¼ teaspoon hot pepper sauce
- ⅛ teaspoon pepper
- 1 cup (4 ounces) shredded fontina cheese
- 1 cup (4 ounces) shredded cheddar cheese
- ½ cup shredded Swiss cheese
- ½ cup grated Parmesan cheese
- ¼ teaspoon paprika

1. Cook pasta according to package directions. Drain and transfer to a greased 13-in. x 9-in. baking dish; add melted butter and toss to coat.

2. In a large skillet, saute garlic in butter until tender. Place bread cubes in a large bowl. Drizzle with butter mixture and sprinkle with seasoned salt; toss to coat.

3. In the same skillet, saute onion in butter until tender. Add garlic; cook 1 minute longer. Stir in flour until blended; gradually add cream. Bring to a boil; cook and stir for 2 minutes or until thickened. Add the process cheese, sugar, seasoned salt, mustard, pepper sauce and pepper; stir until cheese is melted.

4. In a bowl, combine the fontina, cheddar and Swiss cheeses. Add 2 cups cheese mixture to sauce; stir until melted. Pour over pasta; stir to combine. Sprinkle with remaining cheese mixture. Top with bread cubes, Parmesan cheese and paprika.

5. Bake at 350° for 30-35 minutes or until bubbly and bread is lightly browned.

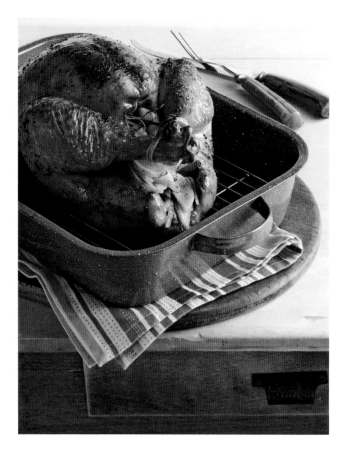

GOLDEN ROASTED TURKEY

Forget about dealing with a dry turkey—brining the bird overnight and stuffing with apples results in juicy, tender meat.
—**MICHAEL WILLIAMS** MORENO VALLEY, CA

PREP: 40 MIN. + MARINATING • **BAKE:** 2¾ HOURS + STANDING
MAKES: 14 SERVINGS

- 4 cartons (32 ounces each) vegetable broth
- 1 cup kosher salt
- ½ cup packed brown sugar
- 1 tablespoon whole peppercorns
- 1½ teaspoons whole allspice
- 1½ teaspoons minced fresh gingerroot
- 4 quarts cold water
- 2 turkey-size oven roasting bags
- 1 turkey (14 to 16 pounds)
- 1 cup water
- 1 medium apple, sliced
- 1 small onion, sliced
- 1 cinnamon stick (3 inches)
- 4 fresh rosemary sprigs
- 6 fresh sage leaves
- 1 tablespoon canola oil
- ½ teaspoon pepper

1. In a stockpot, combine the first six ingredients. Bring to a boil. Cook and stir until salt and brown sugar are dissolved. Remove from the heat. Add the cold water to cool the brine to room temperature.

2. Place a turkey-size oven roasting bag inside a second roasting bag; add turkey. Carefully pour cooled brine into bag. Squeeze

out as much air as possible; seal bags and turn to coat. Place in a roasting pan. Refrigerate for 18-24 hours, turning occasionally.

3. In a microwave-safe bowl, combine the water, apple, onion and cinnamon. Microwave on high for 3-4 minutes or until apples are tender; drain water.

4. Drain and discard brine. Rinse turkey under cold water; pat dry. Place cooked apple mixture, rosemary and sage in turkey cavity. Skewer turkey openings; tie drumsticks together.

5. Place turkey breast side up on a rack in a roasting pan. Rub with oil and pepper. Bake, uncovered, at 325° for 2¾ to 3¼ hours or until a thermometer reads 180°. (Cover loosely with foil if turkey browns too quickly.) Cover and let stand for 15 minutes before carving; discard apple mixture and herbs.

LINGUINE WITH ARTICHOKE-TOMATO SAUCE

Haven't got a clue what to make for dinner? Grab a box of pasta, a can of tomatoes and a jar of artichoke hearts, and you're well on your way to a 30-minute dinner.
—**MARY ANN LEE** CLIFTON PARK, NY

START TO FINISH: 30 MIN. • **MAKES:** 6 SERVINGS

- 12 ounces uncooked linguine
- 1 can (28 ounces) whole tomatoes with basil
- 1 jar (7½ ounces) marinated quartered artichoke hearts
- 1 cup chopped sweet onion
- 2 garlic cloves, minced
- 3 tablespoons olive oil, divided
- ¼ cup capers
- ¼ cup tomato paste
- 8 fresh basil leaves, torn
- 2 teaspoons sugar
- ½ teaspoon salt
- ¼ teaspoon pepper
  Grated Parmesan cheese

1. Cook linguine according to package directions.

2. Meanwhile, coarsely chop tomatoes, reserving liquid. Drain artichokes, reserving ¼ cup marinade. In a large skillet, saute onion and garlic in 2 tablespoons oil until tender. Add the tomatoes, artichokes, capers, tomato paste, basil, sugar, salt, pepper and reserved tomato liquid and artichoke marinade.

3. Bring to a boil. Reduce heat; simmer, uncovered, for 10 minutes or until slightly thickened. Drain linguine and transfer to a large bowl. Toss with tomato mixture and remaining oil. Sprinkle with cheese.

PARMESAN POINTERS

When a recipe calls for grated Parmesan cheese, use the finely grated cheese sold in containers with shaker tops. If a recipe calls for shredded Parmesan, use the bagged shredded cheese found in the grocery store dairy section. You can usually sub one for the other in most recipes.

CHEESE & CRAB BRUNCH BAKE

Who doesn't love an easy, cheesy seafood casserole that can be pulled together quickly, refrigerated overnight and baked up the next morning?

—**JOYCE CONWAY** WESTERVILLE, OH

PREP: 30 MIN. + CHILLING • **BAKE:** 50 MIN. • **MAKES:** 12 SERVINGS

- 2 tablespoons Dijon mustard
- 6 English muffins, split
- 8 ounces lump crabmeat, drained
- 2 tablespoons lemon juice
- 2 teaspoons grated lemon peel
- 2 cups (8 ounces) shredded white cheddar cheese
- 12 eggs
- 1 cup half-and-half cream
- 1 cup 2% milk
- ½ cup mayonnaise
- 1 teaspoon salt
- ½ teaspoon cayenne pepper
- ½ teaspoon pepper
- 2 cups (8 ounces) shredded Swiss cheese
- 1 cup grated Parmesan cheese
- 4 green onions, chopped
- ¼ cup finely chopped sweet red pepper
- ¼ cup finely chopped sweet yellow pepper

1. Spread mustard over bottom half of muffins. Place in a greased 13-in. x 9-in. baking dish. Top with crab, lemon juice and peel. Sprinkle with cheddar cheese. Top with muffin tops; set aside.

2. In a large bowl, whisk the eggs, cream, milk, mayonnaise, salt, cayenne and pepper. Pour over muffins; sprinkle with Swiss cheese, Parmesan cheese, onions and peppers. Cover and refrigerate overnight.

3. Remove dish from the refrigerator 30 minutes before baking. Cover and bake at 375° for 30 minutes. Uncover; bake 20-25 minutes longer or until set. Let stand for 5 minutes before serving.

SWEET & TENDER BEEF RIBS

Wondering if this recipe tastes as good as it looks? The answer is yes! These satisfying ribs are finger-licking good. Another plus is that it requires very little effort. For the majority of the prep time, the ribs are in the oven, giving you plenty of opportunities to make the sauce and take care of other things.

—**HEATHER BATES** ATHENS, ME

PREP: 1½ HOURS • **BROIL:** 5 MIN. • **MAKES:** 5 SERVINGS

- 5 pounds beef back ribs
- 1½ cups maple syrup
- ⅓ cup molasses
- 3 tablespoons orange marmalade
- 2 tablespoons ketchup
- 1½ teaspoons dried minced onion
- 1 teaspoon prepared mustard
- 1 garlic clove, minced
- ¼ teaspoon salt
- ¼ teaspoon onion powder
- ¼ teaspoon pepper

1. Cut ribs into serving size portions. Place in a greased 15-in. x 10-in. x 1-in. baking pan. Cover and bake at 350° for 1¼ hours or until tender.

2. In a small saucepan, combine the remaining ingredients. Bring to a boil; cook and stir for 10-15 minutes or until thickened. Drain ribs; place on a broiler pan. Brush with some of the barbecue sauce. Broil 4-5 in. from the heat for 5-10 minutes or until sauce is bubbly. Serve with remaining sauce.

RIGATONI & SAUSAGE

To serve a dozen people without much extra effort, simply make two of these filling pasta casseroles.

—ELAINE NEUKIRCH GENOA, IL

PREP: 20 MIN. • **BAKE:** 15 MIN. • **MAKES:** 6 SERVINGS

- 3¾ cups uncooked rigatoni
- 5 Italian sausage links (4 ounces each), sliced
- 1 jar (24 ounces) spaghetti sauce
- ¼ cup dry red wine
- 2 cups (8 ounces) shredded Italian cheese blend

1. Cook rigatoni according to package directions. Meanwhile, in a Dutch oven, cook sausage over medium heat until no longer pink; drain. Add spaghetti sauce and wine.

2. Drain rigatoni; add to sausage mixture and toss to coat. Transfer to a greased 13-in. x 9-in. baking dish; sprinkle with cheese. Bake, uncovered, at 350° for 15-20 minutes or until cheese is melted.

HAM AND AVOCADO SCRAMBLE

Featuring hearty ham, creamy avocado and a hint of garlic, this winning egg dish can serve as breakfast, lunch or dinner!

—ELISABETH LARSEN PLEASANT GROVE, UT

START TO FINISH: 15 MIN. • **MAKES:** 4 SERVINGS

- 8 eggs
- ¼ cup 2% milk
- 1 teaspoon garlic powder
- ¼ teaspoon pepper
- 1 cup cubed fully cooked ham
- 1 tablespoon butter
- 1 medium ripe avocado, peeled and cubed
- 1 cup (4 ounces) shredded Colby-Monterey Jack cheese

In a large bowl, whisk the eggs, milk, garlic powder and pepper; stir in ham. In a large skillet, melt butter over medium-high heat. Add egg mixture; cook and stir until almost set. Stir in avocado and cheese. Cook and stir until completely set.

PORK MEDALLIONS WITH CRANBERRY SAUCE

A little bit tangy, a little bit smoky, this special weeknight recipe takes pork medallions from ordinary to extraordinary.
—**CATHERINE HIGGINS** BOUNTIFUL, UT

START TO FINISH: 25 MIN. • **MAKES:** 4 SERVINGS

- 1 pork tenderloin (1 pound), cut into 1-inch slices
- ⅛ teaspoon salt
- ⅛ teaspoon pepper
- ½ cup whole-berry cranberry sauce
- 2 tablespoons barbecue sauce
- 1 tablespoon water
- 2 garlic cloves, minced
- ½ teaspoon Chinese five-spice powder

1. Sprinkle pork with salt and pepper. In a large nonstick skillet coated with cooking spray, cook pork in batches over medium heat for 3-5 minutes on each side or until juices run clear. Remove and keep warm.

2. Add the cranberry sauce, barbecue sauce, water, garlic and five-spice powder to the skillet. Bring to a boil. Reduce heat; simmer, uncovered, for 1-2 minutes or until thickened. Serve with pork.

CHICKEN WITH GARLIC-CAPER SAUCE

Treat your taste buds to my Mediterranean-inspired dish. The elegant sauce is lovely served over pasta or rice.
—**MARILEE ANKER** CHATSWORTH, CA

START TO FINISH: 30 MIN. • **MAKES:** 4 SERVINGS

- 4 boneless skinless chicken breast halves (6 ounces each)
- ½ teaspoon salt
- ½ teaspoon coarsely ground pepper
- 1 tablespoon olive oil
- 5 garlic cloves, minced
- ½ cup heavy whipping cream
- ⅓ cup white wine
- ¼ cup chopped oil-packed sun-dried tomatoes
- 2 tablespoons capers, drained
  Hot cooked bow tie pasta

1. Flatten chicken slightly; sprinkle with salt and pepper. In a large skillet over medium heat, cook chicken in oil for 5-7 minutes on each side or until juices run clear. Add garlic; cook 1 minute longer.

2. Stir in the cream, wine, tomatoes and capers; cook until sauce is slightly thickened. Serve with pasta.

BLUE CHEESE QUICHE WITH CARAMELIZED PEARS

The flavors of sweet sauteed onions, pears and blue cheese come together in this decadent version of a brunch classic. Pop it in the oven, and you'll have just enough time to whip up a fruit salad or a side to pair with it.

—**MAGGIE CARRICK** GAITHERSBURG, MD

PREP: 25 MIN. • **BAKE:** 30 MIN. • **MAKES:** 8 SERVINGS

- 1 sheet frozen puff pastry, thawed
- 8 turkey bacon strips, diced
- 1 cup (4 ounces) crumbled blue cheese
- 8 eggs
- 1 cup heavy whipping cream
- ½ cup shredded Parmesan cheese
- ¾ teaspoon salt
- ½ teaspoon ground nutmeg
- ½ teaspoon pepper

TOPPING

- 1 medium onion, thinly sliced
- 2 teaspoons olive oil
- 3 medium pears, thinly sliced
- 1 tablespoon brown sugar

1. Unfold puff pastry; press into a greased 9-in. fluted tart pan with removable bottom. In a large skillet, cook bacon over medium heat until crisp. Spoon bacon into crust and sprinkle with blue cheese. In a large bowl, whisk the eggs, cream, Parmesan cheese, salt, nutmeg and pepper; pour over top.
2. Bake at 350° for 30-35 minutes or until a knife inserted near the center comes out clean. Meanwhile, in a large skillet, saute onion in oil until tender. Add pears and brown sugar; cook 4 minutes longer. Serve with quiche.

QUESO PORK ENCHILADAS

My husband took this dish to work, and now his co-workers always ask for it. You can prepare the enchiladas with cooked chicken or beef, too.

—**ANNA RODRIGUEZ** BETHPAGE, NY

PREP: 30 MIN. • **BAKE:** 30 MIN. • **MAKES:** 6 SERVINGS

- 1 jar (15½ ounces) salsa con queso dip, divided
- 1 can (10 ounces) enchilada sauce, divided
- 1 can (4 ounces) chopped green chilies
- ⅓ cup water
- 2 tablespoons reduced-sodium taco seasoning
- 4 cups cubed cooked country-style pork ribs
- 12 flour tortillas (6 inches), warmed
- 2½ cups (10 ounces) shredded Mexican cheese blend, divided
  Shredded lettuce and chopped tomatoes, optional

1. In a large skillet, combine ¾ cup queso dip, ½ cup enchilada sauce, green chilies, water and taco seasoning. Bring to a boil. Reduce heat; simmer, uncovered, for 3 minutes.
2. Spread ⅔ cup sauce mixture into a greased 13-in. x 9-in. baking dish. Stir pork into remaining sauce mixture. Place ⅓ cup pork mixture down the center of each tortilla; top with 2 tablespoons cheese. Roll up and place seam side down in prepared dish. Combine remaining queso dip and enchilada sauce; pour over enchiladas.
3. Cover and bake at 350° for 20 minutes. Uncover; sprinkle with remaining cheese; bake 10-15 minutes longer or until heated through. Serve with lettuce and tomatoes if desired.

TURKEY MASHED POTATO CHIMIS

Bet you've never had a chimichanga quite like this! A homemade sauce of pumpkin puree and chipotle peppers gives these delicious chimis a spicy-sweet finish.
—**SHERRI GORDON** OLMSTED FALLS, OH

PREP: 30 MIN. • **BAKE:** 35 MIN. • **MAKES:** 12 SERVINGS

- 4 medium potatoes, peeled and cut into ½-inch cubes
- ¼ cup butter, cubed
- ¼ cup half-and-half cream
- ¼ teaspoon salt
- ⅛ teaspoon pepper
- 4 cups cubed cooked turkey breast
- 2 cups (8 ounces) shredded Monterey Jack cheese
- 12 flour tortillas (8 inches), warmed
- 5 tablespoons butter, melted

CHIPOTLE PUMPKIN SAUCE
- 1 cup canned pumpkin
- 1 teaspoon minced chipotle pepper in adobo sauce
- 1 cup salsa
- ½ cup shredded Parmesan cheese
- ½ cup heavy whipping cream

1. Place potatoes in a large saucepan and cover with water. Bring to a boil. Reduce heat; cover and cook for 10-15 minutes or until tender. Drain.

2. Mash potatoes with butter, cream, salt and pepper. Stir in the turkey and cheese.

3. Brush tortillas with melted butter. Place ⅔ cup potato mixture down the center of each tortilla. Fold sides and ends over filling and roll up. Place seam side down in two greased 13-in. x 9-in. baking dishes. Brush with leftover melted butter.

4. Bake, uncovered, at 375° for 35-40 minutes or until edges are lightly browned.

5. In a saucepan, combine the sauce ingredients; heat through (do not boil). Drizzle over chimichangas before serving.

CRAB IMPERIAL CASSEROLE

The recipe serves eight, but plan to double it if you're having guests over. Fresh mushrooms and lump crabmeat make it hard to turn down second helpings.
—**BARBARA CARLUCCI** ORANGE PARK, FL

PREP: 20 MIN. • **BAKE:** 25 MIN. • **MAKES:** 8 SERVINGS

- 3 cups uncooked spiral pasta
- 1¾ cups sliced fresh mushrooms
- 5 tablespoons butter, cubed
- 2 tablespoons all-purpose flour
- ¾ teaspoon pepper
- ½ teaspoon salt
- 1½ cups 2% milk
- 4 cans (6 ounces each) lump crabmeat, drained
- 1 can (10¾ ounces) condensed cream of mushroom soup, undiluted
- ¼ cup crushed butter-flavored crackers

1. Cook pasta according to package directions. Meanwhile, in a large skillet, saute mushrooms in butter until tender. Stir in the flour, pepper and salt until blended; gradually add milk. Bring to a boil. Cook and stir for 2 minutes or until thickened. Stir in crab and soup until blended.

2. Drain pasta and transfer to a large bowl. Add crab mixture; toss to coat. Transfer to a greased 13-in. x 9-in. baking dish; sprinkle with cracker crumbs. Bake, uncovered, at 350° for 25-30 minutes or until bubbly.

ORANGE BBQ BABY BACK RIBS

I avoid long and complicated recipes during the summer months (I'd rather be out by the pool with my family!), so I came up with this simple citrus twist on barbecue. I also use the sauce when I make chicken fondue.

—**KELLIE SEAMANS** CHANDLER, AZ

PREP: 2¼ HOURS • **GRILL:** 15 MIN. • **MAKES:** 4 SERVINGS

- 4 **pounds pork baby back ribs**
- 1 **bottle (18 ounces) honey barbecue sauce**
- 1 **cup orange juice**
- 2 **tablespoons grated orange peel**

1. Place ribs bone side down on a rack in a shallow roasting pan. Cover and bake at 325° for 2 to 2½ hours or until ribs are tender; drain.

2. In a small bowl, combine the barbecue sauce, orange juice and peel; set aside 1 cup for serving. Moisten a paper towel with cooking oil; using long-handled tongs, lightly coat the grill rack.

3. Place ribs over direct heat; baste with some of the sauce. Grill, covered, over medium heat for 15-20 minutes or until browned, turning and basting occasionally. Serve with reserved sauce.

SAUSAGE FLORENTINE POTPIE

You won't find a meal like this in the freezer aisle, but you'll be surprised how easily you can make a potpie from scratch at home.

—**KENDRA DOSS** COLORADO SPRINGS, CO

PREP: 30 MIN. • **BAKE:** 25 MIN. + STANDING • **MAKES:** 6 SERVINGS

- 1 **pound bulk Italian sausage**
- 2½ **cups sliced fresh mushrooms**
- 1 **medium red onion, chopped**
- 3 **garlic cloves, minced**
- 1 **can (10¾ ounces) reduced-fat reduced-sodium condensed cream of mushroom soup, undiluted**
- 1 **package (10 ounces) frozen chopped spinach, thawed and squeezed dry**
- 1 **cup half-and-half cream**
- 1 **cup shredded part-skim mozzarella cheese**
- ½ **cup shredded Parmesan cheese**

TOPPING
- 5 **sheets phyllo dough (14 inches x 9 inches)**
- 2 **tablespoons butter, melted**
- 1 **egg**
- 1 **tablespoon water**

1. In a large skillet, cook the sausage, mushrooms, onion and garlic over medium heat until no longer pink; drain. Stir in the soup, spinach, cream and cheeses; cook and stir until the cheese is melted.

2. Transfer to a greased 11-in. x 7-in. baking dish. Place a phyllo sheet over top; brush with some of the butter. Repeat with remaining phyllo dough and butter. Crimp edges of dough.

3. Whisk egg and water; brush over top. Bake, uncovered, at 350° for 25-30 minutes or until golden brown. Let stand for 10 minutes before serving.

USING PHYLLO DOUGH

Because phyllo is thin and fragile, be careful when handling it so it doesn't tear. Phyllo also dries out quickly, so once the dough is unwrapped and unrolled, cover it with plastic wrap, then a damp kitchen towel. Work with one phyllo sheet at a time and keep the others covered until you're ready to use them.

CHICKEN & BACON TART

If you're one of those folks who consider bacon a basic food group, you'll love this weeknight-friendly twist with a sweet and spicy kick from jalapeno jelly.

—TASTE OF HOME TEST KITCHEN

PREP: 25 MIN. • **BAKE:** 15 MIN. • **MAKES:** 4 SERVINGS

- ¼ **pound bacon strips, cut into thirds**
- 2 **medium onions, halved and thinly sliced**
- 2 **medium apples, peeled and thinly sliced**
- 1 **package (9 ounces) ready-to-serve roasted chicken breast strips**
- ¼ **cup jalapeno pepper jelly**
- ½ **teaspoon dried thyme**
- ¼ **teaspoon salt**
- 1 **sheet frozen puff pastry, thawed**
- ¾ **cup shredded cheddar cheese**
- ¼ **teaspoon pepper**
- 1 **tablespoon minced fresh parsley**

1. In a large skillet, cook bacon over medium heat until crisp. Remove to paper towels with a slotted spoon. Saute onions and apples in drippings until tender. Stir in the chicken, jelly, thyme and salt.

2. On a lightly floured surface, unfold puff pastry. Roll into a 10-in. x 9-in. rectangle. Transfer to a 15-in. x 10-in. x 1-in. parchment paper-lined baking sheet. Prick with a fork.

3. Spread chicken mixture over pastry to within 1 in. of edges. Sprinkle with cheese and pepper. Press edges with a fork, forming a decorative border.

4. Bake at 425° for 10 minutes. Sprinkle with bacon; bake 5-10 minutes longer or until golden brown. Sprinkle with parsley.

SANTA FE STRIP STEAKS

We love a little dose of Southwestern flavor with our meals, and this recipe definitely provides it.

—JOAN HALLFORD NORTH RICHLAND HILLS, TX

START TO FINISH: 25 MIN. • **MAKES:** 4 SERVINGS

- ½ cup chopped onion
- 1 tablespoon olive oil
- 2 cans (4 ounces each) chopped green chilies
- ½ cup fresh cilantro leaves
- 1 jalapeno pepper, seeded
- 2 teaspoons red currant jelly
- 1 teaspoon chicken bouillon granules
- 1 teaspoon Worcestershire sauce
- 1 garlic clove, peeled
- ½ teaspoon seasoned salt
- ¼ teaspoon dried oregano
- 4 boneless beef top loin steaks (1 inch thick and 8 ounces each)
  Salt and pepper to taste
- ½ cup shredded Monterey Jack cheese, optional

1. In a saucepan, cook and stir onion in oil over medium-high heat until tender. Transfer to a blender. Add the green chilies, cilantro, jalapeno, jelly, bouillon, Worcestershire sauce, garlic, seasoned salt and oregano; cover and process until smooth.

2. Return mixture to the same pan; cook over medium heat until heated through, stirring occasionally. Set aside and keep warm.

3. Sprinkle steaks with salt and pepper to taste. Broil 4-6 in. from heat for 5-8 minutes on each side or until meat reaches desired doneness (for medium-rare, a thermometer should read 145°; medium, 160°; well-done, 170°). Sprinkle steaks with cheese if desired; serve with green chili sauce.

NOTES *Steaks may also be grilled, covered, over medium heat. Top loin steak may be labeled as strip steak, KS City steak, NY strip steak, ambassador steak or boneless club steak in your region. When cutting hot peppers, disposable gloves are recommended. Avoid touching your face.*

LEMON & SAGE ROASTED CHICKEN

You first soak the chicken in marinade, then bake it in the oven, which allows for lots of time to do other things.

—JAN VALDEZ CHICAGO, IL

PREP: 20 MIN. + MARINATING • **BAKE:** 2¼ HOURS + STANDING
MAKES: 6 SERVINGS

- ¼ cup lemon juice
- ¼ cup plus 3 tablespoons olive oil, divided
- 5 garlic cloves, minced
- 2 tablespoons minced fresh sage
- 1 roasting chicken (6 to 7 pounds)
- 2 tablespoons butter, softened
- 1 medium lemon, cut into wedges
- 8 medium potatoes, quartered
- 2 medium onions, quartered
- ½ teaspoon salt
- ¼ teaspoon pepper

1. In a 2-gallon resealable plastic bag, combine the lemon juice, ¼ cup oil, garlic and sage. Add the chicken; seal bag and turn to coat. Refrigerate for at least 4 hours. Drain and discard marinade.

2. With fingers, carefully loosen skin from the chicken; rub butter under the skin. Fill cavity with lemon wedges. Place chicken breast side up on a rack in a roasting pan.

3. In a large bowl, combine the potatoes, onions, salt, pepper and remaining oil. Arrange around chicken. Bake, uncovered, at 350° for 2¼ to 2¾ hours or until a thermometer reads 180°. Cover loosely with foil if chicken browns too quickly. Let stand for 15 minutes before carving.

BAKED SPAGHETTI

You'll get requests for this yummy spaghetti casserole again and again. It's especially popular with my grandchildren, who love all the cheese.

—LOUISE MILLER WESTMINSTER, MD

PREP: 25 MIN. • **BAKE:** 1 HOUR • **MAKES:** 10 SERVINGS

- 1 package (16 ounces) spaghetti
- 1 pound ground beef
- 1 medium onion, chopped
- 1 jar (24 ounces) meatless spaghetti sauce
- ½ teaspoon seasoned salt
- 2 eggs
- ⅓ cup grated Parmesan cheese
- 5 tablespoons butter, melted
- 2 cups (16 ounces) 4% cottage cheese
- 4 cups (16 ounces) part-skim shredded mozzarella cheese

1. Cook spaghetti according to package directions. Meanwhile, in a large skillet, cook beef and onion over medium heat until meat is no longer pink; drain. Stir in spaghetti sauce and seasoned salt; set aside.

2. In a large bowl, whisk the eggs, Parmesan cheese and butter. Drain spaghetti; add to egg mixture and toss to coat.

3. Place half of the spaghetti mixture in a greased 3-qt. baking dish. Top with half of the cottage cheese, meat sauce and mozzarella cheese. Repeat layers.

4. Cover and bake at 350° for 40 minutes. Uncover; bake 20-25 minutes longer or until cheese is melted.

TLC (THANKSGIVING LEFTOVER CASSEROLE)

Turkey, stuffing and veggies come together in this fabulous casserole made from leftovers. There's comfort in every bite!

—BARBARA LENTO HOUSTON, PA

PREP: 20 MIN. • **BAKE:** 65 MIN. • **MAKES:** 8 SERVINGS

- 4 cups seasoned stuffing cubes
- 4 cups cubed cooked turkey
- 2 celery ribs, finely chopped
- 1 cup frozen peas
- 1 cup fresh or frozen cranberries
- ½ cup chopped sweet onion
- ¼ cup all-purpose flour
- 4 eggs
- 3 cups 2% milk
- 1 can (8¼ ounces) cream-style corn
- ½ teaspoon salt
- ½ teaspoon pepper
- 2 tablespoons butter
- ⅓ cup coarsely chopped pecans

1. Preheat oven to 350°. Layer first six ingredients in a greased 13x9-in. baking dish. In a large bowl, whisk flour, eggs and milk until smooth. Add corn, salt and pepper; mix well. Pour over top; let stand 15 minutes. Dot with butter and sprinkle with pecans.

2. Cover and bake 35 minutes. Uncover and bake 30-35 minutes more or until a knife inserted near the center comes out clean.

1. In a small skillet, cook sausage over medium heat until no longer pink; drain. Unroll dough and pat into a 14-in. x 12-in. rectangle. Sprinkle the sausage, cheddar cheese and spinach lengthwise down the center of the dough. Bring edges of dough to the center over filling; pinch seams to seal.

2. Place seam side down on a greased baking sheet. Brush top with butter; sprinkle with Parmesan cheese. Bake at 350° for 20-25 minutes or until golden brown. Serve warm with pizza sauce if desired.

POTLUCK HAM AND PASTA

Because this casserole bakes in two pans, you could freeze one for later, depending on your needs.

—NANCY FOUST STONEBORO, PA

PREP: 40 MIN. • **BAKE:** 25 MIN. • **MAKES:** 12 SERVINGS

- 1 package (16 ounces) elbow macaroni
- 4 cups fresh broccoli florets
- ½ cup finely chopped onion
- ½ cup butter, cubed
- ½ cup all-purpose flour
- 1 teaspoon ground mustard
- 1 teaspoon salt
- ¼ teaspoon pepper
- 6 cups 2% milk
- 1 jar (15 ounces) process cheese sauce
- 2 cups (8 ounces) shredded cheddar cheese, divided
- 4 cups cubed fully cooked ham

1. Cook macaroni according to package directions, adding broccoli during the last 3-4 minutes; drain.

2. In a large Dutch oven, saute onion in butter for 2 minutes. Stir in the flour, mustard, salt and pepper until blended. Gradually stir in milk. Bring to a boil; cook and stir for 2 minutes or until thickened. Stir in cheese sauce and 1 cup cheddar cheese until blended.

3. Remove from the heat; stir in the ham, macaroni and broccoli. Divide between a greased 13-in. x 9-in. baking dish and a greased 8-in. square baking dish. Sprinkle with remaining cheese.

4. Bake, uncovered, at 350° for 25-35 minutes or until bubbly and heated through. Serve immediately or before baking, cover and freeze casseroles for up to 3 months.

TO USE FROZEN CASSEROLES *Thaw in the refrigerator overnight. Remove from the refrigerator 30 minutes before baking. Cover and bake at 350° for 50-60 minutes or until bubbly.*

CHILI-SPICED PORK CHOPS

I like my food spicy, and my husband likes his mild. This pleasantly seasoned dish makes us both happy—and our son enjoys it, too!

—ANDREA KEITH KENTWOOD, MI

START TO FINISH: 30 MIN. • **MAKES:** 6 SERVINGS

- ¾ cup seasoned bread crumbs
- 3 tablespoons chili powder
- ½ teaspoon seasoned salt
- 1 egg
- ¼ cup fat-free milk
- 6 bone-in pork rib chops (7 ounces each, ¾ inch thick)

1. Preheat oven to 350°. In a shallow bowl, combine the bread crumbs, chili powder and seasoned salt. In another shallow bowl, combine the egg and milk. Dip chops in egg mixture, then coat with crumb mixture.

2. Transfer to a 15x10x1-in. baking pan coated with cooking spray. Bake 20-25 minutes or until meat reaches desired doneness (for medium-rare, a thermometer should read 145°; medium, 160°). Let stand 5 minutes before serving.

HEARTY SAUSAGE-STUFFED LOAF

My family devours this every time I make it. The best part? It's so simple to put together!

—JUDY LEARNED BOYERTOWN, PA

PREP: 20 MIN. • **BAKE:** 20 MIN. • **MAKES:** 6 SERVINGS

- ¾ pound bulk pork sausage
- 1 tube (11 ounces) refrigerated crusty French loaf
- 2 cups (8 ounces) shredded cheddar cheese
- 1 package (10 ounces) frozen chopped spinach, thawed and squeezed dry
- 1 tablespoon butter, melted
- 1 tablespoon grated Parmesan cheese
  Pizza sauce, optional

WHEN TO RINSE PASTA

When it comes to rinsing pasta, it depends on what you're using the pasta for. If you're using it in a baked dish, just drain the pasta in a colander. Rinsing would remove the starch and any sauce you add won't stick as well. If you're using the pasta cold in a salad, you can rinse it.

COUNTRY CHUCK ROAST WITH MUSHROOM GRAVY

This savory roast practically melts in your mouth. It looks complex, but the easiness makes it my go-to company recipe on cold-weather days.
—**MARY KAY LABRIE** CLERMONT, FL

PREP: 30 MIN. • **COOK:** 1¾ HOURS • **MAKES:** 8 SERVINGS

- 1 boneless beef chuck roast (2½ to 3 pounds)
- 3 garlic cloves, halved
- 1 tablespoon brown sugar
- 1½ teaspoons kosher salt
- ½ teaspoon pepper
- 2 tablespoons olive oil
- 1 large sweet onion, quartered
- 1 can (10½ ounces) condensed beef consomme, undiluted
- 2 tablespoons Worcestershire sauce
- 1 tablespoon stone-ground mustard
- 1 bay leaf
- 3 to 4 drops browning sauce, optional
- ½ pound sliced fresh mushrooms
- 1 bottle (12 ounces) light beer or nonalcoholic beer
- 1 teaspoon dried thyme
- 3 tablespoons cornstarch
- 3 tablespoons cold water

1. With a sharp knife, cut six 1-in.-long slits in meat; insert a garlic clove half into each slit. Combine the brown sugar, salt and pepper; rub over roast.

2. In an ovenproof Dutch oven, brown roast in oil on all sides. Add the onion, beef consomme, Worcestershire sauce, mustard, bay leaf and browning sauce if desired.

3. Cover and bake at 350° for 1¾ to 2¼ hours or until meat is tender. Remove roast to a serving platter; keep warm.

4. Discard bay leaf. Add the mushrooms, beer and thyme to the pan. Bring to a boil. Cook until liquid is reduced by half. Combine cornstarch and water until smooth; gradually stir into pan. Bring to a boil; cook and stir for 2 minutes or until thickened. Serve with roast.

TURKEY POTPIE CUPS

My children look forward to turkey or chicken leftovers just because they know this recipe will soon make an appearance. Refrigerated flaky biscuits make perfect individual potpie crusts.
—**KAREN WOODARD** MUSTANG, OK

PREP: 25 MIN. • **BAKE:** 20 MIN. • **MAKES:** 8 SERVINGS

- 1 tube (16.3 ounces) large refrigerated flaky biscuits
- 3 cups cubed cooked turkey
- 3 cups turkey gravy
- 2¼ cups frozen mixed vegetables
- ½ teaspoon salt
- ½ teaspoon pepper
- 1 cup French-fried onions
- 2¼ cups mashed potatoes
- ⅓ cup 2% milk
- ½ cup shredded cheddar cheese

1. On a lightly floured surface, roll each biscuit into an 8-in. circle. Press onto the bottoms and up the sides of eight greased 8-oz. ramekins.

2. In a large saucepan, combine the turkey, gravy, vegetables, salt and pepper. Bring to a boil. Reduce heat; simmer, uncovered, for 5 minutes. Sprinkle onions into ramekins; top with turkey mixture. In a small bowl, combine potatoes and milk; spread over tops. Sprinkle with cheese.

3. Bake at 375° for 18-22 minutes or until golden brown.

CARAMEL-APPLE PORK CHOPS

If you're searching for a unique way to serve pork chops, look no further. Bacon, apples, spinach, walnuts and seasonings create a scrumptious skillet supper.

—TASTE OF HOME TEST KITCHEN

PREP: 15 MIN. • **COOK:** 20 MIN. • **MAKES:** 4 SERVINGS

- 4 bacon strips, chopped
- 4 boneless pork loin chops (6 ounces each)
- 3 small tart apples, peeled and thinly sliced
- 1 medium onion, chopped
- 4 teaspoons brown sugar
- 1 tablespoon butter
- ¼ teaspoon salt
- ¼ teaspoon ground cinnamon
- ¼ teaspoon pepper
- ½ cup chicken broth
- 2 packages (6 ounces each) fresh baby spinach
- 3 tablespoons chopped walnuts, toasted

1. Cook bacon in a large skillet over medium heat until crisp. Remove to paper towels; drain, reserving 3 teaspoons drippings. In the same skillet, cook pork chops in 2 teaspoons reserved drippings over medium heat for 2-3 minutes on each side or until lightly browned. Remove and keep warm.

2. Saute apples and onion in 1 teaspoon reserved drippings in the same skillet until apples are crisp-tender. Stir in the brown sugar, butter, salt, cinnamon and pepper. Add broth; bring to a boil. Add pork chops. Reduce heat; cover and simmer for 4-5 minutes or until a thermometer reads 145°.

3. Remove chops to serving platter; let stand for 5 minutes. Add spinach to skillet and cook until wilted. Serve with chops. Sprinkle with bacon and walnuts.

CREAMY CHICKEN LASAGNA ROLL-UPS

I love to experiment with new pasta dishes. I used ingredients I had on hand to make these tasty lasagna roll-ups.

—CYNDY GERKEN NAPLES, FL

PREP: 35 MIN. • **BAKE:** 45 MIN. • **MAKES:** 10 SERVINGS

- 10 lasagna noodles
- ¾ pound boneless skinless chicken breasts, cubed
- 1½ teaspoons herbes de Provence
- ½ teaspoon salt, divided
- ½ teaspoon pepper, divided
- 1 tablespoon olive oil
- 2 cups ricotta cheese
- ½ cup grated Parmesan cheese, divided
- ¼ cup 2% milk
- 2 tablespoons minced fresh parsley
- 4 cups spaghetti sauce
- 8 ounces fresh mozzarella cheese, thinly sliced

1. Cook lasagna noodles according to package directions.

2. Meanwhile, sprinkle chicken with herbes de Provence, ¼ teaspoon salt and ¼ teaspoon pepper. In a large skillet, cook chicken in oil over medium heat for 5-7 minutes or until no longer pink; set aside.

3. In a bowl, combine the ricotta, ¼ cup Parmesan cheese, milk, parsley and remaining salt and pepper. Add chicken.

4. Drain noodles. Spread 1 cup spaghetti sauce into a greased 13-in. x 9-in. baking dish. Spread ⅓ cup chicken mixture over each noodle; carefully roll up. Place seam side down over sauce. Top with remaining sauce and Parmesan cheese.

5. Cover and bake at 375° for 30 minutes. Uncover; top with mozzarella cheese. Bake 15-20 minutes longer or until bubbly and cheese is melted.

NOTE *Look for herbes de Provence in the spice aisle.*

ITALIAN-STYLE SALISBURY STEAKS

This is my husband's favorite recipe. If you like, you can top each serving with mozzarella or Parmesan cheese.
—**HEATHER NALLEY** EASLEY, SC

START TO FINISH: 25 MIN. • **MAKES:** 4 SERVINGS

- 1 egg, beaten
- 1 teaspoon Worcestershire sauce
- ½ cup seasoned bread crumbs
- ½ teaspoon garlic powder
- ½ teaspoon pepper
- 1 pound ground beef
- 1 tablespoon canola oil
- 1 can (14½ ounces) diced tomatoes with basil, oregano and garlic, undrained
- 1 can (8 ounces) Italian tomato sauce

1. In a large bowl, combine the first five ingredients. Crumble beef over mixture and mix well. Shape into four oval patties. In a large skillet, brown patties in oil on both sides. Drain.

2. In a small bowl, combine diced tomatoes and tomato sauce. Pour over patties. Bring to a boil. Reduce heat; cover and simmer for 10-15 minutes or until meat is no longer pink.

CRUNCHY-HERBED CHICKEN BREASTS

I often get requests to make this chicken recipe for family and friends. It's a winner—and so easy!
—**LUCIA JOHNSON** MASSENA, NY

PREP: 15 MIN. • **BAKE:** 25 MIN. • **MAKES:** 6 SERVINGS

- ⅔ cup panko (Japanese) bread crumbs
- ½ cup grated Parmesan cheese
- ½ cup grated Romano cheese
- 1 tablespoon minced fresh oregano or 1 teaspoon dried oregano
- 1 tablespoon minced fresh basil or 1 teaspoon dried basil
- 2 teaspoons minced fresh parsley
- 2 garlic cloves, minced
- ½ teaspoon salt
- ½ teaspoon pepper
- ½ cup all-purpose flour
- 2 eggs, lightly beaten
- 6 boneless skinless chicken breast halves (5 ounces each)
  Olive oil-flavored cooking spray

1. In a bowl, mix the first nine ingredients. Place flour and eggs in separate shallow bowls. Dip both sides of chicken in the flour, eggs, then crumb mixture, patting to help coating adhere.

2. Place on a greased baking sheet. Spritz tops with cooking spray. Bake at 375° for 25-30 minutes or until a thermometer reads 170°.

SLOW COOKER

Who said comfort food takes a lot of effort? When your schedule's packed, turn here for a simple fix. From soups to sides and from main dishes to desserts, simply set your slow cooker for a no-fuss sensation tonight!

SIMPLE SPARERIB & SAUERKRAUT SUPPER

This recipe simplifies my busy life. It lets me get a hearty home-cooked meal on the table for my family without hours of work.

—**DONNA HARP** CINCINNATI, OH

PREP: 30 MIN. • **COOK:** 6 HOURS • **MAKES:** 4 SERVINGS

- 1 pound fingerling potatoes
- 1 medium onion, chopped
- 1 medium Granny Smith apple, peeled and chopped
- 3 slices thick-sliced bacon strips, cooked and crumbled
- 1 jar (16 ounces) sauerkraut, undrained
- 2 pounds pork spareribs
- ½ teaspoon salt
- ¼ teaspoon pepper
- 1 tablespoon vegetable oil
- 3 tablespoons brown sugar
- ¼ teaspoon caraway seeds
- ½ pound smoked Polish sausage, cut into 1-inch slices
- 1 cup beer

1. In a 6-qt. slow cooker, place the potatoes, onion, apple and bacon. Drain sauerkraut, reserving ⅓ cup of the liquid; add sauerkraut and reserved liquid to slow cooker.

2. Cut spareribs into serving-size portions; sprinkle with salt and pepper. In a large skillet, heat oil over medium-high heat; brown ribs in batches. Transfer to slow cooker; sprinkle with brown sugar and caraway seeds.

3. Add sausage; pour in beer. Cover and cook on low for 6-7 hours or until ribs are tender.

CREAMY ONION PORK CHOPS

Wine adds delectable flavor to these chops, and the meat falls from the bone. This dish is sure to initiate family members into the clean-plate club!

—**KRISTINA WYATT** CATAWBA, VA

PREP: 10 MIN. • **COOK:** 8 HOURS • **MAKES:** 6 SERVINGS

- 6 bone-in pork loin chops (8 ounces each)
- ¼ teaspoon pepper
- ⅛ teaspoon salt
- 1¼ cups 2% milk
- 1 can (10¾ ounces) condensed cream of onion soup, undiluted
- 1 can (10¾ ounces) reduced-fat reduced-sodium condensed cream of mushroom soup, undiluted
- ⅔ cup white wine or chicken broth
- 1 envelope ranch salad dressing mix
- 3 tablespoons cornstarch
- 2 tablespoons water
   Minced fresh parsley, optional

1. Sprinkle chops with pepper and salt; transfer to a 4-qt. slow cooker. In a large bowl, combine the milk, soups, wine and dressing mix; pour over pork. Cover and cook on low for 8-10 hours or until pork is tender.

2. Remove pork to a serving platter and keep warm. Skim fat from cooking juices; transfer to a large saucepan. Bring liquid to a boil. Combine cornstarch and water until smooth; gradually stir into the pan. Bring to a boil; cook and stir for 2 minutes or until thickened. Serve with pork and sprinkle with parsley if desired.

BEST EVER ROAST BEEF

This is the best roast beef I've ever had, and it's great for family dinners! Cube leftover meat and save any extra sauce to add to fried rice for another meal.

—CAROLINE FLYNN TROY, NY

PREP: 15 MIN. • **COOK:** 7 HOURS • **MAKES:** 6 SERVINGS

- 1 boneless beef chuck roast (4 pounds), trimmed
- 1 large sweet onion, chopped
- 1⅓ cups plus 3 tablespoons water, divided
- 1 can (10½ ounces) condensed French onion soup
- 1 cup packed brown sugar
- ⅓ cup reduced-sodium soy sauce
- ¼ cup cider vinegar
- 6 garlic cloves, minced
- 1 teaspoon ground ginger
- ¼ teaspoon pepper
- 3 tablespoons cornstarch

1. Cut roast in half. Transfer to a 5-qt. slow cooker; add onion and 1⅓ cups water. In a small bowl, combine the soup, brown sugar, soy sauce, vinegar, garlic, ginger and pepper; pour over top. Cover and cook on low for 7-8 hours or until meat is tender.
2. Remove meat to a serving platter and keep warm. Skim fat from cooking juices; transfer to a small saucepan. Bring liquid to a boil. Combine cornstarch and remaining water until smooth; gradually stir into the pan. Bring to a boil; cook and stir for 2 minutes or until thickened. Serve with roast.

SCALLOPED POTATOES & HAM

I adapted an oven recipe to cook itself while I'm away. Now it's ready to serve when I get home, making it a good pick in my book!

—JONI HILTON ROCKLIN, CA

PREP: 25 MIN. • **COOK:** 8 HOURS
MAKES: 16 SERVINGS (¾ CUP EACH)

- 1 can (10¾ ounces) condensed cheddar cheese soup, undiluted
- 1 can (10¾ ounces) condensed cream of mushroom soup, undiluted
- 1 cup 2% milk
- 10 medium potatoes, peeled and thinly sliced
- 3 cups cubed fully cooked ham
- 2 medium onions, chopped
- 1 teaspoon paprika
- 1 teaspoon pepper
  Minced green chives, optional

1. In a small bowl, combine the soups and milk. In a greased 5-qt. slow cooker, layer half of the potatoes, ham, onions and soup mixture. Repeat layers. Sprinkle with paprika and pepper.
2. Cover and cook on low for 8-10 hours or until the potatoes are tender.
3. Remove ribs and keep warm. Skim fat from cooking juices; serve with ribs.

HOW TO CHOP AN ONION

To quickly chop an onion, peel and cut in half from the root to the top. Leaving root attached, place flat side down on work surface. Cut vertically through the onion, leaving the root end uncut. Cut across the onion, discarding root end. The closer the cuts, the finer the onion will be chopped.

FAMILY-FAVORITE SPAGHETTI SAUCE

I've been sharing this at our campers' potluck ever since my friend gave the recipe to me. It's wonderful!

—HELEN ROWE SPRING LAKE, MI

PREP: 30 MIN. • **COOK:** 6 HOURS
MAKES: 9 SERVINGS (2¼ QUARTS)

- 1 pound bulk Italian sausage
- ½ pound ground beef
- 1 large onion, chopped
- 1 celery rib, chopped
- 3 garlic cloves, minced
- 1 tablespoon olive oil
- 1 can (28 ounces) diced tomatoes
- 1 can (10¾ ounces) condensed tomato soup, undiluted
- 1 can (8 ounces) mushroom stems and pieces, drained
- 1 can (8 ounces) tomato sauce
- 1 can (6 ounces) tomato paste
- 1 tablespoon sugar
- ½ teaspoon pepper
- ½ teaspoon dried basil
- ¼ teaspoon dried oregano
  Hot cooked spaghetti

1. In a large skillet, cook the sausage, beef, onion, celery and garlic in oil over medium heat until meat is no longer pink; drain. In a 4-qt. slow cooker, combine the diced tomatoes, tomato soup, mushrooms, tomato sauce, tomato paste, sugar and seasonings. Stir in sausage mixture.

2. Cover and cook on low for 6-8 hours or until flavors are blended. Serve with spaghetti.

MUSHROOM STEAK

This recipe originally was for the oven, but I was running tight on time one day and transformed it to a slow cooker dish! I let it simmer all day—with great results.

—SANDY PETTINGER LINCOLN, NE

PREP: 20 MIN. • **COOK:** 7 HOURS • **MAKES:** 6 SERVINGS

- ⅓ cup all-purpose flour
- ½ teaspoon salt
- ½ teaspoon pepper, divided
- 1 beef top round steak (2 pounds), cut into 1½-inch strips
- 2 cups sliced fresh mushrooms
- 1 small onion, cut into thin wedges
- 1 can (10¾ ounces) condensed golden mushroom soup, undiluted
- ¼ cup sherry or beef broth
- ½ teaspoon dried oregano
- ¼ teaspoon dried thyme
  Hot cooked egg noodles

1. In a large resealable plastic bag, combine the flour, salt and ¼ teaspoon pepper. Add beef, a few pieces at a time, and shake to coat.

2. In a 3-qt. slow cooker, combine the mushrooms, onion and beef. Combine the soup, sherry, oregano, thyme and remaining pepper; pour over top. Cover and cook on low for 7-9 hours or until beef is tender. Serve with noodles.

RICH FRENCH ONION SOUP

When entertaining guests, I bring out this savory soup while we're waiting for the main course. Just saute the onions early in the day and let the soup simmer until it's time to eat.

—LINDA ADOLPH EDMONTON, AB

PREP: 10 MIN. • **COOK:** 5 HOURS • **MAKES:** 10 SERVINGS

- 6 large onions, chopped
- ½ cup butter
- 6 cans (10½ ounces each) condensed beef broth, undiluted
- 1½ teaspoons Worcestershire sauce
- 3 bay leaves
- 10 slices French bread, toasted
  Shredded Parmesan and shredded part-skim mozzarella cheese

1. In a large skillet, saute onions in butter until crisp-tender. Transfer to a 5-qt. slow cooker. Add the broth, Worcestershire sauce and bay leaves.

2. Cover and cook on low for 5-7 hours or until the onions are tender. Discard bay leaves.

3. Ladle soup into ovenproof bowls. Top each with a slice of toast; sprinkle with desired amount of cheese. Place the bowls on a baking sheet. Broil for 2-3 minutes or until the cheese is lightly golden.

MOCHA MINT COFFEE

My sweet coffee contains hints of mint, cocoa and cinnamon. Top each cup with marshmallows for a little extra fun and bring out the youngster in anyone! The recipe is ideal when you're venturing out in the cold and want a warmer-upper when you return.

—MINDIE HILTON SUSANVILLE, CA

PREP: 10 MIN. • **COOK:** 2 HOURS • **MAKES:** 8 SERVINGS

- 6 cups hot brewed coffee
- 2 packets instant hot cocoa mix
- ½ cup dulce de leche
- ¼ cup peppermint crunch baking chips or mint chocolate chips
- 4 teaspoons sugar
- 1 cup miniature marshmallows
- ½ teaspoon ground cinnamon

1. In a 3-qt. slow cooker, combine the coffee, hot cocoa mix, dulce de leche, baking chips and sugar. Cover and cook on low for 2-3 hours or until hot.

2. Ladle into mugs. Top with marshmallows; sprinkle with cinnamon.

NOTE *This recipe was tested with Nestle La Lechera dulce de leche; look for it in the international foods section. If using Eagle Brand dulce de leche (caramel flavored sauce), thicken according to package directions before using.*

LEMON CHICKEN BREASTS WITH VEGGIES

Why bake chicken when my slow-cooked version is so fuss-free? Topped with herbs, these chicken breasts are nestled with crisp-tender veggies in a subtle lemon sauce.
—**AMBER OTIS** MORRIS, OK

PREP: 25 MIN. • **COOK:** 8 HOURS • **MAKES:** 6 SERVINGS

- 1 **pound fresh baby carrots**
- 3 **cups cubed red potatoes**
- 1 **package (14 ounces) frozen pearl onions, thawed**
- 2 **celery ribs, thinly sliced**
- 6 **bone-in chicken breast halves (10 ounces each), skin removed**
- 1 **can (10¾ ounces) condensed cream of chicken soup, undiluted**
- ½ **cup water**
- ½ **cup lemon juice**
- 1 **teaspoon dried parsley flakes**
- 1 **teaspoon dried thyme**
- ½ **teaspoon pepper**
- ¼ **teaspoon salt**

1. In a 5- or 6-qt. slow cooker, combine the carrots, potatoes, onions and celery. Top with chicken.

2. Combine the soup, water, lemon juice, parsley, thyme, pepper and salt; pour over chicken and vegetables. Cover and cook on low for 8-9 hours or until the chicken and vegetables are tender.

SWEET & SAVORY SLOW-COOKED BEEF

There's plenty of sweet and a little heat from the chipotle pepper in this family-friendly shredded beef. Use your favorite bottled barbecue sauce to speed up prep time.
—**DAVID KLEIMAN** NEW BEDFORD, MA

PREP: 20 MIN. • **COOK:** 8 HOURS • **MAKES:** 16 SERVINGS

- 1 **beef top round roast (4 pounds)**
- 1 **bottle (18 ounces) barbecue sauce**
- ½ **cup water**
- ¼ **cup packed brown sugar**
- 1 **chipotle pepper in adobo sauce, chopped**
- 2 **tablespoons Worcestershire sauce**
- 2 **tablespoons steak sauce**
- 1½ **teaspoons reduced-sodium soy sauce**
- 1 **teaspoon celery salt**
- 1 **teaspoon garlic salt**
- 1 **teaspoon seasoned salt**
- 1 **teaspoon pepper**
- 16 **onion rolls, split**

1. Cut roast in half; place in a 6-qt. slow cooker. Combine the barbecue sauce, water, brown sugar, chipotle pepper, Worcestershire sauce, steak sauce, soy sauce and seasonings. Pour over meat.

2. Cover and cook on low for 8-10 hours or until meat is tender. Remove roast and cool slightly. Skim fat from cooking juices. Shred meat with two forks and return to slow cooker; heat through. Serve on rolls.

NOTE *Wear disposable gloves when cutting hot peppers; the oils can burn skin. Avoid touching your face.*

POTLUCK CANDIED SWEET POTATOES

I love bringing this traditional Southern staple to potlucks, so I found a way to prepare it in the slow cooker. You can't go wrong with candied sweet potatoes. Folks rave about the side dish, and the slow cooker makes it easy to tote.
—**DEIRDRE COX** KANSAS CITY, MO

PREP: 20 MIN. • **COOK:** 5 HOURS
MAKES: 12 SERVINGS (¾ CUP EACH)

- 1 **cup packed brown sugar**
- 1 **cup sugar**
- 8 **medium sweet potatoes, peeled and cut into ½-inch slices**
- ¼ **cup butter, melted**
- 2 **teaspoons vanilla extract**
- ¼ **teaspoon salt**
- 2 **tablespoons cornstarch**
- 2 **tablespoons cold water**
  Minced fresh parsley, optional

1. In a small bowl, combine sugars. In a greased 5-qt. slow cooker, layer a third of the sweet potatoes; sprinkle with a third of the sugar mixture. Repeat layers twice. In a small bowl, combine the butter, vanilla and salt; drizzle over potatoes. Cover and cook on low for 5-6 hours or until sweet potatoes are tender.

2. Using a slotted spoon, transfer potatoes to a serving dish; keep warm. Pour cooking juices into a small saucepan; bring to a boil. In a small bowl, combine cornstarch and water until smooth; stir into pan. Return to a boil, stirring constantly; cook and stir for 1-2 minutes or until thickened. Spoon over the sweet potatoes. Sprinkle with parsley if desired.

SLOW COOKER HULA CHICKEN

As long as you're cooking bacon for breakfast, save some for the slow cooker. In 4 short hours, you'll be saying aloha to lunch!
—**CINDY LUND** VALLEY CENTER, CA

PREP: 15 MIN. • **COOK:** 4 HOURS • **MAKES:** 6 SERVINGS

- 6 **bacon strips, divided**
- 6 **boneless skinless chicken thighs (about 1½ pounds)**
- ¼ **teaspoon salt**
- ⅛ **teaspoon pepper**
- ½ **cup chopped red onion**
- 1 **cup crushed pineapple, drained**
- ¾ **cup barbecue sauce**

1. Cut three bacon strips in half; cook until partially cooked but not crisp. Drain on paper towels.

2. Season chicken with salt and pepper; place in a 3-qt. slow cooker. Top each thigh with a half piece of bacon. Top with onion, pineapple and barbecue sauce.

3. Cover and cook on low for 4-5 hours or until chicken is tender. Cook remaining bacon until crisp; drain and crumble. Sprinkle over each serving.

Soup's On

Brimming with the down-home comfort everyone craves, these soup and stew recipes promise to warm hearts each time they're served. Simmer one up tonight for a soothing meal that can't be beat.

CREAM OF POTATO & CHEDDAR SOUP

My daughter shares Yukon Gold potatoes from her garden, and they give this soup incredible flavor. With sharp cheese and croutons, it's heavenly!

—CINDI BAUER MARSHFIELD, WI

PREP: 25 MIN. • **COOK:** 7½ HOURS
MAKES: 11 SERVINGS (2¾ QUARTS)

- 8 medium Yukon Gold potatoes, peeled and cubed
- 1 large red onion, chopped
- 1 celery rib, chopped
- 2 cans (14½ ounces each) reduced-sodium chicken broth
- 1 can (10¾ ounces) condensed cream of celery soup, undiluted
- 1 teaspoon garlic powder
- ½ teaspoon white pepper
- 1½ cups (6 ounces) shredded sharp cheddar cheese
- 1 cup half-and-half cream
  Optional toppings: salad croutons, crumbled cooked bacon and additional shredded sharp cheddar cheese

1. Combine the first seven ingredients in a 4- or 5-qt. slow cooker. Cover and cook on low for 7-9 hours or until potatoes are tender.

2. Stir in cheese and cream. Cover and cook 30 minutes longer or until cheese is melted. Garnish servings with toppings of your choice.

SPINACH WHITE BEAN SOUP

I work as a college nursing professor, and I needed a delicious soup recipe that was easy and full of nutrients. This fits the bill!

—BRENDA JEFFERS OTTUMWA, IA

PREP: 20 MIN. • **COOK:** 6¼ HOURS
MAKES: 8 SERVINGS (2 QUARTS)

- 3 cans (14½ ounces each) vegetable broth
- 1 can (15½ ounces) great northern beans, rinsed and drained
- 1 can (15 ounces) tomato puree
- ½ cup finely chopped onion
- ½ cup uncooked converted long grain rice
- 2 garlic cloves, minced
- 1 teaspoon dried basil
- ½ teaspoon salt
- ¼ teaspoon pepper
- 1 package (6 ounces) fresh baby spinach, coarsely chopped
- ¼ cup shredded Parmesan cheese

In a 4-qt. slow cooker, combine the first nine ingredients. Cover and cook on low for 6-7 hours or until heated through. Stir in spinach. Cover and cook for 15 minutes or until spinach is wilted. Sprinkle with cheese.

FREEZE OPTION *Before adding cheese, cool soup. Freeze soup in freezer containers. To use, partially thaw in refrigerator overnight. Heat through in a saucepan, stirring occasionally and adding a little broth or water if necessary. Sprinkle each serving with cheese.*

PORK AND GREEN CHILI STEW

Pork, green chilies and hominy have roots in Southwestern cuisine. An easily adaptable stew, this is ready in 4 hours if cooked on high in a slow cooker or in 8 hours if cooked on low.
—**PAUL SEDILLO** PLAINFIELD, IL

PREP: 40 MIN. • **COOK:** 7 HOURS • **MAKES:** 8 SERVINGS (2 QUARTS)

- 2 pounds boneless pork shoulder butt roast, cut into ¾-inch cubes
- 1 large onion, cut into ½-in. pieces
- 2 tablespoons canola oil
- 1 teaspoon salt
- 1 teaspoon coarsely ground pepper
- 4 large potatoes, peeled and cut into ¾-inch cubes
- 3 cups water
- 1 can (16 ounces) hominy, rinsed and drained
- 2 cans (4 ounces each) chopped green chilies
- 2 tablespoons quick-cooking tapioca
- 2 garlic cloves, minced
- ½ teaspoon dried oregano
- ½ teaspoon ground cumin
- 1 cup minced fresh cilantro
  Sour cream, optional

1. In a large skillet, brown pork and onion in oil in batches. Sprinkle with salt and pepper. Transfer to a 4-qt. slow cooker.
2. Stir in the potatoes, water, hominy, chilies, tapioca, garlic, oregano and cumin. Cover and cook on low for 7-9 hours or until meat is tender, stirring in cilantro during the last 30 minutes of cooking. Serve with sour cream if desired.

MOMMA'S TURKEY STEW WITH DUMPLINGS

My mother used to make turkey stew every year with our Thanksgiving leftovers. To this day, it is one of my favorite meals.
—**STEPHANIE RABBITT-SCHAPP** CINCINNATI, OH

PREP: 20 MIN. • **COOK:** 6½ HOURS • **MAKES:** 6 SERVINGS

- 3 cups shredded cooked turkey
- 1 large sweet onion, chopped
- 1 large potato, peeled and cubed
- 2 large carrots, chopped
- 2 celery ribs, chopped
- 2 bay leaves
- 1 teaspoon salt
- ½ teaspoon poultry seasoning
- ½ teaspoon dried thyme
- ¼ teaspoon pepper
- 1 carton (32 ounces) chicken broth
- ⅓ cup cold water
- 3 tablespoons cornstarch
- ½ cup frozen corn, thawed
- ½ cup frozen peas, thawed
- 1 cup biscuit/baking mix
- ⅓ cup 2% milk

1. In a 6-qt. slow cooker, combine the first 10 ingredients; stir in broth. Cover and cook on low for 6-7 hours.
2. Remove bay leaves. In a bowl, mix water and cornstarch until smooth; stir into turkey mixture. Add corn and peas. Cover and cook on high until mixture reaches a simmer.
3. Meanwhile, in a bowl, mix baking mix and milk just until moistened. Drop by rounded tablespoonfuls on top of simmering liquid. Reduce heat to low; cover and cook for 20-25 minutes or until a toothpick inserted in a dumpling comes out clean.

CHOCOLATE-COVERED CHERRY PUDDING CAKE

I remember how much my grandfather cherished the chocolate-covered cherries we brought him for Christmas. After he passed away, I came up with this rich recipe in his honor. It's delicious served with whipped topping.

—MEREDITH COE CHARLOTTESVILLE, VA

PREP: 20 MIN. • **COOK:** 2 HOURS + STANDING • **MAKES:** 8 SERVINGS

- ½ cup reduced-fat sour cream
- 2 tablespoons canola oil
- 1 tablespoon butter, melted
- 2 teaspoons vanilla extract
- 1 cup all-purpose flour
- ¼ cup sugar
- ¼ cup packed brown sugar
- 3 tablespoons baking cocoa
- 2 teaspoon baking powder
- ½ teaspoon ground cinnamon
- ⅛ teaspoon salt
- 1 cup fresh or frozen pitted dark sweet cherries, thawed
- 1 cup fresh or frozen pitted tart cherries, thawed
- ⅓ cup 60% cacao bittersweet chocolate baking chips

PUDDING
- ½ cup packed brown sugar
- 2 tablespoons baking cocoa
- 1¼ cups hot water

1. In a large bowl, beat the sour cream, oil, butter and vanilla until blended. Combine the flour, sugars, cocoa, baking powder, cinnamon and salt. Add to sour cream mixture just until combined. Stir in cherries and chips. Pour into a 3-qt. slow cooker coated with cooking spray.

2. In a small bowl, combine brown sugar and cocoa. Stir in hot water until blended. Pour over the batter (do not stir). Cover and cook on high for 2 to 2½ hours or until set. Let stand for 15 minutes. Serve warm.

SOUTHWEST PULLED PORK

I made this on a whim one morning when I knew friends were dropping by later in the day. Not only does the recipe make a lot, but the seasonings and green chilies give the meat a real kick. Cool sour cream and fresh salsa make fantastic additions.

—DEB LEBLANC PHILLIPSBURG, KS

PREP: 20 MIN. • **COOK:** 8 HOURS • **MAKES:** 14 SERVINGS

- 1 boneless pork shoulder butt roast (4 pounds)
- 2 tablespoons chili powder
- 1 tablespoon brown sugar
- 1½ teaspoons ground cumin
- 1 teaspoon salt
- ½ teaspoon pepper
- ½ teaspoon cayenne pepper
- 1 large sweet onion, coarsely chopped
- 2 cans (4 ounces each) chopped green chilies
- 1 cup chicken broth
- 14 kaiser rolls, split

1. Cut roast in half. In a small bowl, combine the chili powder, brown sugar, cumin, salt, pepper and cayenne; rub over meat. Transfer to a 5-qt. slow cooker. Top with onion and chilies. Pour broth around meat.

2. Cover and cook on low for 8-10 hours or until tender. Remove roast; cool slightly. Skim fat from cooking juices. Shred pork with two forks and return to slow cooker; heat through. Serve on rolls.

BLACK BEAN, CHORIZO & SWEET POTATO CHILI

I just love chili. This recipe takes it to the next level by changing up the flavors and adding a surprise—sweet potatoes!
—**JULIE MERRIMAN** COLD BROOK, NY

PREP: 20 MIN. • **COOK:** 6 HOURS
MAKES: 16 SERVINGS (4 QUARTS)

- 1 pound uncooked chorizo, casings removed, or spicy bulk pork sausage
- 1 large onion, chopped
- 2 poblano peppers, finely chopped
- 2 jalapeno peppers, seeded and finely chopped
- 3 tablespoons tomato paste
- 3 large sweet potatoes, peeled and cut into ½-inch cubes
- 4 cans (14½ ounces each) fire-roasted diced tomatoes, undrained
- 2 cans (15 ounces each) black beans, rinsed and drained
- 2 cups beef stock
- 2 tablespoons chili powder
- 1 tablespoon dried oregano
- 1 tablespoon ground coriander
- 1 tablespoon ground cumin
- 1 tablespoon smoked paprika
- ¼ cup lime juice

1. In a large skillet, cook and stir the chorizo, onion, poblanos and jalapenos over medium heat for 8-10 minutes or until chorizo is cooked. Using a slotted spoon, transfer to a 6-qt. slow cooker.
2. Stir in tomato paste. Add the sweet potatoes, tomatoes, beans, stock and spices; stir to combine. Cover and cook on low for 6-7 hours or until potatoes are tender. Stir in lime juice.

CITRUS-HERB PORK ROAST

You simply can't beat the mixture of seasonings and citrus in this tender pork roast.
—**LAURA BRODINE** COLORADO SPRINGS, CO

PREP: 25 MIN. • **COOK:** 8 HOURS • **MAKES:** 8 SERVINGS

- 1 boneless pork sirloin roast (3 to 4 pounds)
- 1 teaspoon dried oregano
- ½ teaspoon ground ginger
- ½ teaspoon pepper
- 2 medium onions, cut into thin wedges
- 1 cup plus 3 tablespoons orange juice, divided
- 1 tablespoon sugar
- 1 tablespoon white grapefruit juice
- 1 tablespoon steak sauce
- 1 tablespoon reduced-sodium soy sauce
- 1 teaspoon grated orange peel
- ½ teaspoon salt
- 3 tablespoons cornstarch
  Hot cooked egg noodles

1. Cut roast in half. In a small bowl, combine the oregano, ginger and pepper; rub over pork. In a large nonstick skillet coated with cooking spray, brown roast on all sides. Transfer to a 4-qt. slow cooker; add onions.
2. In a small bowl, combine 1 cup orange juice, sugar, grapefruit juice, steak sauce and soy sauce; pour over top. Cover and cook on low for 8-10 hours or until meat is tender. Remove meat and onions to a serving platter; keep warm.
3. Skim fat from cooking juices; transfer to a small saucepan. Add orange peel and salt. Bring to a boil. Combine cornstarch and the remaining orange juice until smooth. Gradually stir into the pan. Bring to a boil; cook and stir for 2 minutes or until thickened. Serve with pork and noodles.

HAWAIIAN BARBECUE BEANS

Guests rave and wonder about the unique taste of this side—fresh ginger is the hidden surprise. It's a hit at every barbecue.

—**HELEN REYNOLDS** QUINCY, CA

PREP: 10 MIN. • **COOK:** 5 HOURS • **MAKES:** 9 SERVINGS

- 4 cans (15 ounces each) black beans, rinsed and drained
- 1 can (20 ounces) crushed pineapple, drained
- 1 bottle (18 ounces) barbecue sauce
- 1½ teaspoons minced fresh gingerroot
- ½ pound bacon strips, cooked and crumbled

In a 4-qt. slow cooker, combine the beans, pineapple, barbecue sauce and ginger. Cover and cook on low for 5-6 hours. Stir in bacon before serving.

PULLED BRISKET SANDWICHES

The sauce for these sandwiches is quite special—it's basically ketchup, brown sugar and a little butter that's drizzled over tender beef brisket.

—**JANE GUILBEAU** NEW ORLEANS, LA

PREP: 25 MIN. • **COOK:** 8 HOURS • **MAKES:** 12 SERVINGS

- 1 fresh beef brisket (4 to 5 pounds)
- 1½ cups water
- ½ cup Worcestershire sauce
- 2 tablespoons cider vinegar
- 2 garlic cloves, minced
- 1½ teaspoons beef bouillon granules
- 1½ teaspoons chili powder
- 1 teaspoon ground mustard
- ½ teaspoon cayenne pepper
- ¼ teaspoon garlic salt
- ½ cup ketchup
- 2 tablespoons brown sugar
- 2 tablespoons butter
- ½ teaspoon hot pepper sauce
- 12 kaiser rolls, split

1. Cut brisket in half; place in a 5-qt. slow cooker. In a small bowl, combine the water, Worcestershire sauce, vinegar, garlic, bouillon, chili powder, mustard, cayenne and garlic salt. Cover and refrigerate ½ cup mixture for sauce; pour remaining mixture over beef. Cover and cook on low for 8-10 hours or until meat is tender.

2. Remove beef; cool slightly. Skim fat from cooking juices. Shred the meat with two forks and return to the slow cooker; heat through.

3. In a small saucepan, combine the ketchup, brown sugar, butter, pepper sauce and reserved water mixture. Bring to a boil; reduce heat. Simmer, uncovered, for 2-3 minutes to allow flavors to blend. Using a slotted spoon, place beef on rolls; drizzle with sauce.

NOTE *This is a fresh beef brisket, not corned beef.*

SLOW COOKED BBQ PORK RIBS

You probably already have everything you need for this entree! The ribs turn out so sweet and tangy.

—**ANNETTE THOMPSON** WOODBURY, VT

PREP: 20 MIN. • **COOK:** 7 HOURS • **MAKES:** 8 SERVINGS

- 4 pounds boneless country-style pork ribs
- 2 cups ketchup
- ¼ cup packed brown sugar
- ¼ cup maple syrup
- ¼ cup prepared mustard
- ¼ cup reduced-sodium soy sauce
- 2 tablespoons lemon juice
- 2 teaspoons dried minced garlic
- ⅛ teaspoon pepper

1. Place ribs in a 5- or 6-qt. slow cooker. Combine remaining ingredients; pour over top. Cover and cook on low for 7-9 hours or until meat is tender.

2. Remove ribs and keep warm. Skim fat from cooking juices; serve with ribs.

LUCKY CORNED BEEF

It's not really lucky—but it's an amazing Irish recipe! Set the slow cooker in the morning and look forward to a delightful dinner.
—**HEATHER PARRAZ** ROCHESTER, WA

PREP: 20 MIN. • **COOK:** 9 HOURS
MAKES: 5 SERVINGS PLUS LEFTOVERS

- 6 medium red potatoes, quartered
- 2 medium carrots, cut into chunks
- 1 large onion, sliced
- 2 corned beef briskets with spice packets (3 pounds each)
- ¼ cup packed brown sugar
- 2 tablespoons sugar
- 2 tablespoons coriander seeds
- 2 tablespoons whole peppercorns
- 4 cups water

1. In a 6-qt. slow cooker, combine the potatoes, carrots and onion. Add briskets (discard spice packets from corned beef or save for another use). Sprinkle the brown sugar, sugar, coriander and peppercorns over meat. Pour water over top.
2. Cover and cook on low for 9-11 hours or until meat and vegetables are tender.
NOTE *Remove meat and vegetables to a serving platter. Thinly slice one brisket across the grain and serve with vegetables. Save the remaining brisket for another use.*

SLOW-COOKED FRUITED OATMEAL WITH NUTS

The beauty of this breakfast is that you can assemble the key ingredients in your slow cooker overnight and spoon out bowls of comfort in the morning. I'd call that a pleasant way to start any day, wouldn't you?
—**TRISHA KRUSE** EAGLE, ID

PREP: 15 MIN. • **COOK:** 6 HOURS • **MAKES:** 6 SERVINGS

- 3 cups water
- 2 cups old-fashioned oats
- 2 cups chopped apples
- 1 cup dried cranberries
- 1 cup fat-free milk
- 2 teaspoons butter, melted
- 1 teaspoon pumpkin pie spice
- 1 teaspoon ground cinnamon
- 6 tablespoons chopped almonds, toasted
- 6 tablespoons chopped pecans, toasted
  Additional fat-free milk

1. In a 3-qt. slow cooker coated with cooking spray, combine the first eight ingredients. Cover and cook on low for 6-8 hours or until liquid is absorbed.
2. Spoon oatmeal into bowls. Sprinkle with almonds and pecans; drizzle with additional milk if desired.

BREADS, ROLLS & MORE

Start a pot of coffee, because once these goodies come out of the oven, you'll want to settle in and enjoy. Choose from biscuits, muffins, rolls, scones and loaves, then wrap a few extras to share the goodness with others.

CHIPOTLE FOCACCIA WITH GARLIC-ONION TOPPING

Chipotle peppers leave some people tongue-tied; others can't get enough of the smoky heat. I came up with this recipe to fit right in the middle. Add more chipotle if you crave the fire.

—FRANCES "KAY" BOUMA TRAIL, BC

PREP: 1¼ HOURS + RISING • **BAKE:** 20 MIN. • **MAKES:** 16 SERVINGS

- 1 **cup water (70° to 80°)**
- 2 **tablespoons olive oil**
- 2½ **cups all-purpose flour**
- 1 **teaspoon salt**
- 1 **tablespoon chopped chipotle pepper in adobo sauce**
- 1½ **teaspoons active dry yeast**

TOPPING

- 6 **garlic cloves, peeled**
- ¼ **teaspoon plus 7 tablespoons olive oil, divided**
- 4 **large onions, cut into ¼-inch slices**
- 2 **tablespoons chopped chipotle peppers in adobo sauce**
- ¼ **teaspoon salt**

1. In a bread machine pan, place the first six ingredients in order suggested by manufacturer. Select dough setting (check dough after 5 minutes of mixing; add 1 to 2 tablespoons of water or flour if needed).

2. When cycle is completed, turn dough onto a lightly floured surface. Punch down dough; cover and let rest for 15 minutes.

3. Meanwhile, place garlic in a small microwave-safe bowl. Drizzle with ¼ teaspoon oil. Microwave garlic on high for 20-60 seconds or until softened. Mash the garlic.

4. Roll dough into a 12x10-in. rectangle. Transfer to a well-greased baking sheet. Cover and let rise in a warm place until slightly risen, about 20 minutes.

5. With fingertips, make several dimples over top of dough. Brush dough with 1 tablespoon oil. Bake at 400° for 10 minutes or until lightly browned.

6. Meanwhile, in a large skillet, saute onions in remaining oil until tender. Add the chipotle peppers, salt and mashed garlic; saute 2-3 minutes longer. Sprinkle over dough.

7. Bake 10-15 minutes longer or until golden brown. Cut into squares; serve warm.

PRALINE SWEET POTATO BREAD

I like to give these pretty loaves as gifts. You can make and freeze a big batch ahead of time, which helps out a lot when life gets especially busy.
—**MARINA CASTLE** CANYON COUNTRY, CA

PREP: 25 MIN. • **BAKE:** 1 HOUR + COOLING
MAKES: 2 LOAVES (16 SLICES EACH)

- 4 **cups all-purpose flour**
- 2 **teaspoons baking soda**
- 1½ **teaspoons salt**
- 1 **teaspoon baking powder**
- 2 **cups packed light brown sugar**
- 1½ **cups sugar**
- 1 **teaspoon ground cinnamon**
- 1 **teaspoon ground nutmeg**
- ½ **teaspoon ground cloves**
- ½ **teaspoon ground allspice**
- ¼ **teaspoon ground ginger**
- 4 **eggs**
- 2 **cups mashed sweet potatoes**
- 1 **cup canola oil**
- ⅔ **cup water**
- 1 **teaspoon rum extract**
- 1 **cup chopped pecans**

TOPPING
- 3 **tablespoons dark brown sugar**
- 3 **tablespoons dark corn syrup**
- 4 **teaspoons butter**
- ½ **teaspoon vanilla extract**
- ½ **cup chopped pecans**

1. Grease and flour two 9x5-in. loaf pans. Line bottoms of pans with waxed paper and grease the paper; set aside.

2. In a large bowl, combine the first 11 ingredients. In another large bowl, whisk eggs, sweet potatoes, oil, water and extract. Stir into the dry ingredients just until moistened; fold in the pecans.

3. Transfer to prepared pans. Bake at 350° for 60-70 minutes or until a toothpick inserted near the center comes out clean. Cool for 10 minutes before removing from pans to wire racks. Carefully peel off waxed paper.

4. For topping, in a small saucepan, combine the brown sugar, corn syrup, butter and vanilla. Cook and stir over medium heat until butter is melted. Remove from the heat; stir in pecans.

MASHING SWEET POTATOES

To make mashed sweet potatoes, you'll first need to place whole scrubbed sweet potatoes in a large kettle; cover potatoes with water. Cover kettle and boil gently for 30-45 minutes or until potatoes can be easily pierced with the tip of a sharp knife. Drain. When potatoes are cool enough to handle, peel and mash.

BACON SCONES

I grew up in Scotland where this scone recipe was very popular. The savory bites are great with a salad.
TERESA ROYSTON SEABECK, WA

PREP: 20 MIN. • **BAKE:** 15 MIN. • **MAKES:** 8 SCONES

- 1¾ **cups all-purpose flour**
- 2¼ **teaspoons baking powder**
- 1 **teaspoon ground mustard**
- ½ **teaspoon salt**
- ¼ **teaspoon pepper**
- 6 **tablespoons cold butter**
- 2 **eggs**
- ⅓ **cup 2% milk**
- ½ **cup chopped onion**
- ¼ **cup shredded cheddar cheese**
- 6 **bacon strips, cooked and crumbled, divided**

1. Preheat oven to 400°. In a large bowl, combine first five ingredients. Cut in butter until mixture resembles coarse crumbs. In a small bowl, whisk eggs and milk. Stir into dry ingredients just until moistened. Fold in onion, cheese and two-thirds of the bacon.

2. Transfer dough to a greased baking sheet. Pat into a 7½-in. circle. Cut into eight wedges, but do not separate. Sprinkle with remaining bacon. Bake 15-20 minutes or until golden brown. Serve warm.

JAZZED-UP FRENCH BREAD

Fire up the grill for this recipe! It takes only minutes to prepare, and then cooks over indirect heat, giving you plenty of time to assemble the rest of the meal.
—**LORI LECROY** EAST TAWAS, MI

PREP: 10 MIN. • **GRILL:** 30 MIN. + STANDING • **MAKES:** 10 SERVINGS

- 2 cups (8 ounces) shredded Colby-Monterey Jack cheese
- ⅔ cup mayonnaise
- 6 green onions, chopped
- 1 loaf (1 pound) French bread, halved lengthwise

1. In a bowl, combine the cheese, mayonnaise and onions. Spread over cut sides of bread and reassemble loaf. Wrap bread in double thickness of heavy-duty foil (about 28x18 in.); seal tightly.
2. Grill, covered, over indirect medium heat for 25-30 minutes or until cheese is melted, turning once. Let stand for 5 minutes before cutting into slices.

GRANDMA'S PUMPKIN BREAD

You just can't beat the aroma of a pumpkin bread fresh out of the oven. This classic recipe makes two moist loaves, each with a sugary crust around its edges.
—**KATHLEENE BAKER** PLANO, TX

PREP: 25 MIN. • **BAKE:** 55 MIN. + COOLING
MAKES: 2 LOAVES (16 SLICES EACH)

- ⅔ cup shortening
- 2⅔ cups sugar
- 4 eggs
- 1 can (15 ounces) solid-pack pumpkin
- ⅔ cup water
- 3⅓ cups all-purpose flour
- 1 teaspoon baking soda
- 1 teaspoon ground cinnamon
- ½ teaspoon baking powder
- ½ teaspoon salt
- ⅛ teaspoon ground nutmeg
- ⅔ cup chopped pecans or walnuts

1. In a large bowl, cream shortening and sugar until light and fluffy. Beat in the eggs, pumpkin and water (mixture will appear curdled). Combine the flour, baking soda, cinnamon, baking powder, salt and nutmeg; gradually beat into pumpkin mixture until blended. Stir in nuts.
2. Transfer to two greased 9x5-in. loaf pans. Bake at 350° for 55-65 minutes or until a toothpick inserted near the center comes out clean. Cool for 10 minutes before removing from pans to wire racks.

JALAPENO CHEDDAR BISCUITS

These tender, cheesy biscuits have a moderate heat level that won't overpower you. Kids like them, too!
—**FLORENCE MCNULTY** MONTEBELLO, CA

START TO FINISH: 25 MIN. • **MAKES:** 15 BISCUITS

- 2 cups all-purpose flour
- 3 teaspoons baking powder
- ½ teaspoon salt
- ½ teaspoon dried thyme
- ½ teaspoon paprika
- 5 tablespoons cold butter
- ¾ cup 2% milk
- 1 cup (4 ounces) shredded sharp cheddar cheese
- 3 tablespoons diced pickled jalapeno slices

1. In a large bowl, combine the flour, baking powder, salt, thyme and paprika. Cut in butter until mixture resembles coarse crumbs. Stir in the milk, cheese and jalapeno.
2. Turn onto a lightly floured surface; knead 8-10 times. Pat or roll out to ½-in. thickness; cut with a floured 2½-in. biscuit cutter. Place 2 in. apart on an ungreased baking sheet.
3. Bake at 450° for 12-14 minutes or until golden brown. Serve biscuits warm.
NOTE *Wear disposable gloves when cutting hot peppers; the oils can burn skin. Avoid touching your face.*

CHEDDAR GOUGERES

Gougeres are usually made with Gruyere cheese but I often substitute the sharpest cheddar I can find for a bolder taste. Experiment to find your personal preference.

—BRIDGET KLUSMAN OTSEGO, MI

PREP: 30 MIN. • **BAKE:** 15 MIN. • **MAKES:** 3 DOZEN

- 1 cup water
- ¼ cup butter, cubed
- 2½ teaspoons kosher salt, divided
- 1 cup all-purpose flour
- 4 eggs
- 1½ cups shredded sharp cheddar cheese
- ½ cup minced fresh chives
- 2 garlic cloves, minced

1. In a saucepan, bring the water, butter and ½ teaspoon salt to a boil. Add flour all at once and stir until a smooth ball forms. Remove from the heat; let stand for 5 minutes. Add eggs, one at a time, beating well after each addition. Continue beating until mixture is smooth and shiny. Stir in cheese, chives and garlic.

2. Drop by tablespoonfuls 1 in. apart onto greased baking sheets. Sprinkle with the remaining salt. Bake at 375° for 14-16 minutes or until golden brown. Serve warm.

WHOLE WHEAT CRESCENT ROLLS

Store-bought rolls are no match for the sweet flavor and soft texture of these homemade crescents.

—FANCHEON RESLER ALBION, IN

PREP: 30 MIN. + RISING • **BAKE:** 10 MIN. • **MAKES:** 2 DOZEN

- 2 packages (¼ ounce each) active dry yeast
- ½ cup warm water (110° to 115°)
- 1 cup 2% milk (110° to 115°)
- ½ cup butter, softened
- 2 eggs
- 2 cups whole wheat flour
- 2 cups all-purpose flour
- 1 cup mashed potato flakes
- ½ cup packed brown sugar
- 1 teaspoon salt
- ¼ cup butter, melted

1. In a large bowl, dissolve yeast in warm water. Add the milk, softened butter, eggs, whole wheat flour, 1 cup all-purpose flour, potato flakes, brown sugar and salt. Beat on medium speed for 3 minutes. Stir in enough remaining all-purpose flour to form a soft dough (dough will be sticky).

2. Turn onto a floured surface; knead until smooth and elastic, about 6-8 minutes. Place in a greased bowl, turning once to grease the top. Cover and let rise in a warm place until doubled, about 1 hour. Punch dough down.

3. Turn onto a lightly floured surface; divide into thirds. Roll each portion into a 12-in. circle; cut each circle into 8 wedges. Roll up wedges from the wide ends and place point side down 2 in. apart on greased baking sheets. Curve the ends to form crescents. Cover and let rise in a warm place for 1 hour or until dough has doubled.

4. Bake at 350° for 8-10 minutes or until golden brown. Brush with melted butter. Serve warm.

1. Place squash in a large saucepan and cover with water. Bring to a boil. Reduce heat; cover and cook for 15-20 minutes or until tender. Drain and mash squash (you will need 2 cups); cool to 110°-115°.

2. In a small bowl, dissolve yeast in warm milk and water. In a large bowl, combine the pepitas, butter, egg, brown sugar, salt, cooked squash, yeast mixture and 2 cups flour; beat on medium speed for 3 minutes. Stir in enough remaining flour to form a soft dough (dough will be sticky).

3. Turn onto a floured surface; knead until smooth and elastic, about 6-8 minutes. Place in a greased bowl, turning once to grease the top. Cover with plastic wrap and let rise in a warm place until doubled, about 1 hour.

4. Punch dough down. Turn onto a lightly floured surface; divide into thirds. Shape each into a 26-in. rope; braid ropes. Transfer to a greased baking sheet; form into a circle, pinching ends together to seal. Cover with a clean kitchen towel; let rise in a warm place until doubled, about 45 minutes.

5. For topping, beat egg and water; brush over braid. Sprinkle with pepitas. Bake at 350° for 18-23 minutes or until golden brown. Remove from pan to wire rack.

CHIVE GARLIC BREAD

Start with a French bread loaf and dress it up with garlic and chives to make it irresistible. We like to serve this with lasagna, and we don't stop eating until the last crumbs have vanished.

—**KIM ORR** WEST GROVE, PA

START TO FINISH: 20 MIN. • **MAKES:** 12 SERVINGS

- ¼ **cup butter, softened**
- ¼ **cup grated Parmesan cheese**
- 2 **tablespoons minced chives**
- 1 **garlic clove, minced**
- 1 **loaf (1 pound) French bread, cut into 1-inch slices**

In a small bowl, combine the butter, cheese, chives and garlic; spread on one side of each slice of bread. Wrap in a large piece of heavy-duty foil; seal tightly. Place on a baking sheet. Bake at 350° for 15-20 minutes or until heated through.

SEEDED BUTTERNUT SQUASH BRAID

Green hulled pumpkin seeds (also known as pepitas) add a slightly nutty taste to this rich bread. Because of their high oil content, pepitas can spoil quickly. Store them in the freezer to keep them fresh.

—**CHERYL PERRY** HERTFORD, NC

PREP: 45 MIN. + RISING • **BAKE:** 20 MIN.
MAKES: 1 LOAF (18 SLICES)

- 2¾ **cups uncooked cubed peeled butternut squash**
- 1 **package (¼ ounce) active dry yeast**
- ⅓ **cup warm 2% milk (110° to 115°)**
- 2 **tablespoons warm water (110° to 115°)**
- ½ **cup pepitas or sunflower kernels**
- ¼ **cup butter, softened**
- 1 **egg**
- 3 **tablespoons brown sugar**
- ½ **teaspoon salt**
- 3½ **to 4 cups all-purpose flour**

TOPPING
- 1 **egg**
- 1 **tablespoon water**
- ¼ **cup pepitas or sunflower kernels**

FARMHOUSE BARBECUE MUFFINS

Tangy barbecue sauce, fluffy biscuits and cheddar cheese combine to make these hearty muffins. Try them with ground turkey or other shredded cheeses to vary the flavor.

—KAREN KENNEY HARVARD, IL

PREP: 20 MIN. • **BAKE:** 20 MIN. • **MAKES:** 10 SERVINGS

- 1 tube (10 ounces) refrigerated buttermilk biscuits
- 1 pound ground beef
- ½ cup ketchup
- 3 tablespoons brown sugar
- 1 tablespoon cider vinegar
- ½ teaspoon chili powder
- 1 cup (4 ounces) shredded cheddar cheese

1. Separate dough into 10 biscuits; flatten into 5-in. circles. Press each onto the bottom and up the sides of a greased muffin cup; set aside.

2. In a skillet, cook beef over medium heat until no longer pink; drain. In a small bowl, combine ketchup, brown sugar, vinegar and chili powder; add to beef and mix well.

3. Divide the meat mixture among biscuit-lined muffins cups, using about ¼ cup for each. Sprinkle with cheese. Bake at 375° for 18-20 minutes or until golden brown. Cool for 5 minutes before serving.

SWEET POTATO BISCUITS WITH HONEY BUTTER

Why not give sweet potatoes a starring role at your breakfast table? Served with cinnamon-honey butter, these biscuits are delicious morning surprise.

—CATHY BELL JOPLIN, MO

START TO FINISH: 30 MIN.
MAKES: 10 BISCUITS (ABOUT ½ CUP HONEY BUTTER)

- 2 cups all-purpose flour
- 4 teaspoons sugar
- 3 teaspoons baking powder
- 1 teaspoon salt
- 1 teaspoon ground cinnamon
- ½ teaspoon ground nutmeg
- ¼ cup shortening
- 1 cup mashed sweet potatoes
- ½ cup half-and-half cream

HONEY BUTTER

- ½ cup butter, softened
- 2 tablespoons honey
- 1 teaspoon ground cinnamon

1. In a small bowl, combine the first six ingredients. Cut in shortening until mixture resembles coarse crumbs. Combine sweet potatoes and cream; stir into crumb mixture just until moistened. Turn onto a lightly floured surface; gently knead 8-10 times.

2. Pat or roll out to ½-in. thickness; cut with a floured 2½-in. biscuit cutter. Place 1 in. apart on a greased baking sheet.

3. Bake at 400° for 9-11 minutes or until golden brown. Meanwhile, in a small bowl, beat the butter, honey and cinnamon until blended. Serve with warm biscuits.

Sweet Sunrise Specialties

Start your day off on a delicious note! Pick from these sweet loaves when planning your next brunch. You may even want to enjoy them for dessert—the recipes are that special!

CHOCOLATE MONKEY BREAD

We enjoy this bread while opening Christmas gifts, but it's perfect year-round. With chocolate inside each bite, this pull-apart delight is impossible to resist.
—HEATHER DETERDING ODENTON, MD

PREP: 20 MIN. • **BAKE:** 40 MIN. • **MAKES:** 16 SERVINGS

- 1 cup packed brown sugar
- ¾ cup butter, cubed
- 2 cans (16.3 ounces each) large refrigerated buttermilk biscuits
- 64 milk chocolate kisses
- ½ cup sugar
- 2 teaspoons ground cinnamon

1. In a small saucepan, combine brown sugar and butter. Cook and stir over medium-low heat for 10-12 minutes or until sugar is melted; set aside.

2. Cut each biscuit into quarters. Shape each piece around a chocolate kiss; pinch seams to seal. In a large resealable plastic bag, combine the sugar and cinnamon. Add biscuits, a few pieces at a time, and shake to coat.

3. Spoon ¼ cup caramel into a well-greased 10-in. fluted tube pan. Arrange a third of the biscuits in the pan and drizzle with ¼ cup caramel. Repeat layers twice.

4. Bake, uncovered, at 350° for 40-45 minutes or until golden brown. Cover loosely with foil if biscuits brown too quickly. Immediately invert onto a serving plate. Let monkey bread stand for 10 minutes before serving.

RASPBERRY BREAKFAST BRAID

We like using blackberries, marionberries or a mixture of raspberries and blackberries in this quick and easy pastry.
—TRESSA NICHOLLS SANDY, OR

PREP: 20 MIN. • **BAKE:** 15 MIN. • **MAKES:** 12 SERVINGS

- 2 cups biscuit/baking mix
- 1 package (3 ounces) cream cheese, cubed
- ¼ cup cold butter, cubed
- ⅓ cup 2% milk
- 1¼ cups fresh raspberries
- 3 tablespoons sugar
- ¼ cup vanilla frosting

1. Place biscuit mix in a large bowl. Cut in cream cheese and butter until mixture resembles coarse crumbs. Stir in the milk just until moistened. Turn onto a lightly floured surface; knead gently 8-10 times.

2. On a greased baking sheet, roll dough into an 18x12-in. rectangle. Spoon raspberries down center third of dough; sprinkle with sugar.

3. On each long side, cut 1-in.-wide strips about 2½ in. into center. Starting at one end, fold alternating strips at an angle across raspberries; seal ends.

4. Bake at 425° for 15-20 minutes or until golden brown. Remove to a wire rack to cool slightly. In a microwave-safe dish, microwave frosting on high for 5-10 seconds or until of desired consistency; drizzle over pastry.

COCONUT-PECAN COFFEE CAKE

I've learned to keep copies of the recipe on hand because this satisfying cake usually generates requests. The coconut-flavored pudding mix is a unique twist.
—**BETH TROPEANO** CHARLOTTE, NC

PREP: 15 MIN. • **BAKE:** 35 MIN. • **MAKES:** 15 SERVINGS

- 1 package yellow cake mix (regular size)
- 1 package (3.4 ounces) instant coconut cream pudding mix
- 1 teaspoon vanilla extract

FILLING
- ½ cup chopped pecans
- ⅓ cup sugar
- ½ teaspoon ground cinnamon

GLAZE
- 1 cup confectioners' sugar
- 1 to 2 tablespoons 2% milk
- ½ teaspoon vanilla extract

1. Prepare cake mix batter according to package directions, adding pudding mix and vanilla; set aside. In a small bowl, combine the pecans, sugar and cinnamon.

2. Spread half of the cake batter into a greased 13x9-in. baking pan. Sprinkle with half of filling. Top with the remaining batter and filling.

3. Bake at 350° for 34-38 minutes or until a toothpick inserted near the center comes out clean. Cool on a wire rack. In a small bowl, combine the glaze ingredients until smooth. Drizzle over warm coffee cake.

BRUNCH CINNAMON ROLLS

This family-friendly breakfast bun is glazed with maple and vanilla to accent the cinnamon and nuts.
—**RITA VOGEL** MALCOM, IA

PREP: 30 MIN. • **BAKE:** 20 MIN. • **MAKES:** 1 DOZEN

- ¾ cup 4% small-curd cottage cheese
- ⅓ cup reduced-fat plain yogurt
- ¼ cup sugar
- ¼ cup butter, melted
- 1 teaspoon vanilla extract
- 2 cups all-purpose flour
- 2 teaspoons baking powder
- ¼ teaspoon baking soda
- ½ teaspoon salt

FILLING
- 2 tablespoons butter, melted
- 1 cup chopped pecans
- ⅔ cup packed brown sugar
- 1½ teaspoons ground cinnamon

MAPLE GLAZE
- ⅔ cup confectioners' sugar
- 3 tablespoons maple syrup
- 1 teaspoon vanilla extract

1. In a food processor, combine the first five ingredients; cover and process until smooth. Add the flour, baking powder, baking soda and salt; cover and pulse until mixture forms a soft dough.

2. Transfer to a lightly floured surface; knead 4-5 times. Roll into a 15x12-in. rectangle. Brush butter to within ½ in. of edges. Combine the pecans, brown sugar and cinnamon; sprinkle over dough. Roll up jelly-roll style, starting with a long side; pinch seam to seal. Cut into 12 slices. Place cut side down in a greased 9-in. round baking pan.

3. Bake at 400° for 20-25 minutes or until golden brown. Cool for 5 minutes before inverting onto a serving plate. Combine glaze ingredients; drizzle over rolls. Serve warm.

APRICOT CREAM BISCUITS

Melt-in-your-mouth good, these biscuits with a hint of orange prove that you can use shortcuts to bake treats with wonderful homemade taste.

—BETTY SAINT TURNER ATTALLA, AL

START TO FINISH: 30 MIN. • **MAKES:** 1 DOZEN

- 3 **cups biscuit/baking mix**
- 2 **teaspoons grated orange peel**
- 1 **cup heavy whipping cream**
- ¼ **cup apricot preserves**
- 2 **tablespoons cream cheese, softened**
- 2 **teaspoons sugar**

1. In a large bowl, combine baking mix and orange peel. Stir in cream just until moistened. Turn onto a lightly floured surface; knead 8-10 times. Roll out to ½-in. thickness; cut with a floured 2½-in. biscuit cutter.

2. Place 2 in. apart on an ungreased baking sheet. Using the end of a wooden spoon handle, make an indentation 1¼ in. wide and ¼ in. deep in the center of each biscuit.

3. In a small bowl, beat apricot preserves and cream cheese until blended. Drop by teaspoonfuls into the center of each biscuit. Sprinkle with sugar.

4. Bake at 400° for 10-15 minutes or until golden brown. Serve biscuits warm.

SUN-DRIED TOMATO GARLIC BREAD

You need only 10 minutes to put this bread together. It's easy enough for a weekday, but special enough for a weekend meal with guests.

—NADINE MESCH MOUNT HEALTHY, OH

START TO FINISH: 10 MIN. • **MAKES:** 6 SERVINGS

- ¼ **cup butter, softened**
- ¼ **cup grated Parmesan cheese**
- 2 **tablespoons chopped oil-packed sun-dried tomatoes**
- 1 **to 2 garlic cloves, minced**
- ½ **loaf Italian bread, halved lengthwise**

1. In a small bowl, combine the butter, cheese, tomatoes and garlic. Spread over cut sides of bread. Transfer to an ungreased baking sheet.

2. Broil 4 in. from the heat for 3-4 minutes or until golden brown. Cut into slices and serve warm.

WHAT KIND OF SUN-DRIED TOMATOES?

Sun-dried tomatoes have been dried to remove most of their water content, resulting in a chewy tomato product with an intense flavor. Sun-dried tomatoes are available packed in oil or dry-packed. Make sure you use the specific type that the recipe calls for.

RAISIN RICOTTA BREAD WITH CHIVE BUTTER

With golden raisins and ricotta cheese, this loaf is something special. Don't skip the accompanying herb butter—it's the perfect touch.

—KATHLEEN GILL PAHRUMP, NV

PREP: 15 MIN. • **BAKE:** 40 MIN. + COOLING
MAKES: 1 MINI LOAF (6 SLICES) AND ¼ CUP BUTTER

- 1¼ cups all-purpose flour
- 1¼ teaspoons baking powder
- ¼ teaspoon salt
- ⅓ cup coarsely chopped golden raisins
- 1 egg
- ⅓ cup whole-milk ricotta cheese
- ¼ cup canola oil
- ¼ cup heavy whipping cream
- 3 tablespoons honey
- ¼ cup plus 1 tablespoon unsalted sunflower kernels, toasted, divided

CHIVE BUTTER
- ¼ cup butter, softened
- 4 teaspoons minced chives

1. In a large bowl, combine the flour, baking powder and salt. Stir in the raisins. In a large bowl, whisk the egg, ricotta cheese, oil, cream and honey. Stir into dry ingredients just until moistened; fold in ¼ cup sunflower seeds.

2. Transfer to a greased 5¾x3x2-in. loaf pan (pan will be full). Sprinkle with remaining sunflower seeds.

3. Bake at 350° for 38-42 minutes or until a toothpick inserted near the center comes out clean. Cool for 10 minutes before removing from pan to a wire rack.

4. Meanwhile, combine the butter and chives. Serve with warm bread.

SEEDED HONEY WHEAT BREAD

I usually have to double this recipe because my family loves the poppy and sunflower seed combination so much. Bread bakers will appreciate its shape and soft texture.

—RACHEL HEIDENREICH MARSHALL, MI

PREP: 45 MIN. + RISING • **BAKE:** 25 MIN. + COOLING
MAKES: 2 LOAVES (12 SLICES EACH)

- 1 cup whole wheat flour
- 2 packages (¼ ounce each) quick-rise yeast
- 1 teaspoon salt
- 3½ to 4 cups all-purpose flour
- 1½ cups water
- ¼ cup butter, cubed
- ¼ cup honey
- ⅓ cup flaxseed
- ¼ cup unsalted sunflower kernels
- 1 tablespoon poppy seeds
- 1 egg

1. In a large bowl, combine the whole wheat flour, yeast, salt and 1 cup all-purpose flour; set aside. In a small saucepan,

heat the water, butter and honey to 120°-130°. Add to the dry ingredients. Stir in the flax, sunflower kernels, poppy seeds and enough remaining flour to form a stiff dough.

2. Turn onto a floured surface; knead until smooth and elastic, about 6-8 minutes. Cover with plastic wrap and let rest 10 minutes. Punch down dough; divide in half. Shape into loaves. Place loaves in two greased 8x4-in. loaf pans, seam side down. Cover and let loaves rise in a warm place until doubled, about 15 minutes.

3. In a small bowl, beat egg; brush over loaves. Bake at 350° for 25-30 minutes or until golden brown. Remove from pans to wire racks to cool.

CHEDDAR BREAD TWISTS

Serve these flaky breadsticks as a side dish, or with dip for an impressive appetizer.

—TRACY TRAVERS FAIRHAVEN, MA

START TO FINISH: 25 MIN. • **MAKES:** 10 BREADSTICKS

- 1 sheet frozen puff pastry, thawed
- 1 egg white
- 1 tablespoon cold water
- ½ cup shredded cheddar cheese
  Dash salt

1. Unfold puff pastry onto a lightly floured surface. In a small bowl, beat egg white and water; brush over pastry. Sprinkle with cheese and salt.

2. Cut into ten 1-in. strips; twist each strip three times. Place on a greased baking sheet. Bake at 400° for 10-13 minutes or until golden brown.

MINI CARAMEL ROLLS

Your family will gravitate to the kitchen when they smell these rolls baking. These treats come together very quickly, thanks to a tube of refrigerated crescent rolls—and they will disappear just as fast.

—**KAYLA WIEGAND** CONGERVILLE, IL

PREP: 20 MIN. • **BAKE:** 15 MIN. • **MAKES:** 12 SERVINGS

- ⅓ cup packed brown sugar
- ⅓ cup butter, cubed
- 2 tablespoons light corn syrup
- 1½ teaspoons 2% milk
- 1 tube (8 ounces) refrigerated crescent rolls
- 2 teaspoons sugar
- ½ teaspoon ground cinnamon

1. In a small saucepan, combine the brown sugar, butter, corn syrup and milk. Cook and stir over medium heat until butter is melted and sugar is dissolved. Pour into a greased 9-in. pie plate; set aside.

2. Separate crescent dough into four rectangles; gently press perforations to seal. In a small bowl, combine sugar and cinnamon; sprinkle evenly over rectangles. Roll up jelly-roll style, starting with a long side; pinch seams to seal.

3. Cut each roll into nine slices; place cut side down in prepared pie plate. Bake at 375° for 15-18 minutes or until golden brown. Cool in pie plate for 1 minute before inverting onto a serving plate.

HERB & SUN-DRIED TOMATO MUFFINS

Mom often served these muffins instead of bread or buns. Now I enjoy them alongside soup or chili.

—**BETSY KING** DULUTH, MN

PREP: 15 MIN. • **BAKE:** 20 MIN. • **MAKES:** 1 DOZEN

- 2 cups all-purpose flour
- 2 teaspoons baking powder
- 1 teaspoon snipped fresh dill or ¼ teaspoon dill weed
- 1 teaspoon minced fresh thyme or ¼ teaspoon dried thyme
- ½ teaspoon baking soda
- ½ teaspoon salt
- ½ teaspoon pepper
- 1 egg
- 1¼ cups 2% milk
- ¼ cup olive oil
- ½ cup shredded cheddar cheese
- ½ cup oil-packed sun-dried tomatoes, finely chopped

1. In a large bowl, mix the first seven ingredients. In another bowl, whisk the egg, milk and oil. Add to flour mixture; stir just until moistened. Fold in cheese and tomatoes.

2. Fill greased muffin cups three-fourths full. Bake at 375° for 18-20 minutes or until a toothpick inserted in center comes out clean. Cool for 5 minutes before removing from pan to a wire rack. Serve warm.

DUTCH APPLE PIE MUFFINS

Wake up loved ones with a fresh batch of these cinnamon-spiced muffins. The crumbly streusel-like topping makes them so special, they could even double as dessert.

—SUZANNE PAULEY RENTON, WA

PREP: 25 MIN. • **BAKE:** 20 MIN. • **MAKES:** 1 DOZEN

- 2 **cups finely chopped peeled tart apples**
- 3 **tablespoons sugar**
- 3 **tablespoons water**
- 2 **tablespoons brown sugar**
- 1 **tablespoon all-purpose flour**
- 2 **tablespoons butter**
- 1 **teaspoon lemon juice**
- 1 **teaspoon vanilla extract**

TOPPING
- 3 **tablespoons brown sugar**
- 2 **tablespoons all-purpose flour**
- 2 **tablespoons quick-cooking oats**
- 2 **tablespoons cold butter**

BATTER
- 1¾ **cups all-purpose flour**
- ½ **cup sugar**
- 2 **teaspoons baking powder**
- 1 **teaspoon ground cinnamon**
- ½ **teaspoon salt**
- 1 **egg**
- ¾ **cup 2% milk**
- ¼ **cup canola oil**

GLAZE
- ¼ **cup confectioners' sugar**
- 1 **to 2 teaspoons 2% milk**

1. In a small saucepan, combine the apples, sugar, water and brown sugar. Bring to a boil over medium heat. Sprinkle with flour; cook and stir for 2 minutes or until thickened. Stir in butter and lemon juice. Remove from the heat; add vanilla. Set aside to cool.

2. For topping, combine the brown sugar, flour and oats. Cut in butter until mixture resembles coarse crumbs; set aside.

3. In a large bowl, combine the flour, sugar, baking powder, cinnamon and salt. In another bowl, beat the egg, milk and oil. Stir into dry ingredients just until moistened. Fill greased or paper-lined muffin cups three-fourths full. Drop the apple mixture by tablespoonfuls into the center of each muffin. Sprinkle with topping.

4. Bake at 400° for 20-24 minutes or until a toothpick inserted in a muffin comes out clean. Cool for 5 minutes before removing from pan to a wire rack. Combine glaze ingredients; drizzle over muffins. Serve warm.

SUPER-FAST CORN BREAD

Slather some butter on this corn bread when it's fresh from the oven. You just can't beat it!

—BECKY BUTLER KELLER, TX

START TO FINISH: 20 MIN. • **MAKES:** 8 SERVINGS

1¼ cups biscuit/baking mix
1¼ cups yellow cornmeal
2 eggs
1½ cups 2% milk

1. Combine biscuit mix and cornmeal in a large bowl. Whisk eggs and milk; stir into dry ingredients. Transfer to a greased 9-in. ovenproof skillet.

2. Bake at 400° for 15-20 minutes or until a toothpick inserted near the center comes out clean. Cut into wedges. Serve warm.

CHERRY-PECAN STREUSEL ROLLS

It's a treat just watching guests enjoy these rolls. The tart cherries, sweet almond paste and crisp streusel topping have people reaching for seconds every time.

—JEANNE HOLT MENDOTA HEIGHTS, MN

PREP: 35 MIN. + RISING • **BAKE:** 20 MIN. • **MAKES:** 1 DOZEN

½ cup warm 2% milk (70° to 80°)
¼ cup butter, melted
¼ cup sugar
1 egg
½ teaspoon salt
1¾ cups all-purpose flour
⅔ cup quick-cooking oats
2¼ teaspoons bread machine yeast

FILLING

⅔ cup chopped pecans
½ cup sugar
⅓ cup quick-cooking oats
⅓ cup butter, melted
1½ teaspoons ground cinnamon
½ cup dried tart cherries, chopped
⅓ cup almond paste, finely chopped
2 tablespoons all-purpose flour

GLAZE

1 cup confectioners' sugar
4 teaspoons 2% milk
¼ teaspoon almond extract

1. In a bread machine pan, place the first eight ingredients in order suggested by manufacturer. Select dough setting (check dough after 5 minutes of mixing; add 1 to 2 tablespoons of water or flour if needed).

2. When cycle is completed, turn dough onto a lightly floured surface. Roll into a 16x8-in. rectangle.

3. In a small bowl, combine the pecans, sugar, oats, butter and cinnamon. Set aside ⅓ cup for topping. To the remaining filling, stir in cherries and almond paste. Sprinkle over dough to within ¼ in. of edges. Roll up jelly-roll style, starting with a long side; pinch seam to seal. Cut into 12 slices.

4. Place cut side down in a greased 13x9-in. baking pan. Cover and let rise until doubled, about 1 hour.

5. Preheat oven to 350°. Stir flour into the reserved topping; sprinkle over rolls. Bake 20-25 minutes or until golden brown. In a small bowl, beat the confectioners' sugar, milk and extract until smooth. Drizzle over warm rolls.

BRAIDED ONION-POTATO LOAF

Mashed potato in a bread recipe? Absolutely! The potato's starch absorbs liquid during kneading, so the bread finishes with a crusty brown exterior and a flavorful, moist interior that helps the bread keep longer.

—**JOAN RANZINI** WAYNESBORO, VA

PREP: 20 MIN. + RISING • **BAKE:** 25 MIN.
MAKES: 1 LOAF (16 SLICES)

- 1 large Yukon Gold potato, peeled and cubed
- 1 small onion, chopped
- 1 cup warm 2% milk (70° to 80°)
- 1 egg
- 2 tablespoons butter
- 1 tablespoon honey
- ¼ cup grated Parmesan cheese
- ¼ cup chopped fresh parsley
- 1½ teaspoons salt
- ¼ teaspoon pepper
- 4 cups bread flour
- 1 package (¼ ounce) active dry yeast

TOPPING

- 1 egg, lightly beaten
  Additional grated Parmesan cheese

1. Place potato and onion in a small saucepan and cover with water. Bring to a boil. Reduce heat; cover and cook for 10-15 minutes or until vegetables are tender. Drain; mash until potatoes are smooth (about ¾ cup); set aside.

2. In a bread machine pan, place the milk, mashed potato, egg, butter, honey, cheese, parsley, salt, pepper, flour and yeast in order suggested by manufacturer. Select dough setting (check dough after 5 minutes of mixing; add 1 to 2 tablespoons of water or flour if needed).

3. When cycle is completed, turn dough onto a lightly floured surface. Divide into thirds. Shape each into an 18-in. rope. Place ropes on a greased baking sheet and braid; pinch ends to seal and tuck under.

4. Cover with a clean kitchen towel and let rise in a warm place until doubled, about 1 hour. Uncover; brush top with beaten egg. Sprinkle with additional cheese. Bake at 350° for 25-35 minutes or until golden brown. Remove from pan to a wire rack.

CHIMICHURRI MONKEY BREAD

My favorite herb sauce, chimichurri, stands out in this nostalgic bread recipe that comes together quickly, thanks in part to refrigerated biscuits.

—**EDEN DRANGER** LOS ANGELES, CA

PREP: 20 MIN. • **BAKE:** 20 MIN. • **MAKES:** 12 SERVINGS

- ¼ cup minced fresh parsley
- ¼ cup olive oil
- 2 tablespoons minced fresh oregano
- 1 tablespoon white wine vinegar
- 2 garlic cloves
- ¾ teaspoon kosher salt
- ¼ teaspoon ground cumin
- ¼ teaspoon pepper
- ⅛ teaspoon crushed red pepper flakes
- 2 tubes (12 ounces each) refrigerated buttermilk biscuits

1. In a shallow bowl, combine the first nine ingredients. Cut each biscuit in half and shape into a ball. Roll in herb mixture.

2. Place the biscuit pieces in a greased 10-in. fluted tube pan. Bake at 375° for 18-22 minutes or until golden brown. Cool for 5 minutes before inverting onto a serving plate.

MEALS IN MINUTES

Think you're too busy to prepare a homemade meal? Think again! If you're crunched for time, you'll find plenty of meal options here. That's because they're all ready—start to finish—in just 30 minutes or less!

FIESTA SWEET POTATO SOUP

Here's a simple soup with plenty of taste and just a little heat. Loaded with sweet potatoes, black beans and sausage, it tastes even better the next day—if you have leftovers.

—GILDA LESTER MILLSBORO, DE

START TO FINISH: 30 MIN. • **MAKES:** 6 SERVINGS (2¼ QUARTS)

- 1 package (9 ounces) fully cooked spicy chicken sausage links, chopped
- 2 medium sweet potatoes, peeled and cubed
- 1 large onion, chopped
- 1 small green pepper, diced
- 2 tablespoons olive oil
- 2 teaspoons ground cumin
- 2 cans (14½ ounces each) reduced-sodium chicken broth
- 1 can (14½ ounces) diced tomatoes with mild green chilies, undrained
- 1 can (15 ounces) black beans, rinsed and drained
- 2 tablespoons minced fresh cilantro
  Sour cream and thinly sliced green onions

1. In a large saucepan, saute the sausage, sweet potatoes, onion and pepper in oil until onion is tender. Add cumin; cook 1 minute longer. Stir in the broth, tomatoes and beans. Bring to a boil. Reduce heat; cover and simmer for 10 minutes or until potatoes are tender. Stir in cilantro.

2. Garnish servings with sour cream and green onions.

PEPPERONI PENNE CARBONARA

Sun-dried tomatoes and turkey pepperoni top this creamy, hearty pasta dish. It's a great change of pace from everyday spaghetti.

—TASTE OF HOME TEST KITCHEN

START TO FINISH: 30 MIN. • **MAKES:** 6 SERVINGS

- 3 cups uncooked penne pasta
- 2 cups chopped sun-dried tomatoes (not packed in oil)
- 3 cups boiling water
- ¼ cup butter
- ½ teaspoon minced garlic
- 1 cup chopped turkey pepperoni
- 1 cup shredded Parmesan cheese
- 1 cup heavy whipping cream
- 3 tablespoons minced fresh basil
- ½ teaspoon salt
- ¼ teaspoon pepper

1. Cook pasta according to package directions. Meanwhile, soak tomatoes in boiling water for 10 minutes; drain well.

2. In a large skillet, saute tomatoes in butter for 3 minutes. Add garlic; cook 1 minute longer.

3. Stir in the pepperoni, cheese, cream, basil, salt and pepper. Cook over low heat until heated through. Drain the pasta; toss with sauce.

CHUNKY CHICKEN NOODLE SOUP

Marjoram and thyme add nice flavors to an old-fashioned soup that tastes just like Grandma used to make. You can also modify the recipe to include whatever veggies your family enjoys. For instance, my kids love carrots, so I always toss in a few extra.
—**COLEEN MARTIN** BROOKFIELD, WI

START TO FINISH: 25 MIN. • **MAKES:** 6 SERVINGS

- ½ cup finely chopped carrot
- ¼ cup finely chopped celery
- ¼ cup finely chopped onion
- 1 teaspoon butter
- 6 cups chicken broth
- 1½ cups cubed cooked chicken
- 1 teaspoon salt
- ½ teaspoon dried marjoram
- ½ teaspoon dried thyme
- ⅛ teaspoon pepper
- 1¼ cups uncooked medium egg noodles
- 1 tablespoon minced fresh parsley

Saute the carrot, celery and onion in butter in a Dutch oven until tender. Stir in the broth, chicken and seasonings. Bring to a boil. Reduce heat. Add noodles; cook for 10 minutes or until noodles are tender. Sprinkle with parsley.

SUPER-STUFFED MEXICAN POTATOES

Yum, yum, these taters are packed! Everyone will enjoy customizing the potatoes with their favorite toppings.
—**STEVE WESTPHAL** WIND LAKE, WI

START TO FINISH: 25 MIN. • **MAKES:** 4 SERVINGS

- 4 large baking potatoes
- 1 jar (16 ounces) black bean and corn salsa
- 1 package (6 ounces) ready-to-use grilled chicken breast strips
- 1 cup cubed process cheese (Velveeta)
- 1 medium tomato, chopped
  Optional toppings: chopped green onions, sliced ripe olives and sour cream

1. Scrub and pierce potatoes; place on a microwave Microwave, uncovered, on high for 15-17 minutes o tender, turning once.
2. Meanwhile, in a large saucepan, combine the salsa, chicken and cheese. Cook and stir over medium heat until the cheese is melted.
3. Cut an "X" in the top of each potato; fluff pulp with a fork. Spoon salsa mixture over potatoes and sprinkle with tomato. Serve with toppings of your choice.
NOTE *This recipe was tested in a 1,100-watt microwave.*

CHILI HASH

You'll need your microwave and stovetop for only a few minutes to make this satisfying meal.
—**TASTE OF HOME TEST KITCHEN**

START TO FINISH: 30 MIN. • **MAKES:** 4 SERVINGS

- 1 pound medium potatoes, cubed
- ½ cup water
- 1 pound ground beef
- 1 medium onion, chopped
- 1 can (15½ ounces) chili starter
- 1 cup frozen peas
- 2 tablespoons minced fresh parsley
- ¼ teaspoon salt
  Sour cream, optional

1. Place potatoes and water in a microwave-safe dish. Cover and microwave on high for 7 minutes or until tender.
2. Meanwhile, in a large skillet, cook beef and onion over medium heat until meat is no longer pink; drain. Drain the potatoes and add to the skillet. Stir in the chili starter, peas, parsley and salt. Bring to a boil. Reduced heat; simmer, uncovered, for 5 minutes. Serve with sour cream if desired.

GRILLED RIBEYES WITH BLUE CHEESE BUTTER

Fire up the grill for steaks that practically melt in your mouth. With this recipe on hand, weeknight menus are sure to sizzle. The steaks are perfect for a weekened barbecue, too. They're garlic-infused, and the grilled flavor is off the charts.

—**JIM MOODY** WICHITA, KS

START TO FINISH: 25 MIN. • **MAKES:** 8 SERVINGS

- 8 beef ribeye steaks (10 ounces each)
- 12 garlic cloves, sliced
- ¼ cup olive oil
- 1 teaspoon salt
- ¾ teaspoon cayenne pepper
- ½ teaspoon pepper
- ½ cup crumbled blue cheese
- ¼ cup butter, softened

1. Cut slits into each steak; insert garlic slices. Brush with oil and sprinkle with salt, cayenne and pepper.

2. Grill, covered, over medium heat or broil 4 in. from the heat for 4-6 minutes on each side or until meat reaches desired doneness (for medium-rare, a thermometer should read 145°; medium, 160°; well-done, 170°).

3. Combine blue cheese and butter. Serve with steaks.

POLENTA ROUNDS WITH SAUSAGE RAGOUT

Fried polenta is fabulous with an endless variety of toppings from different cuisines. Make it Mexican with black beans and corn, French with mushroom ragout or Creole with spicy shrimp.

—**LISA SPEER** PALM BEACH, FL

START TO FINISH: 25 MIN. • **MAKES:** 4 SERVINGS

- 1 pound bulk Italian sausage
- 1 garlic clove, minced
- 2 cans (14½ ounces each) diced tomatoes with basil, oregano and garlic, drained
- ⅛ teaspoon pepper
- ¼ cup minced fresh basil
- 1 tube (1 pound) polenta, cut into ½-inch slices
- ¼ cup olive oil
- ½ cup grated Parmesan cheese

1. In a large skillet, cook sausage and garlic over medium heat until no longer pink; drain. Stir in tomatoes and pepper. Cook and stir for 4-5 minutes or until heated through. Remove from the heat; stir in basil.

2. In another skillet, cook polenta slices in oil over medium-high heat for 3-4 minutes on each side or until lightly browned. Serve with sausage mixture; sprinkle with cheese.

FIESTA TURKEY TORTILLA SOUP

Need to throw together a delicious soup in under 30 minutes? Here's the answer to your busy-night dinner problems!
—**AMY MCFADDEN** CHELSEA, AL

START TO FINISH: 25 MIN. • **MAKES:** 8 SERVINGS

- 4 cans (14½ ounces each) chicken broth
- 3 cups shredded cooked turkey or rotisserie chicken
- 1 can (15 ounces) black beans, rinsed and drained
- 1 can (15¼ ounces) whole kernel corn, drained
- ½ cup medium salsa
- 5 corn tortillas (6 inches), cut into ¼-inch strips
- ¼ cup chopped fresh cilantro
  Additional salsa, optional

1. In a Dutch oven, combine the first five ingredients; bring to a boil. Reduce heat; simmer for 10 minutes, stirring occasionally.
2. Meanwhile, spread tortilla strips in a single layer on a baking sheet. Bake at 400° for 4-6 minutes or until golden brown and crisp.
3. Stir cilantro into soup. Top servings with tortilla strips. If desired, serve with additional salsa.

BAKED PEANUT CHICKEN

Try a Thai dinner that's a little nutty, with a bit of spice. Add a steamed veggie and you'll have a complete meal in half an hour.
—**BRENDA HENDRICKSON** DANVILLE, KY

START TO FINISH: 30 MIN. • **MAKES:** 4 SERVINGS

- 1 can (13.66 ounces) coconut milk
- 1 package (3½ ounces) Thai peanut sauce mix
- 4 boneless skinless chicken breast halves (6 ounces each)
- 1 package (8½ ounces) ready-to-serve jasmine rice
- 2 green onions, thinly sliced
  Spanish peanuts, optional

1. Combine coconut milk and sauce mix in a small saucepan. Bring to a boil; cook and stir for 2-3 minutes or until thickened.
2. Arrange chicken in a greased 11x7-in. baking dish. Pour sauce over top. Bake, uncovered, at 350° for 20-25 minutes or until a thermometer reads 170°. Prepare rice according to package directions. Serve with chicken and sprinkle with onions and peanuts if desired.

DETERMINING IF CHICKEN'S DONE

To determine whether chicken is done, insert an instant-read thermometer. It should read 170° for breasts (boneless or bone-in) and boneless thighs, 180° for all other dark meat and whole chickens.

2. In the same skillet, melt butter over medium-high heat. Whisk the eggs, water, salt and pepper. Add egg mixture to skillet (mixture should set immediately at edges).

3. As eggs set, push cooked edges toward the center, letting uncooked portion flow underneath. When the eggs are set, spoon bacon mixture and potato on one side and sprinkle with cheese; fold other side over filling. Slide omelet onto a plate.

HAM & NOODLES WITH VEGGIES

Here, a package of frozen veggies with cheese sauce jazzes up pasta for a surefire success when time is tight.
—**JEANNIE KLUGH** LANCASTER, PA

START TO FINISH: 20 MIN. • **MAKES:** 6 SERVINGS

- 1 **can (14½ ounces) chicken broth**
- 1 **cup water**
- 3 **cups uncooked egg noodles**
- 2 **packages (24 ounces each) frozen broccoli, carrots, cauliflower and cheese sauce**
- 1 **package (16 ounces) cubed fully cooked ham**

1. Bring broth and water to a boil in a large saucepan. Add pasta; return to a boil. Cook for 8-10 minutes or until pasta is tender. Meanwhile, place vegetables and cheese sauce in a Dutch oven. Cover mixture and cook over medium heat for 13-15 minutes or until heated through, stirring occasionally.

2. Pour noodles and cooking liquid into vegetable mixture. Stir in ham and heat through.

POTATO BACON OMELET

Get breakfast off to a quick start with this hearty, yummy omelet. Plus, it's easy to make more than one at a time if necessary.
—**TASTE OF HOME TEST KITCHEN**

START TO FINISH: 20 MIN. • **MAKES:** 1 SERVING

- 2 **bacon strips, chopped**
- 2 **tablespoons chopped onion**
- ½ **cup cubed cooked potato**
- 1 **tablespoon butter**
- 3 **eggs**
- 3 **tablespoons water**
- ⅛ **teaspoon salt**
- ⅛ **teaspoon pepper**
- ¼ **cup shredded sharp cheddar cheese**

1. In a small nonstick skillet, cook bacon and onion over medium heat until bacon is crisp. Add potato; heat through. Drain. Remove from skillet and set aside. Remove to paper towels to drain.

SAUSAGE PINEAPPLE LETTUCE WRAPS

Pineapple adds a sweet surprise to these colorful wraps. After one bite, you'll want to fix this recipe time and again.
—**AYSHA SCHURMAN** AMMON, ID

START TO FINISH: 30 MIN. • **MAKES:** 2½ DOZEN

- 1 can (8 ounces) crushed pineapple
- ¼ cup soy sauce
- 1 tablespoon rice vinegar
- 1 teaspoon cornstarch
- 1 garlic clove, minced
- ½ teaspoon ground ginger
- ½ teaspoon pepper
- 1 pound bulk spicy pork sausage
- 1 can (8 ounces) sliced water chestnuts, drained and finely chopped
- 30 Bibb or Boston lettuce leaves
- 30 pineapple chunks (about 2 cups)
- 1 tablespoon sesame seeds, toasted
  Teriyaki sauce, optional

1. Drain pineapple, reserving 3 tablespoons juice. In a small bowl, combine the soy sauce, vinegar, cornstarch, garlic, ginger, pepper and reserved pineapple juice; set aside.

2. In a large skillet, cook sausage over medium heat until no longer pink; drain. Stir in water chestnuts and crushed pineapple. Gradually stir in soy sauce mixture. Bring to a boil; cook and stir for 2 minutes or until thickened.

3. Place about 2 tablespoons sausage mixture on each lettuce leaf; fold lettuce over filling. Top with a pineapple chunk; secure with a toothpick. Sprinkle with sesame seeds and serve with teriyaki sauce if desired.

ITALIAN PESTO PIZZAS

It's hard to believe these individual pizzas are ready in 30 minutes or less. The pesto base makes the kitchen smell wonderful.
—**KELLY EVANS** DENTON, TX

START TO FINISH: 30 MIN. • **MAKES:** 4 SERVINGS

- 4 whole wheat pita or flat breads
- ¼ cup prepared pesto
- 2 cups shredded part-skim mozzarella cheese
- 2 cups fresh baby spinach
- ½ cup sliced fresh mushrooms
- ½ cup chopped sweet yellow pepper
- 1 plum tomato, halved and sliced
- ¼ cup chopped red onion
- ¼ cup grated Parmesan cheese
- 2 tablespoons sliced ripe olives, optional
- ¼ teaspoon crushed red pepper flakes
- 2 fresh basil leaves, thinly sliced

1. Place pita breads on an ungreased baking sheet; spread with pesto. Layer with mozzarella cheese, spinach, mushrooms, yellow pepper, tomato, onion, Parmesan cheese, olives if desired and pepper flakes.

2. Bake at 425° for 10-12 minutes or until cheese is melted. Top pizzas with basil.

Trip to the Tropics

Need a sunny getaway? Maybe you're looking for a new dish to switch up your routine? These sizzling offerings could be just what you need. Take a bite and enjoy a mini vacation without leaving home!

SOUTHWESTERN PINEAPPLE PORK CHOPS

My husband and I love visiting the Southwest. After a recent trip, I wanted to come up with some dishes with spicy flair. This is one of our fast and healthy go-to recipes.

—LISA VARNER EL PASO, TX

START TO FINISH: 30 MIN. • **MAKES:** 4 SERVINGS

- 4 boneless pork loin chops (5 ounces each)
- ½ teaspoon garlic pepper blend
- 1 tablespoon canola oil
- 1 can (8 ounces) unsweetened crushed pineapple, undrained
- 1 cup medium salsa
  Minced fresh cilantro

Sprinkle pork chops with pepper blend. In a large skillet, brown chops in oil. Remove and keep warm. In the same skillet, combine pineapple and salsa. Bring to a boil. Return chops to the pan. Reduce heat; cover and simmer for 15-20 minutes or until tender. Sprinkle with cilantro.

GRILLED CHICKEN SAUSAGES WITH HARVEST RICE

Try something new on the grill tonight. My husband loves chicken sausage, so I'm always creating new recipes to include it. We prefer the apple-flavored sausages, but any flavor would work well. Experiment to find your own personal favorite.

—PAMELA SHANK PARKERSBURG, WV

START TO FINISH: 25 MIN. • **MAKES:** 4 SERVINGS

- 1¾ cups chicken broth
- 2 cups instant brown rice
- 1 package (12 ounces) frozen cooked winter squash, thawed and drained well
- ⅓ cup dried cranberries
- 1 package (12 ounces) fully cooked apple chicken sausage links or flavor of your choice

1. Bring broth to a boil in a large saucepan. Stir in the rice. Reduce heat; cover and simmer for 3 minutes. Add squash and simmer, uncovered, for 4-6 minutes or until liquid is absorbed. Remove from the heat. Stir in the cranberries; cover and let stand for 5 minutes.

2. Grill sausages, uncovered, over medium heat or broil 4 in. from the heat for 8-10 minutes or until heated through, turning often. Slice sausages and serve with rice mixture.

TROPICAL TILAPIA

Venture into the tropics with this one-skillet dish. Cool mint balances the sweet heat from the jelly.

—ROXANNE CHAN ALBANY, CA

START TO FINISH: 25 MIN. • **MAKES:** 4 SERVINGS

 4 tilapia fillets (4 ounces each)
 1 teaspoon Caribbean jerk seasoning
 1 can (15 ounces) mixed tropical fruit, undrained
 ¼ cup dried tropical fruit
 2 green onions, chopped
 ¼ cup red jalapeno pepper jelly

 2 tablespoons sliced almonds
 2 tablespoons minced fresh mint
 1 tablespoon lime juice
    Hot cooked rice

1. Season fillets with jerk seasoning. In a large nonstick skillet coated with cooking spray, cook fillets over medium-high heat for 3-5 minutes or until fish flakes easily with a fork, turning once. Transfer to a serving platter and keep warm.
2. In the same skillet, combine the fruit, onions, jelly and almonds; heat through. Stir in mint and lime juice. Serve with fish and rice.

SHRIMP PICCATA

I typically serve this succulent pasta with crusty French bread and asparagus. Make it the next time you have company, and guests will beg for the recipe.
—**HOLLY BAUER** WEST BEND, WI

START TO FINISH: 25 MIN. • **MAKES:** 4 SERVINGS

- ½ pound uncooked angel hair pasta
- 2 shallots, finely chopped
- 2 garlic cloves, minced
- 2 tablespoons olive oil
- 1 pound uncooked large shrimp, peeled and deveined
- 1 teaspoon dried oregano
- ⅛ teaspoon salt
- 1 cup chicken broth
- 1 cup white wine or additional chicken broth
- 4 teaspoons cornstarch
- ⅓ cup lemon juice
- ¼ cup capers, drained
- 3 tablespoons minced fresh parsley

1. Cook pasta according to package directions.
2. Meanwhile, in a large skillet, saute shallots and garlic in oil for 1 minute. Add shrimp, oregano and salt; cook and stir until shrimp turn pink. In a small bowl, combine the broth, wine and cornstarch; gradually stir into pan. Bring to a boil; cook and stir for 2 minutes or until thickened. Remove from the heat.
3. Drain pasta. Add the pasta, lemon juice, capers and parsley to the skillet; toss to coat.

ZIPPY ZUCCHINI PASTA

Spoon zucchini and canned tomatoes over quick-cooking angel hair pasta. I like the extra zip from crushed red pepper flakes.
—**KATHLEEN TIMBERLAKE** DEARBORN HEIGHTS, MI

START TO FINISH: 15 MIN. • **MAKES:** 3 SERVINGS

- 1 package (7 ounces) angel hair pasta or thin spaghetti
- 2 small zucchini, cut into ¼-inch pieces
- 2 garlic cloves, minced
- 3 tablespoons olive oil
- 1 can (14½ ounces) Mexican diced tomatoes, undrained
- ¼ cup minced fresh parsley
- 1 teaspoon dried oregano
- ⅛ to ½ teaspoon crushed red pepper flakes

1. Cook pasta according to package directions. Meanwhile, in a large skillet, saute zucchini and garlic in oil until zucchini is crisp-tender.
2. Add the tomatoes, parsley, oregano and pepper flakes; heat through. Drain pasta; serve with zucchini mixture.

PASTA STORAGE MADE EASY
Instead of keeping pasta in opened boxes, I store it in canning jars. The jars keep the pasta fresh longer, and they stack nicely, too. As an added bonus, I can easily see what I need when I'm making my list for grocery shopping.
—**LAURIE S.** GETTYSBURG, PA

PANKO CHICKEN WITH FRESH MARINARA

Bring restaurant fare right to your own home with these crispy, crunchy tenders served with a chunky homemade sauce. You can use this dish as an appetizer, too!

—ALLISON PATON SCARBOROUGH, ME

PREP: 25 MIN. • **COOK:** 5 MIN./BATCH • **MAKES:** 4 SERVINGS

- 1 egg
- 1 cup panko (Japanese) bread crumbs
- 1 tablespoon all-purpose flour
- 1 tablespoon minced fresh parsley
- ½ teaspoon garlic powder
  Dash salt and pepper
- 1 pound chicken tenderloins
- ¼ cup olive oil

MARINARA
- 6 medium tomatoes, seeded and finely chopped
- 1 medium onion, finely chopped
- 8 medium fresh mushrooms, finely chopped
- 2 garlic cloves, minced
- 1 teaspoon Italian seasoning
- ¼ teaspoon salt

1. In a shallow bowl, beat the egg. In another shallow bowl, combine the bread crumbs, flour, parsley, garlic powder, salt and pepper. Dip chicken in egg, then roll in crumb mixture.

2. In a large skillet over medium heat, cook chicken in oil in batches for 2-3 minutes on each side or until juices run clear. Drain on paper towels.

3. Meanwhile, in a small saucepan, combine the marinara ingredients; heat through. Serve with chicken.

GARDEN VEGETABLE PRIMAVERA

Although I enjoy this throughout the year, it's even more special when I use my garden to supply the vegetables in it. A splash of white wine and the addition of fresh basil really add a lot to the recipe. I have also roasted the vegetables and mixed in chicken breasts with scrumptious results.

—CARLY CURTIN ELLICOTT CITY, MD

START TO FINISH: 30 MIN. • **MAKES:** 4 SERVINGS

- 8 ounces uncooked fettuccine
- 2 medium zucchini, coarsely chopped
- 1 medium carrot, sliced
- 1 teaspoon Italian seasoning
- ¼ teaspoon salt
- 1 tablespoon olive oil
- 1 cup grape tomatoes
- 2 garlic cloves, minced
- ½ cup reduced-sodium chicken broth
- ⅓ cup white wine
- ½ cup grated Parmesan cheese
- ¼ cup minced fresh basil

1. Cook fettuccine according to package directions.

2. Meanwhile, in a large skillet, saute the zucchini, carrot, Italian seasoning and salt in oil until vegetables are crisp-tender. Add tomatoes and garlic; cook 1 minute longer. Add broth and wine, stirring to loosen browned bits from pan. Bring to a boil; cook until liquid is reduced by half.

3. Drain fettuccine. Add the fettuccine, cheese and basil to the skillet and toss to coat.

CHICKEN AND SAUSAGE PENNE

Gather the family for a comfy-cozy main dish with two types of meat in a garlic-cream sauce. This recipe's versatile, too. You can use whatever cream soup and cheese you have on hand.
—**SANDRA PERRIN** NEW IBERIA, LA

START TO FINISH: 30 MIN. • **MAKES:** 8 SERVINGS

- 1 package (16 ounces) penne pasta
- 1 pound boneless skinless chicken breasts, cubed
- ¾ pound smoked Polish sausage or fully cooked bratwurst links, cubed
- 1 medium onion, chopped
- 1 medium sweet red pepper, chopped
- 1 medium green pepper, chopped
- 2 tablespoons olive oil
- 6 garlic cloves, minced
- 2 jars (16 ounces each) Parmesan Alfredo sauce
- 1 can (10¾ ounces) condensed cream of mushroom soup, undiluted
- ½ teaspoon pepper
- ¼ teaspoon salt
- 2 cups (8 ounces) shredded cheddar cheese

1. Cook pasta according to package directions. Meanwhile, in a Dutch oven, cook the chicken, sausage, onion and red and green peppers in oil over medium heat for 6-8 minutes or until chicken is no longer pink. Add the garlic; cook and stir 1 minute longer.

2. Stir in the Alfredo sauce, soup, pepper and salt. Bring to a boil. Reduce heat; simmer, uncovered, for 2 minutes. Stir in cheese. Drain pasta; add to chicken mixture and toss to coat.
3. Serve desired amount immediately. Cool remaining mixture; transfer to freezer containers. Freeze for up to 3 months.

BLUEGILL PARMESAN

This seasoned crumb mixture produces a crispy coating that really stays on the fillets.
—**MARGARET GARBERS** VAN HORNE, IA

START TO FINISH: 30 MIN. • **MAKES:** 4 SERVINGS

- ¼ cup butter, melted
- ½ cup dry bread crumbs
- ⅓ cup grated Parmesan cheese
- 2 tablespoons minced fresh parsley
- 1 teaspoon salt
- ½ teaspoon paprika
- ¼ teaspoon dried oregano
- ¼ teaspoon dried basil
- ¼ teaspoon pepper
- 1 pound bluegill

1. Place butter in a shallow bowl. In another shallow bowl, combine the bread crumbs, cheese and seasonings. Dip fish in butter, then coat with crumb mixture.
2. Place in a greased 15x10x1-in. baking pan. Bake, uncovered, at 350° for 20 minutes or until fish flakes easily with a fork.
NOTE *Perch or crappie may be substituted for the bluegill.*

DELI ROAST BEEF SANDWICHES WITH MASHED POTATOES

Just like Mom used to make—but so much quicker and without the fuss. Order up!

—RUTH ANN BOTT LAKE WALES, FL

START TO FINISH: 10 MIN. • **MAKES:** 4 SERVINGS

  1 **pound sliced deli roast beef**
  2 **cans (10¼ ounces each) beef gravy**
  1 **can (4 ounces) mushroom stems and pieces, drained**
  1 **package (3¾ ounces) creamy butter instant mashed potatoes**
  4 **slices Italian bread (½ inch thick)**

1. In a 2-qt. microwave-safe bowl, combine the beef, gravy and mushrooms. Cover and microwave on high for 2-3 minutes or until heated through.

2. Meanwhile, prepare potatoes according to the package directions. Divide bread among four plates. Spoon the beef mixture over bread. Serve with potatoes.

NOTE *This recipe was tested in a 1,100-watt microwave.*

APRICOT-HONEY CHICKEN

My tender chicken has such a short prep time, you'll have it on the table just like that! The apricots and honey add just a bit of sweetness and make an unexpectedly tasty combination to dress up chicken.

—JANET PAVKOV BARBERTON, OH

START TO FINISH: 15 MIN. • **MAKES:** 4 SERVINGS

  4 **boneless skinless chicken breast halves (5 ounces each)**
  ⅓ **cup honey mustard**
  3 **tablespoons apricot preserves**
  ¼ **teaspoon ground ginger**
     Dash each salt and pepper

1. Flatten chicken to ¼-in. thickness. In a small bowl, combine the mustard, apricot preserves, ginger, salt and pepper. Place the chicken on a greased foil-lined baking sheet. Spoon half of the mustard mixture over chicken.

2. Broil 4-6 in. from the heat for 4 minutes. Turn; brush with remaining mustard mixture. Broil 3-4 minutes longer or until juices run clear.

QUICK POACHED SALMON WITH CUCUMBER SAUCE

Don't be afraid of cooking fish at home—this recipe's easy! Try adding dill, fennel or coriander to the basil in the sauce.
—**CRYSTAL JO BRUNS** ILIFF, CO

START TO FINISH: 20 MIN. • **MAKES:** 4 SERVINGS

- 1 cup water
- ½ cup dry white wine or chicken broth
- 1 small onion, sliced
- 2 sprigs fresh parsley
- ¼ teaspoon salt
- 5 peppercorns
- 4 salmon steaks (6 ounces each)

SAUCE

- ½ cup sour cream
- ⅓ cup chopped seeded peeled cucumber
- 1 tablespoon finely chopped onion
- ¼ teaspoon salt
- ¼ teaspoon dried basil

1. In an 11x7-in. microwave-safe dish coated with cooking spray, combine the first six ingredients. Microwave, uncovered, on high for 2-3 minutes or until the mixture comes to a boil.
2. Carefully add salmon to dish. Cover and microwave at 70% power for 5 to 5½ minutes or until the fish flakes easily with a fork.
3. Meanwhile, in a small bowl, combine the sour cream, cucumber, onion, salt and basil. Remove salmon from poaching liquid. Serve with sauce.

BALSAMIC PORK STIR-FRY

The solution to expensive Chinese takeout is right here. I think this stir-fry is much tastier than any takeout I've tried.
—**SUSAN JONES** APPLETON, WI

START TO FINISH: 30 MIN. • **MAKES:** 5 SERVINGS

- 1 pork tenderloin (1 pound), cut into thin strips
- ⅔ cup balsamic vinaigrette, divided
- 1½ cups sliced fresh carrots
- 1 cup sliced fresh mushrooms
- 1 can (8 ounces) sliced water chestnuts, drained
- 2 tablespoons hoisin sauce
  Hot cooked rice

1. In a large skillet or wok, stir-fry pork in 2 tablespoons vinaigrette for 3-4 minutes or until browned. Remove and keep warm.
2. Stir-fry carrots in 2 tablespoons vinaigrette for 2 minutes. Add mushrooms; stir-fry 2 minutes longer. Add water chestnuts and stir-fry 2-3 minutes longer or until vegetables are crisp-tender. Add hoisin sauce and remaining vinaigrette. Bring to a boil; cook for 1 minute. Add the pork and heat through. Serve with rice.

CRANBERRY PANCAKES

Adding a touch of baking powder to pancake mix will take your morning meal to new heights. Flip these towering pancakes onto a plate and then wait for smiles to surround the table.

—TASTE OF HOME TEST KITCHEN

START TO FINISH: 30 MIN. • **MAKES:** 3 SERVINGS

- 1 cup fresh or frozen cranberries
- ⅔ cup cranberry juice
- ½ cup packed brown sugar
- 2 tablespoons honey
- ½ teaspoon lemon juice

PANCAKES
- 2 cups biscuit/baking mix
- 2 tablespoons brown sugar
- 2 teaspoons baking powder
- ½ teaspoon ground cinnamon
- 2 eggs
- 1¼ cups 2% milk
- ½ teaspoon grated lemon peel
- ½ cup chopped fresh or frozen cranberries
  Lemon peel strips, optional

1. In a small saucepan, bring the cranberries, cranberry juice and brown sugar to a boil. Reduce heat; simmer, uncovered, for 5 minutes. Cool slightly. With a slotted spoon, remove ¼ cup cranberries and set aside.

2. In a blender, process the remaining cranberry mixture until smooth. Stir in the honey, lemon juice and reserved cranberries; keep warm.

3. In a large bowl, combine the biscuit mix, brown sugar, baking powder and cinnamon. In another bowl, whisk the eggs, milk and lemon peel. Stir into dry ingredients just until moistened. Stir in cranberries.

4. Drop batter by ¼ cupfuls onto a greased hot griddle; turn when bubbles form on top. Cook until second side is golden brown. Serve with syrup and garnish servings with lemon peel strips if desired.

PASTA PRIMAVERA

Full of veggies, this simple, colorful pasta makes an ideal dinner. It can also work as a side dish.

—STEPHANIE MARCHESE WHITEFISH BAY, WI

START TO FINISH: 25 MIN. • **MAKES:** 4 SERVINGS

- 8 ounces uncooked linguine
- 1 cup thinly sliced fresh broccoli
- 1 medium carrot, thinly sliced
- ½ cup sliced green onions
- ¼ cup butter, cubed
- 1½ cups sliced fresh mushrooms
- 1 garlic clove, minced
- 1 teaspoon dried basil
- ½ teaspoon salt
- ¼ teaspoon pepper
- 6 ounces fresh or frozen snow peas (about 2 cups), thawed
- ¼ cup dry white wine or chicken broth
- ¼ cup shredded Parmesan cheese

1. Cook linguine according to package directions.

2. Meanwhile, in a large skillet, cook the broccoli, carrot and onions in butter for 3 minutes. Add the mushrooms, garlic, basil, salt and pepper; cook 1 minute longer. Add snow peas and wine. Cover and cook for 2 minutes or until the peas are crisp-tender.

3. Drain the linguine; add to skillet and toss to coat. Sprinkle with cheese.

COOKING FOR TWO

Don't worry about scaling down recipes. This chapter features dishes perfect for small households. Searching for a main dish, dessert or side dish? Turn here for tasty options that won't leave you with lots of leftovers!

CHICKEN WITH ROSEMARY BUTTER SAUCE FOR 2

It doesn't require much effort to plate this rich and creamy chicken entree. Give it a try!

—**CONNIE MCDOWELL** GREENWOOD, DE

START TO FINISH: 20 MIN. • **MAKES:** 2 SERVINGS

- 2 **boneless skinless chicken breast halves (4 ounces each)**
- 2 **tablespoons butter, divided**
- ¼ **cup white wine or chicken broth**
- ¼ **cup heavy whipping cream**
- 1½ **teaspoons minced fresh rosemary**

1. In a small skillet over medium heat, cook the chicken in 1 tablespoon butter for 4-5 minutes on each side or until a thermometer reads 170°. Remove and keep warm.

2. Add wine to the pan; cook over medium-low heat, stirring to loosen browned bits from pan. Add cream and bring to a boil. Reduce heat; cook and stir until slightly thickened. Stir in the rosemary and remaining butter until blended. Serve with the chicken.

BLUEBERRY-RHUBARB CRISP

Microwaving this recipe produces a crisp that's just as good as when it's baked in the oven. The warm treat is simply unbeatable with a scoop of vanilla ice cream.

—**LORRI CAMPBELL** MANKATO, MN

START TO FINISH: 25 MIN. • **MAKES:** 6 SERVINGS

- 2½ **cups diced fresh or frozen rhubarb, thawed**
- ⅓ **cup sugar**
- 2 **tablespoons all-purpose flour**
- 1 **can (21 ounces) blueberry pie filling**

TOPPING

- ¾ **cup all-purpose flour**
- ¾ **cup old-fashioned oats**
- ⅓ **cup packed brown sugar**
- ¾ **teaspoon ground cinnamon**
- ½ **cup cold butter, cubed**

1. In a 2-qt. microwave-safe dish, combine the rhubarb, sugar and flour. Cover and microwave on high for 3 minutes; stir. Add the pie filling.

2. In a small bowl, combine the flour, oats, brown sugar and cinnamon. Cut in butter until mixture is crumbly; sprinkle over fruit. Cover and cook 4-5 minutes longer or until bubbly and rhubarb is tender. Serve warm.

NOTES *If using frozen rhubarb, measure rhubarb while still frozen, then thaw completely. Drain in a colander, but do not press liquid out. This recipe was tested in a 1,100-watt microwave.*

SESAME CHICKEN WRAPS

Make these refreshing handhelds in a matter of minutes! A simple Asian dressing gives these sandwiches extra zip.

—**ANDRE HOUSEKNECHT** FEASTERVILLE, PA

START TO FINISH: 10 MIN. • **MAKES:** 2 SERVINGS

- 1 **package (6 ounces) ready-to-use grilled chicken breast strips**
- ¼ **cup plus 2 tablespoons sesame ginger salad dressing, divided**
- 2 **whole wheat tortillas (8 inches)**
- ½ **cup bean sprouts**
- ½ **cup julienned carrot**
- ¼ **cup chopped sweet red pepper**
- 2 **tablespoons chopped red onion**

In a small bowl, combine chicken and ¼ cup salad dressing. Spoon over tortillas. Top with bean sprouts, carrot, pepper and onion. Drizzle with the remaining dressing; roll up and secure with toothpicks.

KIELBASA SPINACH SOUP

I love this meal-in-a-bowl because it's very tasty with little preparation. Collard greens or chopped kale can also be used instead of spinach. The hot pepper sauce adds real kick, so maybe you'll want to let each person spice up their own serving.
—**ANTOINETTE PISICCHIO** EASTON, PA

START TO FINISH: 20 MIN. • **MAKES:** 4 SERVINGS

- 1 carton (32 ounces) chicken broth
- 1 package (10 ounces) frozen chopped spinach
- ½ pound smoked kielbasa or Polish sausage, halved and sliced
- 1 can (15 ounces) white kidney or cannellini beans, rinsed and drained
- ⅔ cup uncooked elbow macaroni
- 8 to 10 drops hot pepper sauce

Combine the broth, spinach and kielbasa in a large saucepan. Bring to a boil. Add beans and macaroni. Reduce heat; simmer, uncovered, for 7-9 minutes or until macaroni is tender. Stir in pepper sauce.

FREEZABLE KIELBASA SKILLET DISHES

When I have two leftover kielbasa links, I cut them into ¼-inch slices and fry them in the skillet. Then I find two large microwave-safe freezer containers and pour a jar of sauerkraut in one and a can of baked beans in the other. I divide the sausage slices between the two and freeze until I need to thaw.
—**KATIE W.** TOPEKA, KS

ORANGE CHOCOLATE RICOTTA PIE

A traditional Italian dessert served during the holidays and for special occasions, this pie boasts a classic pairing of orange and chocolate flavors.
—**TRISHA KRUSE** EAGLE, ID

PREP: 20 MIN. • **BAKE:** 40 MIN. + COOLING • **MAKES:** 8 SERVINGS

- 2 cartons (15 ounces each) whole-milk ricotta cheese
- 2 eggs, lightly beaten
- ½ cup dark chocolate chips
- ⅓ cup sugar
- 1 tablespoon grated orange peel
- 2 tablespoons orange liqueur, optional
  Pastry for double-crust pie (9 inches)

1. In a large bowl, combine the ricotta cheese, eggs, chocolate chips, sugar, orange peel and, if desired, orange liqueur.
2. Roll out half of the pastry to fit a 9-in. pie plate; transfer pastry to pie plate. Fill with ricotta mixture.
3. Roll out remaining pastry into an 11-in. circle; cut into 1-in.-wide strips. Lay half of the strips across the pie, about 1 in. apart. Fold back every other strip halfway. Lay another strip across center of pie at a right angle. Unfold strips over center strip. Fold back the alternate strips; place a second strip across the pie. Continue to add strips until pie is covered with lattice. Trim, seal and flute edges.
4. Bake at 425° for 40-45 minutes or until crust is golden brown. Refrigerate leftovers.

4. Add heated broth, ¼ cup at a time, stirring constantly. Allow the liquid to absorb between additions. Cook just until risotto is creamy and rice is almost tender. (Cooking time is about 20 minutes.) Stir in cheese until melted. Add squash and sage. Serve immediately.

CINNAMON-RAISIN RICE PUDDING

This may be an old-fashioned dessert, but it's oh-so good!
—**IRENE SCHROEDER** HUBBARD, OH

PREP: 15 MIN. • **BAKE:** 35 MIN. • **MAKES:** 2 SERVINGS

- ⅔ cup evaporated milk
- 1 egg
- ½ cup water
- ¼ cup sugar
- ¼ teaspoon ground cinnamon
- ¼ teaspoon ground nutmeg
- ¼ teaspoon vanilla extract
- 1 cup cooked rice
- ¼ cup chopped pecans
- ¼ cup raisins

1. In a small bowl, whisk the first seven ingredients. Stir in the rice, pecans and raisins. Pour into two greased 10-oz. ramekins or custard cups. Place ramekins on a baking sheet.
2. Bake, uncovered, at 350° for 35-40 minutes or until a knife inserted near the center comes out clean.

SHIITAKE & BUTTERNUT RISOTTO

I like to think of this recipe as a labor of love. The risotto takes a bit of extra attention, but once you take your first bite, you'll know it was worth the effort.
—**STEPHANIE CAMPBELL** ELK GROVE, CA

PREP: 25 MIN. • **COOK:** 25 MIN. • **MAKES:** 2 SERVINGS

- 1 cup cubed peeled butternut squash
- 2 teaspoons olive oil, divided
  Dash salt
- 1¼ cups reduced-sodium chicken broth
- ⅔ cup sliced fresh shiitake mushrooms
- 2 tablespoons chopped onion
- 1 small garlic clove, minced
- ⅓ cup uncooked arborio rice
  Dash pepper
- ¼ cup white wine or ¼ cup additional reduced-sodium chicken broth
- ¼ cup grated Parmesan cheese
- 1 teaspoon minced fresh sage

1. Place squash in a greased 9-in. square baking pan. Add 1 teaspoon oil and salt; toss to coat.
2. Bake, uncovered, at 350° for 25-30 minutes or until tender, stirring occasionally.
3. Meanwhile, in a small saucepan, heat broth and keep warm. In a small skillet, saute the mushrooms, onion and garlic in remaining oil for 3-4 minutes or until tender. Add rice and pepper; cook and stir for 2-3 minutes. Reduce heat; stir in wine. Cook and stir until all of the liquid is absorbed.

CREAM CHEESE & CHIVE OMELET

The first bite of creamy filling lets you know this isn't any regular omelet. Make it once, and I suspect you'll be fixing it often.

—**ANNE TROISE** MANALAPAN, NJ

START TO FINISH: 15 MIN. • **MAKES:** 2 SERVINGS

- 1 tablespoon olive oil
- 4 eggs
- 2 tablespoons minced chives
- 2 tablespoons water
- ⅛ teaspoon salt
- ⅛ teaspoon pepper
- 2 ounces cream cheese, cubed
  Salsa

1. In a large nonstick skillet, heat oil over medium-high heat. Whisk the eggs, chives, water, salt and pepper. Add egg mixture to skillet (mixture should set immediately at edges).

2. As eggs set, push cooked edges toward the center, letting uncooked portion flow underneath. When the eggs are set, sprinkle cream cheese on one side; fold other side over filling. Slide omelet onto a plate; cut in half. Serve with salsa.

SHALLOT & BASIL GREEN BEANS

When you have fresh basil on hand, you'll definitely want to utilize it in this tantalizing side dish.

—**SHARON DELANEY-CHRONIS** SOUTH MILWAUKEE, WI

START TO FINISH: 25 MIN. • **MAKES:** 2 SERVINGS

- ½ pound fresh green beans, trimmed
- 2 shallots, chopped
- 1 teaspoon olive oil
- ¼ teaspoon sugar
- ¼ teaspoon salt
- ⅛ teaspoon pepper
- 2 tablespoons minced fresh basil or ½ teaspoon dried basil
- 1 teaspoon grated lemon peel

1. Place beans in a small saucepan and cover with water; bring to a boil. Cook, uncovered, for 8-10 minutes or until crisp-tender.

2. Meanwhile, in a small skillet, saute shallots in oil until tender. Stir in the sugar, salt and pepper.

3. Drain beans and add to skillet. Add basil and lemon peel; toss to coat.

CHOCOLATE CHALLAH FRENCH TOAST

I serve up this decadent breakfast—with pleasure—from the kitchen of my family-run bed and breakfast.
—**MARIE PARKER** MILWAUKEE, WI

PREP: 15 MIN. + SOAKING • **COOK:** 10 MIN. • **MAKES:** 2 SERVINGS

- 4 slices challah or egg bread (¾ inch thick)
- ⅔ cup sugar
- ⅓ cup baking cocoa
- ¼ teaspoon salt
- ⅛ teaspoon baking powder
- 4 eggs
- 1 cup 2% milk
- 1 teaspoon vanilla extract
- 2 tablespoons butter
  Optional toppings: confectioners' sugar, fresh raspberries, sliced fresh strawberries, sliced ripe banana and maple syrup

1. Arrange bread slices in a 13-in. x 9-in. dish. In a small bowl, combine the sugar, cocoa, salt and baking powder. In another bowl, whisk the eggs, milk and vanilla. Gradually whisk into the dry ingredients until smooth. Pour over bread. Let stand 10 minutes, turning once.
2. In a large skillet, melt butter over medium heat. Cook bread for 3-4 minutes each side or until toasted. Serve with toppings of your choice.

ASIAN SPAGHETTI

Pair your main dish with an Asian side that packs some heat. You could substitute any veggies you have on hand for the snow peas.
—**ANNE SMITHSON** CARY, NC

START TO FINISH: 20 MIN. • **MAKES:** 5 SERVINGS

- 8 ounces uncooked angel hair pasta
- 1 cup sliced fresh mushrooms
- 1 cup fresh snow peas
- ¾ cup shredded carrots
- 4 green onions, cut into 1-inch pieces
- 2 tablespoons canola oil
- 1 garlic clove, minced
- ¼ cup reduced-sodium soy sauce
- 1 teaspoon sugar
- ¼ teaspoon cayenne pepper
- 2 tablespoons sesame seeds, toasted

1. Cook pasta according to package directions. Meanwhile, in a large skillet, saute the mushrooms, snow peas, carrots and onions in oil until crisp-tender. Add garlic; cook 1 minute longer.
2. In a small bowl, combine the soy sauce, sugar and cayenne. Drain pasta. Add pasta and soy sauce mixture to skillet and toss to coat. Heat through. Sprinkle with sesame seeds.

QUICKLY CUT GREEN ONIONS

I use kitchen scissors to quickly cut green onions for a recipe. There's no cutting board to clean up when I'm done, so there's more time to prep other dishes in the kitchen!
—**KRISTY B.** KELOWNA, BC

BACON-WRAPPED FILETS WITH SCOTCHED MUSHROOMS

There's elegance in every bite of these bacon-wrapped steaks. Just a half-hour of work produces a meal you will be proud to share with someone special.
—**MARY KAY LABRIE** CLERMONT, FL

START TO FINISH: 30 MIN. • **MAKES:** 2 SERVINGS

- 2 bacon strips
- 2 beef tenderloin steaks (5 ounces each)
- ¼ teaspoon salt
- ¼ teaspoon coarsely ground pepper
- 3 teaspoons olive oil, divided
- 2 cups sliced baby portobello mushrooms
- ¼ teaspoon dried thyme
- 2 tablespoons butter, divided
- ¼ cup Scotch whiskey
- ½ cup diet ginger ale
- 1 tablespoon brown sugar
- 1½ teaspoons reduced-sodium soy sauce
- ¼ teaspoon rubbed sage

1. In a small skillet, cook bacon over medium heat until partially cooked but not crisp. Remove to paper towels to drain.
2. Sprinkle steaks with salt and pepper; wrap a strip of bacon around the sides of each steak and secure with toothpicks.
3. In a small ovenproof skillet coated with cooking spray, cook steaks in 1½ teaspoons oil over medium-high heat for 2 minutes on each side.
4. Bake, uncovered, at 375° for 8-12 minutes or until meat reaches desired doneness (for medium-rare, a thermometer should read 145°; medium, 160°; well-done, 170°).
5. Meanwhile, in a large skillet, saute mushrooms and thyme in 1 tablespoon butter and remaining oil until tender; remove from the heat. Add whiskey, stirring to loosen browned bits from pan. Stir in the ginger ale, brown sugar, soy sauce and sage.
6. Bring to a boil. Reduce heat; simmer, uncovered, for 3-5 minutes or until reduced by half. Stir in remaining butter. Serve with steaks.

CRANBERRY-PECAN SWEET POTATO CASSEROLE

Pecans, cranberries and sweet potatoes, oh my! This side will vanish before your eyes once you put it out.
—**BERNICE MORRIS** MARSHFIELD, MO

PREP: 20 MIN. • **BAKE:** 20 MIN. • **MAKES:** 3 SERVINGS

- 1 cup mashed sweet potato
- 2 tablespoons sugar
- 2 tablespoons dried cranberries
- 2 tablespoons butter, melted
- 2 tablespoons beaten egg
- ¼ teaspoon vanilla extract

TOPPING
- ¼ cup chopped pecans
- ¼ cup packed brown sugar
- 2 tablespoons all-purpose flour
- 2 tablespoons cold butter

1. In a small bowl, combine the sweet potato, sugar, cranberries, butter, egg and vanilla. Transfer to a greased shallow 2-cup baking dish.
2. Combine the pecans, brown sugar and flour. Cut in butter until crumbly. Sprinkle over top.
3. Bake, uncovered, at 350° for 20-25 minutes or until a thermometer reads 160°.

Savoring Summer

*Whether you're tempted by vegetable-stand goodness or tropical tastes, it's easy to enjoy
the flavors of the season with these warm-weather dishes.*

SWEET CORN WITH PARMESAN AND CILANTRO

A little tart and a touch sassy, corn gets an upgrade in this side.
Just a few minutes of pan frying gives it a delightful golden color.

—FAYE SLOAN LAS VEGAS, NV

START TO FINISH: 25 MIN. • **MAKES:** 4 SERVINGS

- 4 large ears sweet corn, husks removed
- ⅓ cup grated Parmesan cheese
- 6 tablespoons olive oil, divided
- 1 tablespoon lime juice
- 1 garlic clove, minced
- 1 teaspoon ground cumin
- ½ teaspoon hot pepper sauce
- ¼ teaspoon salt
- ¼ teaspoon pepper
- ¼ cup minced fresh cilantro

1. Place corn in a stockpot; cover with water. Bring to a boil;
cover and cook for 3-5 minutes or until tender. Drain.
2. In a small bowl, combine the cheese, 5 tablespoons oil, lime
juice, garlic, cumin, pepper sauce, salt and pepper. Brush
1 tablespoon over each ear of corn.
3. In a large skillet, cook corn in remaining oil over medium
heat for 4-6 minutes or until lightly browned, turning
occasionally. Stir cilantro into remaining cheese mixture;
brush over corn.

WARM PINEAPPLE SUNDAES WITH RUM SAUCE

Pineapple, rum, sugar and just a hint of ginger will finish off any
meal with a dreamy touch of tropical flavors.

—JAMIE MILLER MAPLE GROVE, MN

START TO FINISH: 25 MIN. • **MAKES:** 2 SERVINGS

- 4 fresh pineapple spears (about 8 ounces)
- ½ cup packed brown sugar
- 2 tablespoons dark rum
- ¾ teaspoon ground ginger
- 4 teaspoons butter, cut into small pieces
- 2 scoops vanilla ice cream or low-fat frozen yogurt
- 4 gingersnap cookies

1. Place pineapple in 1-qt. baking dish. In a small bowl,
combine the brown sugar, rum and ginger; spoon over
pineapple. Dot with butter.
2. Bake, uncovered, at 425° for 8-10 minutes or until pineapple
is lightly browned and sauce is bubbly. Place ice cream in
two dessert dishes; top with pineapple and sauce. Serve
immediately with cookies.

VEGETABLE TROUT BAKE

I love how easy this entree is to prepare. If you don't care for trout, use salmon or chicken instead—or maybe try eggplant and broccoli florets in place of the green beans and tomatoes.

—**ELIZABETH YARNELL** DENVER, CO

PREP: 35 MIN. • **BAKE:** 35 MIN. • **MAKES:** 2 SERVINGS

- 4   small red potatoes, cut into 1-inch pieces
- 1   cup cut fresh green beans (2-inch pieces)
- 8   to 10 frozen pearl onions
- ½   teaspoon salt, divided
- 4   garlic cloves, minced, divided
- 2   trout fillets (6 ounces each)
- ¼   cup pitted Greek or ripe olives, halved
- 3   teaspoons minced fresh parsley, divided
- ¼   teaspoon pepper
- 2   plum tomatoes, chopped
- ¼   cup white wine or chicken broth

1. In a large saucepan, combine the potatoes, beans and onions; cover with water. Add ¼ teaspoon salt. Bring to a boil; reduce heat. Cover and cook for 10-15 minutes or until beans and onions are crisp-tender; drain.

2. Place vegetables in a single layer in a shallow 2-qt. baking dish coated with cooking spray. Top with half of the garlic. Place trout skin side down over vegetables. Sprinkle with olives, 1½ teaspoons parsley, pepper and remaining salt and garlic. Top with tomatoes and remaining parsley.

3. Pour wine over the top. Cover and bake at 400° for 35-40 minutes or until fish flakes easily with a fork.

ZESTY DILL TUNA SANDWICHES

I absolutely love tuna salad, so I brought together even more of my favorite ingredients to make what just might be the best tuna salad sandwich ever!

—**JENNY DUBINSKY** INWOOD, WV

START TO FINISH: 15 MIN. • **MAKES:** 2 SERVINGS

- 1 **can (5 ounces) light water-packed tuna, drained**
- ¼ **cup reduced-fat mayonnaise**
- 1 **tablespoon grated Parmesan cheese**
- 1 **tablespoon sweet pickle relish**
- 1 **tablespoon minced fresh parsley**
- 1 **teaspoon spicy brown mustard**
- ¼ **teaspoon dill weed**
- ⅛ **teaspoon onion powder**
- ⅛ **teaspoon curry powder**
- ⅛ **teaspoon garlic powder**
- 4 **slices whole wheat bread**

In a small bowl, combine the first 10 ingredients. Spread over two slices of bread. Top with remaining bread.

RHUBARB SUNDAES

Here's a simple dessert sauce with so much versatility. Spoon it over ice cream, pancakes, waffles, pound cake and more!

—**TASTE OF HOME TEST KITCHEN**

START TO FINISH: 15 MIN. • **MAKES:** 1 CUP

- 2 **cups chopped fresh or frozen rhubarb**
- ⅓ **cup sugar**
- ¼ **cup water**
- ¼ **teaspoon ground cinnamon**
- ½ **teaspoon honey**
   Vanilla ice cream
   Chopped walnuts, optional

In a small saucepan, bring the rhubarb, sugar, water and cinnamon to a boil. Reduce heat; simmer, uncovered, for 8-10 minutes or until rhubarb is tender and the sauce has reached desired consistency. Remove from the heat; stir in honey. Serve warm over ice cream. Sprinkle with walnuts if desired.

GINGER PEAR SIPPER

A refreshing treat for brunch or during cocktail hour, this alcohol-free beverage will please any palate.

—**SUSAN WESTERFIELD** ALBUQUERQUE, NM

START TO FINISH: 5 MIN. • **MAKES:** 1 SERVING

- 3 **ounces ginger ale, chilled**
- 3 **ounces pear nectar, chilled**
- 1 **slice fresh pear**

In a tall glass, combine ginger ale and pear nectar; garnish with pear slice.

APPLE ALMOND SALAD

Sweet, tangy and crunchy, this fruit salad brightens up any meal and couldn't be easier to whip up!

—**CRITINA WHEELER** UPTON, KY

START TO FINISH: 10 MIN. • **MAKES:** 8 SERVINGS

- 3 **large apples, chopped**
- 1 **cup sliced almonds, toasted**
- 1 **cup dried cranberries**
- 2½ **cups whipped topping**
- ⅓ **cup mayonnaise**

In a large bowl, combine the apples, almonds and cranberries. Combine whipped topping and mayonnaise. Add to apple mixture and toss to coat; garnish as desired.

CHOCOLATE CHIP ICE CREAM PIE

My mom gave me this pie recipe, but I changed her crust to feature delicious cookie dough. The crust will harden after being frozen, so it's easiest to cut through the pie layers if you first dip a knife in hot water, then wipe the knife off and cut. Repeat the process as needed.

—**LETITIA LANDIS** ROCHESTER, IN

PREP: 10 MIN. • **BAKE:** 15 MIN. + FREEZING • **MAKES:** 8 SERVINGS

- 1 tube (16½ ounces) refrigerated chocolate chip cookie dough
- ¼ cup sour cream
- ¼ cup chocolate syrup
- 1 quart chocolate chip ice cream, softened

1. Cut cookie dough in half widthwise; let one half stand at room temperature for 5-10 minutes to soften (save the other half for another use). Press dough onto the bottom and up the sides of an ungreased 9-in. deep-dish pie plate. Bake at 350° for 12-16 minutes or until lightly browned. Cool on a wire rack.

2. In a small bowl, combine sour cream and syrup. Spoon half of the ice cream into crust. Cover and freeze for 1 hour. Drizzle with ¼ cup of syrup mixture. Repeat layers. Cover and freeze for 8 hours or overnight.

CHICKEN WITH CORN BREAD STUFFING

Make everyday chicken into something spectacular when you add the corn bread stuffing here. Guests are sure to ask for seconds (or copies of the recipe)!

—**JOYCE MARTIN** CAMARILLO, CA

PREP: 20 MIN. • **BAKE:** 20 MIN. • **MAKES:** 2 SERVINGS

- 2 boneless skinless chicken breast halves (5 ounces each)
- 1½ cups crushed corn bread stuffing, divided
- 1 medium tart apple, chopped
- 4 green onions, chopped
- 2 teaspoons canola oil
- ¼ teaspoon celery seed

1. Flatten chicken to ½-in. thickness. Finely crush ¼ cup corn bread stuffing; place in a shallow bowl. Coat chicken with crumbs; set aside.

2. In a small skillet, saute apple and onions in oil until tender. Stir in celery seed and remaining corn bread stuffing. In a greased 11-in. x 7-in. baking dish, shape stuffing mixture into two oval mounds. Top each with a chicken breast.

3. Bake, uncovered, at 350° for 20-25 minutes or until a thermometer reads 170°.

MOCHA CREAM CHEESE MOUSSE

Show your sweetie some tasty TLC and put together this mouthwatering mousse. It satisfies a chocolate-coffee craving, and the cream cheese adds velvety richness you'll both enjoy.

—**BETH ALLARD** BELMONT, NH

PREP: 25 MIN. + CHILLING • **MAKES:** 2 SERVINGS

- ⅔ cup semisweet chocolate chips
- 3 tablespoons plus 1 teaspoon half-and-half cream
- 1 teaspoon instant coffee granules
- ⅔ cup heavy whipping cream
- 3 tablespoons confectioners' sugar
- 1 package (3 ounces) cream cheese, softened
- ½ teaspoon vanilla extract
   Whipped cream and chocolate curls

1. In a bowl, microwave the chocolate chips, half-and-half cream and coffee granules at 80% power for 45-60 seconds or until chips are melted; stir until smooth. Cool to room temperature.

2. In another bowl, beat whipping cream until it begins to thicken. Add confectioners' sugar; beat until stiff peaks form. Add cream cheese and vanilla to cooled chocolate mixture; beat until smooth. Fold in whipped cream.

3. Spoon into serving dishes. Garnish with whipped cream and chocolate curls.

NOTE *This recipe was tested in a 1,100-watt microwave.*

COOKIES, BARS & CANDIES

C'mon, it's time to treat yourself to something sweet—you deserve it! After all, there's nothing like the aroma of fresh-baked cookies. The scent brings back memories...and draws folks to your kitchen like a magnet!

NUTTER BUTTER TRUFFLES

You can prepare these truffles 5 to 7 days in advance and store in the refrigerator for convenience.

—KATHY CARLAN CANTON, GA

PREP: 1 HOUR + CHILLING • **MAKES:** 4 DOZEN

- 1 package (1 pound) Nutter Butter sandwich cookies
- 1 package (8 ounces) cream cheese, softened
- 8 ounces milk chocolate candy coating, melted
- 8 ounces white candy coating, melted
- 3 ounces bittersweet chocolate, melted

1. Place cookies in a food processor; cover and process until finely crushed. Add cream cheese; process until blended. Roll into 1-in. balls.

2. Dip half of the balls in milk chocolate, allowing excess to drip off. Place on waxed paper. Repeat with remaining balls and white coating. Drizzle bittersweet chocolate over truffles. Let stand until set. Store in an airtight container in the refrigerator.

PEANUT BUTTER SWIRLED FUDGE

I give out this homemade fudge to so many people and everyone—from our mail carrier to the neighbors—loves it!

—DAWN STITELY MIFFLIN, PA

PREP: 20 MIN. • **COOK:** 35 MIN. + CHILLING • **MAKES:** 4¾ POUNDS

- 1 teaspoon plus 1 cup butter, divided
- 4 cups sugar
- 1 cup half-and-half cream
- ¾ cup baking cocoa
- ½ cup dark corn syrup
- ⅛ teaspoon salt
- 1 jar (7 ounces) marshmallow creme
- 1 cup creamy peanut butter
- 2 packages (10 ounces each) peanut butter chips, divided

1. Line a 13-in. x 9-in. pan with foil and grease the foil with 1 teaspoon butter; set aside.

2. In a large heavy saucepan, combine the sugar, cream, cocoa, corn syrup, salt and remaining butter. Bring to a boil over medium heat, stirring until sugar is dissolved. Cook over medium-low heat, without stirring until a candy thermometer reads 234° (soft-ball stage). Remove from the heat; stir in the marshmallow creme, peanut butter and 1 package of chips.

3. With a hand mixer, beat until mixture begins to lose its gloss, about 6-8 minutes. Fold in remaining chips. Pour into prepared pan. Refrigerate for 2 hours or until firm.

4. Using foil, lift fudge out of pan. Discard foil; cut fudge into 1-in. squares. Store in an airtight container.

WHOOPIE COOKIES

I don't always have time to make whoopie pies from scratch, so I tweaked a cake mix recipe to create these. Try a bit of peanut butter in the filling, too.

—NUNDI HARRIS LAS VEGAS, NV

PREP: 20 MIN. • **BAKE:** 10 MIN./BATCH + COOLING
MAKES: 2 DOZEN

- 1 package devil's food cake mix (regular size)
- ¼ cup butter, softened
- 2 eggs
- 1 jar (7 ounces) marshmallow creme
- 4 ounces cream cheese, softened

1. In a large bowl, beat cake mix and butter until well combined. Beat in eggs. Shape into 1-in. balls. Place 2 in. apart on ungreased baking sheets.

2. Bake at 350° for 7-10 minutes or until tops are cracked. Cool for 2 minutes before removing to wire racks to cool completely.

3. In a large bowl, beat marshmallow creme and cream cheese until light and fluffy. Spread filling on the bottoms of half of the cookies. Top with remaining cookies. Store in an airtight container in the refrigerator.

BACKWOODS BONFIRE BARK

This chocolaty treat packed with marshmallows and peanuts reminds me of summers at my family's cabin. And it simply disappears at school bake sales!

—JAMIE MCMAHON COLOGNE, MN

PREP: 10 MIN. • **COOK:** 5 MIN. + STANDING
MAKES: ABOUT 1½ POUNDS

- 1 pound semisweet chocolate, chopped
- 1½ cups honey bear-shaped crackers
- 1½ cups miniature marshmallows
- ¾ cup dry roasted peanuts

1. Place chocolate in a microwave-safe bowl. Microwave on high for 1 minute; stir. Microwave 1 minute longer in 20-second intervals until melted; stir until smooth.
2. Spread to ¼-in. thickness on a waxed paper-lined baking sheet. Immediately sprinkle crackers, marshmallows and peanuts over chocolate; press in lightly.
3. Chill until firm. Break or cut bark into pieces. Store in an airtight container.

KEEP MARSHMALLOWS FRESH
When I don't use up all the marshmallows in the bag for a recipe, I freeze the leftovers so they don't go stale. Let the marshmallows thaw before you use them, but they'll still be soft and fresh!

—LYN C. PROVO, UT

HEAVENLY CHOCOLATE-FUDGE CAKE BALLS

Similar to the popular cake pops—but without the stick, these are guaranteed to satisfy any chocolate craving. Best of all, no one will guess how easy they are to make.

—LYNN DAVIS MORENO VALLEY, CA

PREP: 1¾ HOURS + STANDING • **BAKE:** 30 MIN. + COOLING
MAKES: ABOUT 8 DOZEN

- 1 package devil's food cake mix (regular size)
- 2 tablespoons hot water
- 1 teaspoon instant coffee granules
- 1 cup chocolate fudge frosting
- ⅓ cup baking cocoa
- ¼ cup chocolate syrup
- 1⅓ cups miniature semisweet chocolate chips
- 2 pounds white candy coating, chopped
  Optional toppings: milk chocolate English toffee bits, toasted flaked coconut and crushed candy canes

1. Prepare and bake cake according to package directions. Cool completely. Crumble cake into a large bowl.
2. In a small bowl, combine hot water and coffee granules; stir until dissolved. Add the frosting, cocoa and chocolate syrup; stir until combined. Add to cake; beat on low speed until blended. Stir in chocolate chips. Shape into 1-in. balls.
3. In a microwave, melt candy coating; stir until smooth. Dip balls in coating mixture; allow excess to drip off. Place on waxed paper; sprinkle with toppings of your choice. Let stand until set. Store in airtight containers.

APRICOT PINWHEEL COOKIES

My grandmother always made these cookies for the holidays. The recipe has been passed down through generations to me, and now from me to you!

—ROBERT LOGAN CLAYTON, CA

PREP: 45 MIN. + CHILLING • **BAKE:** 10 MIN./BATCH
MAKES: ABOUT 5 DOZEN

- ½ cup butter, softened
- ¾ cup sugar, divided
- ½ cup packed brown sugar
- 1 egg
- 1 teaspoon vanilla extract
- 2 cups all-purpose flour
- ¼ teaspoon baking soda
- ⅛ teaspoon salt
- 1½ cups finely chopped dried apricots or dates
- ⅔ cup water
- 1 tablespoon hazelnut liqueur, optional
- 1 cup finely chopped pecans, optional

1. In a large bowl, cream the butter, ½ cup sugar and brown sugar until light and fluffy. Beat in egg and vanilla. In another bowl, mix the flour, baking soda and salt; gradually beat into creamed mixture. Divide dough in half. Shape each half into a thick rectangle; wrap in plastic wrap. Refrigerate until firm or overnight.

2. In a saucepan, combine the apricots, water, remaining sugar and, if desired, liqueur; bring to a boil, stirring occasionally. Reduce heat to medium; cook until liquid is almost evaporated, about 5 minutes. Stir in pecans if desired; cool completely.

3. On a floured surface, roll each portion of dough into a 12-in. x 9-in. rectangle. Evenly spread half of the apricot mixture over each rectangle to within ½-in. of edges. Roll up jelly-roll style, starting with a long side; wrap in plastic wrap. Refrigerate for 2 hours or until firm.

4. Unwrap and cut into ¼-in. slices. Place 1 in. apart on greased baking sheets. Bake at 350° for 9-12 minutes or until golden brown. Remove from pans to wire racks to cool.

MACADAMIA-COFFEE BEAN COOKIES

Are you a coffee lover? Then you definitely won't be able to resist dunking these java-flavored treats into a cup of joe.

—KATHLEEN SPECHT CLINTON, MT

PREP: 20 MIN. • **BAKE:** 10 MIN./BATCH • **MAKES:** ABOUT 2½ DOZEN

- 1 package (17½ ounces) double chocolate chunk cookie mix
- 1 egg
- ¼ cup canola oil
- 2 tablespoons water
- 1½ cups chocolate-covered coffee beans, finely chopped
- 1 cup macadamia nuts, chopped

1. In a large bowl, beat the cookie mix, egg, oil and water until blended. Stir in coffee beans and nuts.

2. Drop by tablespoonfuls 2 in. apart onto greased baking sheets. Bake at 375° for 8-10 minutes or until set. Remove to wire racks to cool. Store in an airtight container.

SALTED PEANUT SQUARES

Want to give something a little out of the ordinary to loved ones? This recipe makes nearly 10 dozen chewy, nutty, sweet-and-salty bars to enjoy (or share).
—**BARB TIMM** LAKEVILLE, MN

PREP: 20 MIN. + STANDING • **MAKES:** 9¾ DOZEN

- 3½ cups dry roasted peanuts, divided
- 1 package (10 ounces) peanut butter chips
- 2 tablespoons butter
- 1 can (14 ounces) sweetened condensed milk
- 1 jar (7 ounces) marshmallow creme
- 36 miniature Snickers candy bars, chopped

1. Sprinkle half of the peanuts into a greased 13-in. x 9-in. baking pan. In a large microwave-safe bowl, heat chips and butter at 50% power for 1 minute; stir. Microwave in 20-second intervals until melted; stir until smooth. Stir in sweetened condensed milk; cook, uncovered, on high for 1 minute.
2. Stir in marshmallow creme and candy bars. Spread into prepared pan. Sprinkle with remaining peanuts. Cover with plastic wrap; press down lightly.
3. Refrigerate until set. Cut into 1-in. squares. Store in an airtight container.

TRIPLE-LAYER PRETZEL BROWNIES

If you've ever thought about trying a brownie pie with a pretzel crust and peanut butter-chocolate topping, your dreams have come true.
—**CATHIE AYERS** HILTON, NY

PREP: 30 MIN. • **BAKE:** 35 MIN. + COOLING • **MAKES:** 2 DOZEN

- 3 cups crushed pretzels
- ¾ cup butter, melted
- 3 tablespoons sugar
- 1 package fudge brownie mix (13-inch x 9-inch pan size)
- ¾ cup semisweet chocolate chips
- ½ cup creamy peanut butter

1. Preheat oven to 400°. In a small bowl, combine pretzels, butter and sugar. Press into an ungreased 13-in. x 9-in. baking dish. Bake 8 minutes. Cool on a wire rack.
2. Reduce heat to 350°. Prepare brownie mix batter according to package directions. Pour over prepared crust. Bake 35-40 minutes or until a toothpick inserted near the center comes out with moist crumbs (do not overbake). Cool completely on a wire rack.
3. In a microwave, melt chocolate chips and peanut butter; stir until smooth. Spread over top. Refrigerate 30 minutes or until firm. Cut into bars. Store in an airtight container.

DOUBLE WHAMMY EGGNOG COOKIES

I use up extra eggnog when I make these cookies. They've become a new family tradition.

—**TERESA MORRIS** LAUREL, DE

PREP: 30 MIN. + CHILLING • **BAKE:** 15 MIN./BATCH + COOLING
MAKES: 4 DOZEN

1⅓ cups butter, softened
1 cup packed brown sugar
4 egg yolks
2 tablespoons eggnog
½ teaspoon rum extract
3 cups all-purpose flour
EGGNOG FROSTING
4½ cups confectioners' sugar
¾ cup butter, softened
1½ teaspoons rum extract
½ teaspoon ground nutmeg
¼ teaspoon ground cinnamon
2 to 3 tablespoons eggnog
Additional ground nutmeg

1. In a large bowl, cream butter and brown sugar until light and fluffy. Beat in egg yolks, eggnog and extract. Gradually beat in flour. Refrigerate, covered, for at least 2 hours.
2. Shape into 1-in. balls; place 2 in. apart on ungreased baking sheets. Bake at 325° for 13-16 minutes or until bottoms are brown. Remove to wire racks to cool completely.
3. In a large bowl, beat the first five frosting ingredients until blended; beat in enough eggnog to reach desired consistency. Spread over cookies; sprinkle with additional nutmeg. Let stand until set. Store in airtight containers.
NOTE *This recipe was tested with commercially prepared eggnog.*

HAZELNUT-MOCHA BONBON COOKIES

I adapted a cookie recipe from a cookbook I received at my bridal shower. The little glazed balls have been a favorite ever since.
—**NANCY MUELLER** MENOMONEE FALLS, WI

PREP: 40 MIN. • **BAKE:** 10 MIN./BATCH + COOLING
MAKES: 3½ DOZEN

½ cup butter, softened
¾ cup confectioners' sugar
3 teaspoons vanilla extract
2 teaspoons instant espresso powder
1½ cups all-purpose flour
⅛ teaspoon salt
42 whole hazelnuts
ESPRESSO GLAZE
1½ cups confectioners' sugar
¾ teaspoon instant espresso powder
1½ teaspoons vanilla extract
4 to 5 tablespoons heavy whipping cream
CHOCOLATE GLAZE
1½ cups confectioners' sugar
2 ounces unsweetened chocolate, melted
2 tablespoons heavy whipping cream
Chocolate and gold jimmies

1. In a large bowl, cream butter and confectioners' sugar until light and fluffy. Combine vanilla and espresso powder until dissolved. Add to creamed mixture. Combine flour and salt; gradually add to creamed mixture and mix well.
2. Shape a heaping teaspoon of dough around each hazelnut, forming a ball. Place 2 in. apart on ungreased baking sheets. Bake at 350° for 8-10 minutes or until bottoms are browned. Remove to wire racks to cool.
3. For espresso glaze, place confectioners' sugar in a small bowl. Combine the espresso powder and vanilla until dissolved; add to bowl. Stir in enough cream to achieve a dipping consistency; set aside. For chocolate glaze, combine the confectioners' sugar, chocolate and cream.
4. Dip half of the cookies in espresso glaze. Dip remaining cookies in chocolate glaze; allow excess to drip off. Place on waxed paper and sprinkle with jimmies. Let stand until set.

CANDY-LICIOUS FUDGE

A no-fuss fudge prepared in the microwave that tastes like a candy bar? It sounds too good to be true, but it's not! This is melt-in-your-mouth good.

—DEE LANCASTER OZARK, MO

PREP: 15 MIN. + CHILLING • **MAKES:** 2¼ POUNDS

- 1 teaspoon butter
- 1 can (14 ounces) sweetened condensed milk
- 1 package (11 ounces) peanut butter and milk chocolate chips
- 1 cup milk chocolate chips
- ⅔ cup milk chocolate English toffee bits
- 1 cup chopped pecans
- 2 teaspoons vanilla extract

Line a 9-in. square baking pan with foil and grease the foil with butter; set aside. In a large microwave-safe bowl, combine the milk, chips and toffee bits. Microwave, uncovered, on high for 1 minute; stir. Cook 1-2 minutes longer, stirring every minute, or until chips are melted. Stir in pecans and vanilla. Transfer to prepared pan. Cover and refrigerate for at least 1 hour. Using foil, lift fudge out of pan. Gently peel off foil; cut into 1-in. squares. Store in an airtight container.

NOTE *This recipe was tested in a 1,100-watt microwave.*

DRIZZLED NANAIMO BARS

No one knows for sure who invented Nanaimo bars, but nearly everyone who makes these creamy, chocolaty goodies knows how quickly they disappear.

—ALICE MAYSICK BERRIEN CENTER, MI

PREP: 40 MIN. + CHILLING • **MAKES:** 4 DOZEN

- 1 cup butter, cubed
- ½ cup sugar

- 2 ounces unsweetened chocolate, chopped
- 2 eggs, beaten
- 2 teaspoons vanilla extract
- 4 cups graham cracker crumbs
- 2 cups flaked coconut
- 1 cup chopped walnuts

FILLING
- ½ cup butter, softened
- 3 tablespoons 2% milk
- 2 tablespoons instant vanilla pudding mix
- 2 cups confectioners' sugar

GLAZE
- 8 ounces semisweet chocolate, chopped
- 1 tablespoon butter

1. In a large heavy saucepan, combine the butter, sugar and chocolate. Cook and stir over medium-low heat until melted. Whisk a small amount of hot mixture into eggs. Return all to the pan, whisking constantly. Cook and stir over medium-low heat until mixture reaches 160°. Remove from the heat; stir in vanilla.

2. In a large bowl, combine the cracker crumbs, coconut and walnuts. Stir in chocolate mixture until blended. Press into a greased 15-in. x 10-in. x 1-in. pan. Refrigerate for 30 minutes or until set.

3. For filling, in a large bowl, beat the butter, milk and pudding mix until blended. Gradually beat in confectioners' sugar until smooth; spread over crust.

4. For glaze, in a microwave, melt chocolate and butter; stir until smooth. Drizzle over filling. Refrigerate until set. Cut into bars.

Bounty of Bars

Want something simple for dessert? Looking to feed the gang at an upcoming family reunion?
Now's the time to bake up a batch of creative, convenient and crowd-pleasing bars.

RASPBERRY LINZER BARS

Even though they have a touch of sophistication, these bars leave all those who bite into them with a childlike grin of delight.
—HOLLY CAIN ST. PETERSBURG, FL

PREP: 15 MIN. • **BAKE:** 35 MIN. + COOLING • **MAKES:** 18 BARS

- 1⅓ cups butter, softened
- ¾ cup sugar
- 1 egg
- 1 teaspoon grated lemon peel
- 2½ cups all-purpose flour
- 2 cups ground almonds
- 1 teaspoon ground cinnamon
- 1 cup seedless raspberry preserves
  Confectioners' sugar

1. In a large bowl, cream the butter and sugar until light and fluffy. Beat in egg and lemon peel. In another bowl, mix the flour, ground almonds and cinnamon; gradually beat into creamed mixture.
2. Press 2 cups of the dough onto the bottom of a greased 13-in. x 9-in. baking pan. Spread with preserves. Crumble remaining dough over preserves.
3. Bake at 350° for 35-40 minutes or until lightly browned. Cool completely on a wire rack.
4. Sprinkle with confectioners' sugar; cut into bars.

MILLION DOLLAR PECAN BARS

Invest just 15 minutes of your time, and enjoy a big payoff when you pull these rich layered bars of golden goodness from your oven!
—LAURA DAVIS RUSK, TX

PREP: 15 MIN. • **BAKE:** 20 MIN. • **MAKES:** 2 DOZEN

- ¾ cup butter, softened
- ¾ cup packed brown sugar
- 2 eggs
- 2 teaspoons vanilla extract
- 1 package butter pecan cake mix (regular size)
- 2½ cups quick-cooking oats

FILLING

- 1 can (14 ounces) sweetened condensed milk
- 2 cups milk chocolate chips
- 1 cup butterscotch chips
- 1 tablespoon butter
- 1 teaspoon vanilla extract
- 1½ cups chopped pecans

1. In a large bowl, cream butter and brown sugar until light and fluffy. Add eggs, one at a time, beating well after each addition. Beat in vanilla. Add cake mix just until blended. Stir in oats. Press 3 cups onto bottom of a greased 13-in. x 9-in. baking pan.
2. In a large microwave-safe bowl, combine milk and chips. Microwave, uncovered, on high for 2 minutes; stir. Cook 1 to 2½ minutes longer or until chips are melted, stirring every 30 seconds. Stir in butter and vanilla until melted. Stir in pecans. Spread over crust.
3. Crumble remaining oat mixture; sprinkle over top. Bake at 350° for 20-25 minutes or until topping is golden brown. Cool on a wire rack. Cut into bars.

CRANBERRY COCONUT BARS

With equal parts sweet, tart and salty, these bars have something to satisfy just about everyone.

—MARY ANN DELL PHOENIXVILLE, PA

PREP: 40 MIN. • **BAKE:** 30 MIN. + CHILLING • **MAKES:** 2 DOZEN

- 2 cups fresh cranberries
- 1 cup dried cranberries
- ⅔ cup sugar
- ½ cup water
- 2 teaspoons grated lemon peel
- ½ cup butter, softened
- 1 cup packed brown sugar
- 1¼ cups all-purpose flour
- ¾ cup old-fashioned oats
- ½ teaspoon salt
- ½ teaspoon baking soda
- ½ cup flaked coconut
- ½ cup chopped pecans, toasted

1. In a saucepan, combine the cranberries, sugar, water and lemon peel. Cook over medium heat until berries pop, about 15 minutes. Remove from the heat; cool to room temperature.
2. Meanwhile, in a small bowl, beat butter and brown sugar until crumbly, about 2 minutes. Combine the flour, oats, salt and baking soda; gradually add to creamed mixture and mix well. Set aside 1 cup for topping; press remaining crumb mixture into a greased 13-in. x 9-in. baking dish.
3. Bake at 400° for 10-12 minutes or until lightly browned. Spread cranberry mixture over crust. Combine the coconut, pecans and reserved crumb mixture; sprinkle over filling. Bake 18-20 minutes longer or until filling is set.
4. Cool on a wire rack. Refrigerate for 2 hours. Cut into bars.

PUMPKIN CREAM CHEESE BARS

The first time I brought these treats to a church function, there was barely a crumb left on the platter! They really are just too good to resist.

—KIM CHAMBERS LAURELTON, NY

PREP: 25 MIN. • **BAKE:** 35 MIN. + COOLING • **MAKES:** 2 DOZEN

- 1⅓ cups all-purpose flour
- ¾ cup sugar, divided
- ½ cup packed brown sugar
- ¾ cup cold butter, cubed
- 1 cup old-fashioned oats
- ½ cup chopped pecans
- 1 package (8 ounces) cream cheese, softened, cubed
- 2 teaspoons ground cinnamon
- 1 teaspoon ground allspice
- 1 teaspoon ground cardamom
- 1 can (15 ounces) solid-pack pumpkin
- 1 teaspoon vanilla extract
- 3 eggs, lightly beaten

1. Preheat oven to 350°. In a small bowl, mix flour, ¼ cup sugar and brown sugar; cut in butter until crumbly. Stir in oats and pecans. Reserve 1 cup for topping.
2. Press remaining crumb mixture onto bottom of a greased 13-in. x 9-in. baking pan. Bake 15 minutes.
3. In a small bowl, beat cream cheese, spices and remaining sugar until smooth. Beat in pumpkin and vanilla. Add eggs; beat on low speed just until blended. Pour over warm crust; sprinkle with reserved crumb mixture.
4. Bake 20-25 minutes or until a knife inserted near the center comes out clean and filling is set. Cool on a wire rack. Serve or refrigerate, covered, within 2 hours. Cut into bars.

stirring, until a candy thermometer reads 250° (hard-ball stage).

3. Meanwhile, beat egg whites in a heat-proof large bowl until stiff peaks form. With mixer running on high speed, carefully add hot syrup in a slow steady stream, beating constantly at high speed for 5 minutes or until thickened. Cover and set aside.

4. In a large heavy saucepan, combine the remaining sugar, corn syrup and water. Bring to a boil over medium heat, stirring constantly. Reduce heat to medium-low; cook, without stirring, until a candy thermometer reads 290° (soft-crack stage).

5. Gradually pour hot syrup into egg white mixture; stir with a wooden spoon. Stir in the butter, vanilla and salt.

6. Pour mixture over peanuts in pan; press down evenly with buttered fingers.

7. For coating, in a large saucepan, combine sugar, 1/2 cup cream and corn syrup. Bring to a boil over medium heat, stirring constantly; add remaining cream. Reduce heat to medium-low; cook and stir until a candy thermometer reads 242° (soft-ball stage).

8. Remove from the heat; stir in vanilla and salt. Pour over nougat layer in pan. Sprinkle with remaining peanuts, pressing slightly into nougat. Cool for at least 2 hours or until set. Cut into 1½-in. x 1-in. pieces. Roll edges in additional peanuts and shape into logs. Wrap in waxed paper. Store at room temperature.

NOTE *We recommend that you test your candy thermometer before each use by bringing water to a boil; the thermometer should read 212°. Adjust your recipe temperature up or down based on your test.*

CARAMEL NUT LOGS

You'll be glad this recipe makes a lot because these wrapped logs never stick around long! They take a bit of effort to make but are well worth it.

—KAREN HAEN STURGEON BAY, WI

PREP: 30 MIN. • **COOK:** 2½ HOURS • **MAKES:** 4½ POUNDS

- 4 cups (1⅓ pounds) chopped salted peanuts, divided
- 3 cups sugar, divided
- 1⅓ cups light corn syrup, divided
- 1 cup water, divided
- 2 egg whites
- ¼ cup butter, melted
- 2 teaspoons vanilla extract
- ⅛ teaspoon salt

COATING

- 2 cups sugar
- 1½ cups half-and-half cream, divided
- 1¼ cups light corn syrup
- 1 teaspoon vanilla extract
- ¼ teaspoon salt
  Additional chopped salted peanuts

1. Line a 15-in. x 10-in. x 1-in. baking pan with foil; spray foil with cooking spray. Sprinkle with 2 cups peanuts; set aside.

2. In a small heavy saucepan, combine ¾ cup sugar, ⅔ cup corn syrup and ¼ cup water. Bring to a boil over medium heat, stirring constantly. Reduce heat to medium-low. Cook, without

GIANT MONSTER COOKIES

Who can resist a gigantic cookie full of chocolate chips, M&M's and peanut butter? If your appetite isn't quite monster-size, scoop the dough by heaping tablespoonfuls instead.

—JUDY FREDENBERG MISSOULA, MT

PREP: 20 MIN. + CHILLING • **BAKE:** 15 MIN./BATCH
MAKES: ABOUT 2½ DOZEN

- 2 cups creamy peanut butter
- ⅔ cup butter, softened
- 1⅓ cups sugar
- 1⅓ cups packed brown sugar
- 4 eggs
- 2½ teaspoons baking soda
- 1 teaspoon vanilla extract
- 1 teaspoon light corn syrup
- 6 cups old-fashioned oats
- 1 cup semisweet chocolate chips
- 1 cup milk chocolate M&M's

1. In a bowl, cream the peanut butter, butter, sugar and brown sugar until light and fluffy, about 4 minutes. Beat in the eggs, baking soda, vanilla and corn syrup. Add oats and mix well. Stir in chocolate chips and M&M's. Cover and refrigerate for 1 hour.

2. Drop by ¼ cupfuls 3 in. apart onto ungreased baking sheets. Bake at 350° for 14-18 minutes or until edges are lightly browned. Cool for 5 minutes before removing from pans to wire racks to cool completely. Store in an airtight container.

FROSTED RED VELVET COOKIES

I worked in a bakery during my college years, and I like to make this recipe whenever I want to remember the good ol' times.

—**CHRISTINA PETRI** ALEXANDRIA, MN

PREP: 20 MIN. • **BAKE:** 10 MIN./BATCH • **MAKES:** 5 DOZEN

- 2 ounces unsweetened chocolate, chopped
- ½ cup butter, softened
- ⅔ cup packed brown sugar
- ⅓ cup sugar
- 1 egg
- 1 tablespoon red food coloring
- 1 teaspoon vanilla extract
- 2 cups all-purpose flour
- ½ teaspoon baking soda
- ½ teaspoon salt
- 1 cup sour cream
- 1 cup (6 ounces) semisweet chocolate chips
- 1 can (16 ounces) cream cheese frosting

1. In a microwave, melt unsweetened chocolate; stir until smooth. Cool.

2. In a bowl, cream butter and sugars until light and fluffy. Beat in the egg, food coloring and vanilla. Add cooled chocolate; beat until blended. In another bowl, mix the flour, baking soda and salt; add to creamed mixture alternately with sour cream, beating well after each addition. Stir in chocolate chips.

3. Drop by tablespoonfuls 2 in. apart onto parchment paper-lined baking sheets. Bake at 375° for 6-9 minutes or until set. Remove to wire racks to cool completely. Spread with frosting.

TIRAMISU BROWNIES

Tiramisu and brownies—does it get any yummier than this combo? My easy recipe provides traditional tiramisu flavor without all the usual fuss.

—**ANNA-MARIA CARPANZANO** WHITBY, ON

PREP: 25 MIN. • **BAKE:** 45 MIN. + COOLING • **MAKES:** 3 DOZEN

- 12 ounces semisweet chocolate, chopped
- 1 cup butter, softened
- 1⅓ cups plus ¼ cup sugar, divided
- 8 eggs
- 1 cup cake flour
- ¼ cup instant coffee granules or espresso powder
- 2 cartons (8 ounces each) Mascarpone cheese
- 2 teaspoons vanilla extract
- 1 teaspoon baking cocoa

1. In a large microwave-safe bowl, melt chocolate. Stir until smooth; cool slightly. Beat in the butter. Gradually beat in 1⅓ cups sugar. Add six eggs, one at a time, beating well after each addition.

2. Combine flour and coffee granules; add to chocolate mixture. Beat on low speed just until combined; set aside.

3. For filling, in a small bowl, beat the cheese, vanilla and remaining sugar and eggs until smooth.

4. Pour half of the chocolate batter into a greased 13-in. x 9-in. baking pan. Spread with filling. Top with remaining batter, spreading evenly to completely cover filling.

5. Bake at 350° for 45-50 minutes or until center is almost set and brownies begin to pull away from sides of pan.

6. Cool on a wire rack. Dust with cocoa. Cut into squares. Store in the refrigerator.

DAZZLING DESSERTS

What are you in the mood for? Whether you're thinking pies, cakes, tartlets, ice cream, cupcakes or creme brulee, you'll find a lovely finale to any meal here. Your family and friends will love these choices, too.

SPICED CHOCOLATE MOLTEN CAKES

Take time to linger over this decadent dessert. Is there anything better than a chocolate cake with a warm melted center?
—**DEB CARPENTER** HASTINGS, MI

START TO FINISH: 30 MIN. • **MAKES:** 2 SERVINGS

- ¼ cup butter, cubed
- 2 ounces semisweet chocolate, chopped
- 1½ teaspoons dry red wine
- ½ teaspoon vanilla extract
- 1 egg
- 2 teaspoons egg yolk
- ½ cup confectioners' sugar
- 3 tablespoons all-purpose flour
- ⅛ teaspoon ground ginger
- ⅛ teaspoon ground cinnamon
  Additional confectioners' sugar

1. In a microwave, melt butter and chocolate; stir until smooth. Stir in wine and vanilla.

2. In a small bowl, beat the egg, egg yolk and confectioners' sugar until thick and lemon-colored. Beat in the flour, ginger and cinnamon until well blended. Gradually beat in the butter mixture.

3. Transfer to two greased 6-oz. ramekins or custard cups. Place ramekins on a baking sheet. Bake at 425° for 10-12 minutes or until a thermometer inserted near the center reads 160° and sides of cakes are set.

4. Remove from the oven and let stand for 1 minute. Run a knife around edges of ramekins; invert onto dessert plates. Dust with additional confectioners' sugar. Serve immediately.

APPLE-CRANBERRY TART

A treat for all seasons, this one is sweet, tart and nutty—all rolled into a single dessert! Make it during the holidays, for birthdays, or whenever you crave something fabulous and fruity.
—**SONYA LABBE** WEST HOLLYWOOD, CA

PREP: 30 MIN. • **BAKE:** 40 MIN. + COOLING • **MAKES:** 14 SERVINGS

- 1⅔ cups all-purpose flour
- ⅔ cup sugar
- ⅓ cup finely chopped walnuts
- ⅔ cup cold butter

FILLING

- 3 medium tart apples, peeled and thinly sliced
- ½ cup sugar
- 2 tablespoons cornstarch
- 1 teaspoon ground cinnamon
- ¼ teaspoon ground nutmeg
- 2 cups fresh or frozen cranberries

STREUSEL

- ½ cup all-purpose flour
- ½ cup packed brown sugar
- 1 teaspoon grated orange peel
- ¼ cup cold butter
- ⅓ cup chopped walnuts

1. In a small bowl, combine the flour, sugar and walnuts; cut in butter until crumbly. Press onto the bottom and up the sides of an ungreased 11-in. fluted tart pan with removable bottom.

2. In a large bowl, combine the apples, sugar, cornstarch, cinnamon and nutmeg. Gently stir in the cranberries. Transfer to crust.

3. Bake at 425° for 25 minutes. In a small bowl, combine the flour, brown sugar and orange peel. Cut in butter until crumbly. Stir in walnuts. Sprinkle over filling. Bake 15-20 minutes longer or until filling is bubbly and topping is golden brown. Cool on a wire rack.

RED VELVET CHEESECAKE

This cheesecake is likely to become a fixture on your dessert menu. A red velvet filling is spiked with cocoa, topped with cream cheese frosting and baked in a chocolate cookie crumb crust.

—**KAREN DIVELY** CHAPIN, SC

PREP: 30 MIN. • **BAKE:** 1 HOUR + CHILLING • **MAKES:** 16 SERVINGS

- 17 chocolate cream-filled chocolate sandwich cookies, crushed
- ¼ cup butter, melted
- 1 tablespoon sugar

FILLING
- 3 packages (8 ounces each) cream cheese, softened
- 1½ cups sugar
- 1 cup (8 ounces) sour cream
- ½ cup buttermilk
- 3 tablespoons baking cocoa
- 2 teaspoons vanilla extract
- 4 eggs, lightly beaten
- 1 bottle (1 ounce) red food coloring

FROSTING
- 1 package (3 ounces) cream cheese, softened
- ¼ cup butter, softened
- 2 cups confectioners' sugar
- 1 teaspoon vanilla extract

1. Place a greased 9-in. springform pan on a double thickness of heavy-duty foil (about 18 in. square). Securely wrap foil around pan.

2. In a small bowl, combine the cookie crumbs, butter and sugar. Press onto the bottom of prepared pan.

3. In a large bowl, beat cream cheese and sugar until smooth. Beat in the sour cream, buttermilk, cocoa and vanilla. Add eggs; beat on low speed just until combined. Stir in food coloring. Pour over crust. Place springform pan in a large baking pan; add 1 in. of hot water to larger pan.

4. Bake at 325° for 60-70 minutes or until center is just set and top appears dull. Remove springform pan from water bath. Cool on a wire rack for 10 minutes. Carefully run a knife around edge of pan to loosen; cool 1 hour longer. Refrigerate overnight. Remove sides of pan.

5. For frosting, in a small bowl, beat cream cheese and butter until fluffy. Add confectioners' sugar and vanilla; beat until smooth. Frost top of cheesecake. Refrigerate until serving.

BLUEBERRY & GINGER TART

Bring this stunning tart to the table for lots of "oohs" and "aahs." With a hint of mint and lime, juicy blueberries, ginger and a buttery crust—it's tough to stop at just one slice.

—**KAREN HICKS** MABELVALE, AR

PREP: 30 MIN. • **BAKE:** 40 MIN. + COOLING • **MAKES:** 14 SERVINGS

- 1¾ cups all-purpose flour
- ¾ cup packed brown sugar
- ¾ cup cold butter, cubed
- 2 tablespoons lime juice, divided
- ⅔ cup sugar
- 4 teaspoons cornstarch
- 1½ teaspoons minced fresh gingerroot
- 1 teaspoon minced fresh mint
- 3½ cups fresh or frozen blueberries, thawed
  Whipped cream

1. In a food processor, combine the flour, brown sugar and butter; cover and pulse until mixture resembles coarse crumbs. Remove and set aside 1 cup for topping. Stir 1 tablespoon lime juice into remaining pastry. Press onto the bottom and up the sides of a greased 11-in. fluted tart pan with removable bottom.

2. In a large bowl, combine the sugar, cornstarch, ginger and mint. Add blueberries and remaining lime juice; toss to coat. Transfer to crust. Sprinkle with reserved topping.

3. Bake at 400° for 40-45 minutes or until filling is bubbly and topping is golden brown. Cover edges with foil during the last 15 minutes to prevent overbrowning if necessary. Cool completely on a wire rack. Serve with whipped cream.

PEANUT BUTTER BROWNIE CUPCAKES

Folks love brownies and cupcakes, so why not combine them? You'll see these snacks disappear before your very eyes!
—**CAROL GILLESPIE** CHAMBERSBURG, PA

PREP: 15 MIN. • **BAKE:** 15 MIN. + COOLING • **MAKES:** 1 DOZEN

- 1 package fudge brownie mix (8-inch square pan size)
- ½ cup miniature semisweet chocolate chips
- ⅓ cup creamy peanut butter
- 3 tablespoons cream cheese, softened
- 1 egg
- ¼ cup sugar
  Confectioners' sugar

1. Preheat oven to 350°. Prepare the brownie batter according to package directions; stir in chocolate chips. For filling, in a small bowl, beat peanut butter, cream cheese, egg and sugar until smooth.

2. Fill paper-lined muffin cups one-third full with batter. Drop filling by teaspoonfuls into the center of each cupcake. Cover with remaining batter.

3. Bake 15-20 minutes or until a toothpick inserted in brownie portion comes out clean. Cool 10 minutes before removing from pan to a wire rack to cool completely. Dust tops with confectioners' sugar. Store in the refrigerator.

DREAMY ORANGE CHARLOTTE

Once you've finished your main meal, bring out this perfect finale. It has a light, airy texture and refreshing citrus taste.
—**VIOLET GERTSCH** DARLINGTON, WI

PREP: 30 MIN. + CHILLING • **MAKES:** 12 SERVINGS

- 1 envelope unflavored gelatin
- ¼ cup cold water
- ¼ cup boiling water
- 1 cup plus 2 tablespoons orange juice
- ⅔ cup sugar
- 3 tablespoons lemon juice
- 2 tablespoons orange liqueur or additional orange juice
- 1½ teaspoons grated orange peel
- 2 cups heavy whipping cream, whipped
- 1 prepared angel food cake (8 to 10 ounces), cut into 1-inch cubes

1. In a small bowl, sprinkle gelatin over cold water; let stand for 1 minute. Stir in boiling water until gelatin is completely dissolved. Stir in the orange juice, sugar, lemon juice, orange liqueur and orange peel until sugar is dissolved. Refrigerate until thickened, about 1 hour.

2. Fold in whipped cream and cake cubes. Transfer to a greased 11-in. x 7-in. dish. Cover and refrigerate for at least 2 hours before serving.

BOURBON CHOCOLATE-PECAN PIE

Don't have bourbon on hand? Use three tablespoons of melted butter in its place. If you decide to make this pie lighter, leave out the chocolate.

—SARAH VARNER SANTA RITA, GUAM

PREP: 20 MIN. • **BAKE:** 50 MIN. • **MAKES:** 10 SERVINGS

> Pastry for single-crust pie (9 inches)
> ½ cup miniature semisweet chocolate chips
> 4 eggs, lightly beaten
> 1 cup corn syrup
> ½ cup sugar
> 6 tablespoons butter, melted
> ¼ cup packed brown sugar
> 3 tablespoons bourbon
> 1 tablespoon all-purpose flour
> 3 teaspoons vanilla extract
> 1½ cups chopped pecans, divided

1. Roll out pastry to fit a 9-in. pie plate. Transfer pastry to pie plate. Trim pastry to ½ in. beyond edge of plate; flute edges. Sprinkle chocolate chips into pastry shell. Set aside.
2. In a large bowl, whisk the eggs, corn syrup, sugar, butter, brown sugar, bourbon, flour and vanilla until smooth. Stir in 1 cup pecans. Pour into pastry shell; sprinkle with the remaining pecans.
3. Bake at 350° for 50-60 minutes or until set. Cool on a wire rack. Store leftovers in the refrigerator.

VERY RASPBERRY PIE

We live along an old railroad track (our house was once a train station), where wild raspberries pop up for a few weeks every year. I harvest the berries for this incredibly delicious pie.

—KATHY JONES WEST WINFIELD, NY

PREP: 30 MIN. + CHILLING • **MAKES:** 8 SERVINGS

RASPBERRY TOPPING
> 6 cups fresh raspberries, divided
> 1 cup sugar
> 3 tablespoons cornstarch
> ½ cup water

CREAM FILLING
> 1 package (8 ounces) cream cheese, softened
> 1 cup whipped topping
> 1 cup confectioners' sugar
> 1 graham cracker crust (9 inches)
> Fresh mint, optional

1. Mash about 2 cups raspberries to measure 1 cup; place in a small saucepan. Add the sugar, cornstarch and water.
2. Bring to a boil, stirring constantly; cook and stir 2 minutes longer. Strain to remove berry seeds if desired. Cool to room temperature, about 20 minutes.
3. Meanwhile, for filling, beat the cream cheese, whipped topping and confectioners' sugar in a small bowl. Spread in bottom of crust.
4. Top with remaining raspberries. Pour cooled raspberry sauce over top. Refrigerate until set, about 3 hours.
5. Store in the refrigerator. Garnish with mint if desired.

FRESH BERRY SHORTCAKES

Juicy, fresh-picked strawberries can take a place of honor on any table—especially when presented in a buttery, mouthwatering shortcake! You'll want to whip these up every spring and early summer, and be sure to add a swirl of whipped cream on top for the ultimate crowning touch.

—JENNIFER MASTNICK-COOK HARTVILLE, OH

PREP: 35 MIN. • **BAKE:** 20 MIN. • **MAKES:** 10 SERVINGS

- 5 cups sliced fresh strawberries
- ½ cup sugar
- ¼ cup orange juice

SHORTCAKES

- 3 cups all-purpose flour
- ½ cup sugar
- 1 tablespoon baking powder
- 1 tablespoon grated orange peel
- ½ teaspoon salt
- ½ cup cold butter, cubed
- 1½ cups plus 1 tablespoon heavy whipping cream, divided
- 1 egg
- 1 egg yolk
- 1 teaspoon vanilla extract
  Coarse sugar, optional

WHIPPED CREAM

- 2 cups heavy whipping cream
- ¼ cup confectioners' sugar
- ½ teaspoon vanilla extract

1. In a small bowl, combine the strawberries, sugar and orange juice; set aside.

2. For shortcakes, combine the flour, sugar, baking powder, orange peel and salt; cut in butter until mixture resembles coarse crumbs. Whisk 1½ cups cream, egg, egg yolk and vanilla; add to flour mixture, stirring just until moistened. Turn onto a lightly floured surface; gently knead 8-10 times.

3. Pat or roll out to 1-in. thickness; cut with a floured 3-in. scalloped or round biscuit cutter. Place 2 in. apart on a parchment paper-lined baking sheet. Brush tops with 1 tablespoon cream; sprinkle with coarse sugar if desired. Bake at 400° for 15-18 minutes or until golden brown. Cool on a wire rack for 5 minutes.

4. For whipped cream, beat cream in a large bowl until it begins to thicken. Add confectioners' sugar and vanilla; beat until soft peaks form.

5. Just before serving, cut shortcakes in half horizontally. Place bottoms on dessert plates; top with strawberry mixture. Replace tops; dollop with whipped cream.

COWABUNGA ROOT BEER CUPCAKES

I developed these cupcakes for my daughter's first birthday and transported them using dry ice. I got a lot of recipe requests after.
—MINDY CARSWELL WALKER, MI

PREP: 10 MIN. • **BAKE:** 15 MIN. + COOLING • **MAKES:** 24 SERVINGS

- 1 package butter recipe golden cake mix (regular size)
- 4 teaspoons root beer concentrate, divided
- 1 carton (12 ounces) frozen whipped topping, thawed
  Vanilla ice cream

1. Prepare and bake cupcakes according to package directions, adding 2 teaspoons root beer concentrate when mixing batter. Remove to wire racks to cool completely.

2. In a small bowl, mix whipped topping and remaining root beer concentrate until blended; spread over cupcakes. Serve with ice cream.

NOTE *This recipe was tested with McCormick root beer concentrate.*

RASPBERRY-RHUBARB SLAB PIE

"Slab Pie" is a pastry baked in a jelly roll pan and cut in slabs like a bar cookie—or a pie bar, if you will. My grandfather was a professional baker and served pieces of slab pie to his customers back in the day. Here is my spin on that recipe, featuring rhubarb and gorgeous red raspberries.

—JEANNE AMBROSE MILWAUKEE, WI

PREP: 30 MIN. + CHILLING • **BAKE:** 45 MIN. + COOLING
MAKES: 2 DOZEN

- 3¼ cups all-purpose flour
- 1 teaspoon salt
- 1 cup butter
- ¾ cup plus 1 to 2 tablespoons 2% milk, divided
- 1 egg yolk
- 2 cups sugar
- ⅓ cup cornstarch
- 5 cups fresh or frozen unsweetened raspberries, thawed and drained
- 3 cups sliced fresh or frozen rhubarb, thawed and drained

VANILLA ICING

- 1¼ cups confectioners' sugar
- ½ teaspoon vanilla extract
- 5 to 6 teaspoons 2% milk

1. In a large bowl, combine flour and salt; cut in butter until crumbly. Whisk ¾ cup milk and egg yolk; gradually add to flour mixture, tossing with a fork until dough forms a ball. Add additional milk, 1 tablespoon at a time, if necessary.

2. Divide dough in half so that one portion is slightly larger than the other; wrap each in plastic wrap. Refrigerate for 1 hour or until easy to handle.

3. Roll out larger portion of dough between two large sheets of lightly floured waxed paper into an 18-in. x 13-in. rectangle. Transfer to an ungreased 15-in. x 10-in. x 1-in. baking pan. Press onto the bottom and up the sides of pan; trim pastry to edges of pan.

4. In a large bowl, combine sugar and cornstarch. Add raspberries and rhubarb; toss to coat. Spoon into pastry.

5. Roll out remaining dough; place over filling. Fold bottom pastry over edge of top pastry; seal with a fork. Prick top with a fork.

6. Bake at 375° for 45-55 minutes or until golden brown. Cool completely on a wire rack.

7. For icing, combine confectioners' sugar, vanilla and enough milk to achieve a drizzling consistency; drizzle over pie. Cut pie into squares.

NOTE *If using frozen rhubarb, measure rhubarb while still frozen, then thaw completely. Drain in a colander, but do not press liquid out.*

CHOOSING & STORING RHUBARB

Select rhubarb stalks that are brightly colored and crisp, then tightly wrap stalks in a plastic bag and store in the refrigerator for up to 3 days. One pound of rhubarb yields about 3 cups chopped.

TEMPTING CARAMEL APPLE PUDDING WITH GINGERSNAP CRUST

Crunchy apples top cream cheese and butterscotch-caramel pudding layers in this delectable dessert. The gingersnap crust lends a touch of spice.

—MARGARET WILSON SUN CITY, CA

PREP: 30 MIN. + CHILLING • **MAKES:** 15 SERVINGS

- 2 cups crushed gingersnap cookies (about 40 cookies)
- ⅓ cup butter, melted
- 1 package (8 ounces) cream cheese, softened
- ¼ cup sugar
- 3¼ cups cold 2% milk, divided
- 1 carton (8 ounces) frozen whipped topping, thawed, divided
- 2 packages (3.4 ounces each) instant butterscotch pudding mix
- ½ cup hot caramel ice cream topping, divided
- 1 medium Red Delicious, Gala or Cortland apple, chopped
- 1 medium Granny Smith apple, chopped
- ⅓ cup dry roasted peanuts, chopped

1. In a small bowl, mix crushed cookies and butter until blended; press onto the bottom of a greased 13-in. x 9-in. baking dish. Refrigerate for at least 15 minutes.

2. Meanwhile, in a large bowl, beat cream cheese, sugar and ¼ cup milk until smooth. Fold in 1 cup whipped topping; spread over crust.

3. In a large bowl, whisk remaining milk and pudding mixes for 2 minutes; let stand 2 minutes or until soft-set. Stir in ¼ cup caramel topping. Spoon over cream cheese layer. Cover and refrigerate 15 minutes.

4. Spread remaining whipped topping over top. Cover and refrigerate at least 4 hours or until filling is firm.

5. Just before serving, top with apples; drizzle with remaining caramel topping. Sprinkle with peanuts.

Ice Cream Social

I scream, you scream, we all know what comes next! Cool down by hosting a fresh take on a classic theme. Who needs the ice cream truck when you've got these desserts?

PRALINE ICE CREAM CAKE

Mmm...melted ice cream is the key ingredient in this lovely golden cake. It's been a family favorite for years.

—**JOAN HALLFORD** NORTH RICHLAND HILLS, TX

PREP: 20 MIN. • **BAKE:** 25 MIN. + COOLING • **MAKES:** 15 SERVINGS

- 1 cup packed brown sugar
- ½ cup sour cream
- 2 tablespoons plus ½ cup butter, divided
- 2 teaspoons cornstarch
- 1 teaspoon vanilla extract, divided
- 2 cups vanilla ice cream, softened
- 2 eggs
- 1½ cups all-purpose flour
- 1 cup graham cracker crumbs
- ⅔ cup sugar
- 2½ teaspoons baking powder
- ½ teaspoon salt
- ½ cup chopped pecans, toasted
  Whipped cream, optional

1. In a heavy saucepan, combine the brown sugar, sour cream, 2 tablespoons butter and cornstarch; bring to a boil over medium heat, stirring constantly. Remove from the heat; stir in ½ teaspoon vanilla.

2. Melt the remaining butter; place in a large bowl. Add ice cream; stir to blend. Add eggs, one at a time, beating well after each addition; stir in the remaining vanilla. In another bowl, mix the flour, cracker crumbs, sugar, baking powder and salt; gradually stir into ice cream mixture.

3. Pour into a greased 13-in. x 9-in. baking pan. Drizzle with half of the sauce. Bake at 350° for 25-30 minutes or until a toothpick inserted in center comes out clean. Cool slightly in pan on a wire rack.

4. Add pecans to remaining sauce; spoon over warm cake (sauce will not cover cake completely). Cool cake in pan. Serve with whipped cream if desired.

PISTACHIO MERINGUE SUNDAES

Meringue sundaes can be made with any gelato or ice cream, then topped with different sauces, nuts or fresh fruit.

—**LISA SPEER** PALM BEACH, FL

START TO FINISH: 5 MIN. • **MAKES:** 4 SERVINGS

- 2 cups pistachio gelato or pistachio ice cream
- 4 miniature meringue cookies or vanilla wafers
- 4 teaspoons chocolate syrup
- ¼ cup finely chopped pistachios

Scoop gelato into four dessert dishes. Top each with a cookie and drizzle with chocolate syrup. Sprinkle with pistachios.

CARAMEL-MOCHA ICE CREAM DESSERT

You can use any kind of ice cream in this frosty dessert—the possibilities are endless! I personally suggest changing it up by substituting chocolate and vanilla for coffee and dulce de leche.

—SCARLETT ELROD NEWNAN, GA

PREP: 45 MIN. + FREEZING • **MAKES:** 20 SERVINGS

- 10 **whole graham crackers**
- 1 **cup butter, cubed**
- 1 **cup packed brown sugar**
- 1 **cup chopped pecans**

FILLING

- 1 **quart dulce de leche ice cream, softened**
- 1 **jar (16 ounces) hot fudge ice cream topping, warmed**
- 1 **quart coffee ice cream, softened**
- 1½ **cups heavy whipping cream**
- ⅓ **cup coffee liqueur**
  Chocolate curls

1. Preheat oven to 350°. Arrange crackers in a single layer in a greased 15-in. x 10-in. x 1-in. baking pan. In a large saucepan, melt butter over medium heat. Stir in brown sugar. Bring to a gentle boil; cook and stir for 2 minutes. Remove from the heat and stir in pecans. Pour over crackers; spread to cover crackers.

2. Bake 8-10 minutes or until bubbly. Remove to a wire rack to cool completely.

3. Crush cracker mixture into coarse crumbs; sprinkle half into an ungreased 13-in. x 9-in. dish. Spread with dulce de leche ice cream. Cover and freeze for 1 hour or until firm.

4. Drizzle with ice cream topping and sprinkle with remaining crumb mixture. Cover and freeze 30 minutes or until ice cream topping is set.

5. Spread with coffee ice cream; freeze. In a small bowl, beat cream until stiff peaks form. Fold in coffee liqueur. Spread over top of dessert. Cover and freeze 4 hours or until firm.

6. Remove from freezer 15 minutes before serving. Garnish with chocolate curls.

ALLOW ICE CREAM TO SOFTEN

To soften ice cream before using it in a recipe, transfer ice cream from the freezer to refrigerator 20-30 minutes before using. Another option is to allow ice cream to sit out at room temperature for 10-15 minutes or to microwave it at 30-percent power for 30 seconds.

FROZEN KEY LIME DELIGHT

Nothing hits the spot quite like this refreshing Key lime dessert. It will bring smiles with the very first bite.

—**MELISSA MILLWOOD** LYMAN, SC

PREP: 50 MIN. • **BAKE:** 25 MIN. + FREEZING • **MAKES:** 8 SERVINGS

- 1 cup all-purpose flour
- ½ cup salted cashews, chopped
- ½ cup flaked coconut
- ¼ cup packed light brown sugar
- ½ cup butter, melted
- 2 cups heavy whipping cream
- 1½ cups sweetened condensed milk
- 1 cup Key lime juice
- 3 teaspoons grated Key lime peel
- 1 teaspoon vanilla extract
  Whipped cream and Key lime slices

1. In a small bowl, combine the flour, cashews, coconut and brown sugar. Stir in butter. Sprinkle into a greased 15-in. x 10-in. x 1-in. baking pan. Bake at 350° for 20-25 minutes or until golden brown, stirring once. Cool on a wire rack.

2. Meanwhile, in a large bowl, combine the cream, milk, lime juice, peel and vanilla. Refrigerate until chilled.

3. Fill cylinder of ice cream freezer two-thirds full; freeze according to the manufacturer's directions.

4. Sprinkle half of the cashew mixture into an ungreased 11-in. x 7-in. dish. Spread ice cream over top; sprinkle with remaining cashew mixture. Cover and freeze for 4 hours or until firm. Garnish servings with whipped cream and lime slices.

MINT PAPAYA SORBET

While looking for new ways to use fresh mint, I decided to create a frosty treat that was good for me, too. You'll love this one!

—**JESS APFE** BERKELEY, CA

PREP: 15 MIN. + FREEZING • **MAKES:** 5 SERVINGS

- 1 cup water
- ½ cup sugar
- ½ cup fresh mint leaves
- 2 cups chopped peeled papaya
- ¼ cup lime juice
- 3 tablespoons minced fresh mint

1. In a small saucepan, bring the water, sugar and mint leaves to a boil. Cook and stir until sugar is dissolved; set aside to cool. Strain; discard mint leaves.

2. Place the papaya in a food processor; add sugar syrup and lime juice. Cover and process for 2-3 minutes or until smooth. Stir in chopped mint.

3. Fill cylinder of ice cream freezer; freeze according to manufacturer's directions. Transfer to a freezer container; freeze for 4 hours or until firm.

CHOCOLATE-RASPBERRY CREME BRULEE

Creme brulee was already wonderfully decadent, but then I created this version with rich chocolate and sweet raspberries. Cracking through the top of the dessert reveals a smooth custard everyone enjoys.

—**JAN VALDEZ** CHICAGO, IL

PREP: 25 MIN. • **BAKE:** 40 MIN. + CHILLING • **MAKES:** 10 SERVINGS

- 8 ounces semisweet chocolate, chopped
- 4 cups heavy whipping cream
- ½ cup plus 2 tablespoons sugar, divided
- 8 egg yolks, beaten
- 1 tablespoon vanilla extract
- 30 fresh raspberries
- 2 tablespoons brown sugar

1. Place chocolate in a small bowl. In a small saucepan, bring cream and ½ cup sugar just to a boil. Pour over chocolate; whisk until smooth. Stir a small amount of hot cream mixture into egg yolks. Return all to the pan, stirring constantly. Remove from the heat; stir in vanilla.

2. Place 3 raspberries in each of 10 ungreased 6-oz. ramekins or custard cups. Evenly divide custard among ramekins. Place in a baking pan; add 1 in. of boiling water to pan. Bake, uncovered, at 325° for 40-50 minutes or until centers are just set (mixture will jiggle). Remove ramekins from water bath; cool 10 minutes. Cover and refrigerate for at least 4 hours.

3. Combine brown sugar and remaining sugar. If using a creme brulee torch, sprinkle custards with sugar mixture. Heat sugar with the torch until caramelized. Serve immediately.

4. If broiling the custards, place ramekins on a baking sheet; let stand at room temperature for 15 minutes. Sprinkle with sugar mixture. Broil 8 in. from the heat for 4-7 minutes or until sugar is caramelized. Refrigerate for 1-2 hours or until firm.

GRILLED POUND CAKE WITH WARM AMARETTO BANANAS

Adding a lick of almond liqueur to this luscious grilled dessert flavored with bananas and caramel takes it to a whole new level. Elegant enough to serve guests!

—**CAROL TRAUPMAN-CARR** BREINIGSVILLE, PA

START TO FINISH: 25 MIN. • **MAKES:** 4 SERVINGS

    4 teaspoons butter, divided
    2 large bananas, cut into ¼-inch slices
    2 tablespoons brown sugar
    1 tablespoon amaretto
    1 teaspoon lemon juice
    4 slices pound cake (about 1 inch thick)
       Sweetened whipped cream and toasted sliced almonds,
       optional

1. Melt 2 teaspoons butter; drizzle over a double thickness of heavy-duty foil (about 10 in. square). Place bananas on foil; top with brown sugar, amaretto and lemon juice. Dot with remaining butter. Fold foil around mixture and seal tightly.
2. Grill, covered, over medium heat for 8-10 minutes or until heated through. Grill pound cake for 1-2 minutes on each side or until lightly browned. Open foil packets carefully, allowing steam to escape. Spoon bananas over pound cake; top with whipped cream and almonds if desired.
NOTE *To toast nuts, spread in a 15-in. x 10-in. x 1-in. baking pan. Bake at 350° for 5-10 minutes or until lightly browned, stirring occasionally. Or, spread in a dry nonstick skillet and heat over low heat until lightly browned, stirring occasionally.*

CHOCOLATE MALLOW PIE

I've been cooking for more than 60 years and this is THE best chocolate pie recipe I've found.

—**LOUISE GENN** COSMOPOLIS, WA

PREP: 25 MIN. + CHILLING • **MAKES:** 8 SERVINGS

    1¼ cups cream-filled chocolate sandwich cookie crumbs
     ¼ cup butter, melted
     2 tablespoons sugar
     2 packages (one 8 ounces, one 3 ounces) cream cheese,
        softened
     ½ cup chocolate syrup
    1⅓ cups semisweet chocolate chips, melted
     1 carton (8 ounces) frozen whipped topping, thawed, divided
     2 cups miniature marshmallows
        Chocolate curls, optional

1. In a large bowl, combine the cookie crumbs, butter and sugar. Press into a 9-in. pie plate. Bake at 375° for 8-10 minutes or until set; cool completely on a wire rack.
2. In a large bowl, beat cream cheese and chocolate syrup until blended. Beat in melted chips. Set aside ¼ cup of whipped topping. Fold marshmallows and remaining whipped topping into chocolate mixture.
3. Spoon filling into crust. Refrigerate for at least 8 hours or overnight. Top with reserved whipped topping. Garnish with chocolate curls if desired.

GRITS PIE

Simple, Southern and scrumptious, this pie will be a definite hit—even with people who dislike grits! It has the perfect custardy texture.

—VICTORIA HUDSON PICKENS, SC

PREP: 15 MIN. • **BAKE:** 30 MIN. • **MAKES:** 10 SERVINGS

- ¾ cup water
- ⅛ teaspoon salt
- ¼ cup quick-cooking grits
- ½ cup butter, cubed
- ¾ cup sugar
- 2 tablespoons all-purpose flour
- 3 eggs
- ¼ cup buttermilk
- 1 teaspoon vanilla extract
  Pastry for single-crust pie (9 inches)
  Whipped cream, orange slices or sliced fresh strawberries, optional

1. In a small saucepan, bring water and salt to a boil. Slowly stir in grits. Reduce heat; cook and stir for 4-5 minutes or until thickened. Add butter; stir until melted. Remove from the heat; cool to room temperature.

2. In a small bowl, whisk the sugar, flour, eggs, buttermilk and vanilla. Slowly stir into grits. Roll out pastry to fit a 9-in. pie plate. Transfer pastry to pie plate. Trim pastry to ½ in. beyond edge of plate; flute edges. Add filling.

3. Bake at 325° for 30-35 minutes or just until set. Serve warm or cool to room temperature. Garnish with whipped cream and orange or strawberries if desired.

ORANGE-DRIZZLED GRAPE TARTLETS

Sugar cookie dough and cream cheese make it so fast and easy to create these crunchy, tangy tartlets.

—JULIE STERCHI JACKSON, MO

START TO FINISH: 20 MIN. • **MAKES:** 1 DOZEN

- 1 tube (16½ ounces) refrigerated sugar cookie dough
- 1 package (8 ounces) cream cheese, softened
- ½ cup confectioners' sugar
- ½ teaspoon vanilla extract
- ¾ cup seedless red grapes, halved
- ¾ cup green grapes, halved
- ¼ cup orange marmalade

1. Cut cookie dough into 12 slices, about ¾ inch thick. On ungreased baking sheets, pat each slice to form a ½-in.- thick circle. Bake at 350° for 10-12 minutes or until golden brown. Remove to wire racks to cool completely.

2. Meanwhile, in a small bowl, beat the cream cheese, confectioners' sugar and vanilla until blended. Spread over cookie crusts. Top with grapes.

3. In a microwave-safe dish, microwave marmalade, covered, on high for 15-20 seconds or until warmed. Drizzle over grapes.

NECTARINE PLUM CRISPS

Made with a sweet fusion of late-summer fruits, these crisps can also double as breakfast. Look for apple crisp mix in the produce department of your grocery store.
—**NICOLE WERNER** ANN ARBOR, MI

PREP: 20 MIN. • **BAKE:** 25 MIN. • **MAKES:** 4 SERVINGS

- 1 package (9 ounces) apple crisp mix
- 6 tablespoons cold butter, cubed
- 2 cups sliced fresh nectarines
- 2 cups sliced fresh plums
- 2 teaspoons cornstarch
  Vanilla ice cream, optional

1. Place crisp mix in a small bowl; cut in butter until crumbly. Spoon half of the mixture into four 10-oz. ramekins or custard cups coated with cooking spray; reserve remaining mixture for topping.

2. In another bowl, combine the nectarines, plums and cornstarch; toss to coat. Spoon over the crumb layer. Sprinkle with topping.

3. Bake at 375° for 25-30 minutes or until the filling is bubbly and the topping is golden brown. Serve warm; top with ice cream if desired.

NOTE *This recipe was tested with Marzetti apple crisp mix. Look for it in the produce section of your grocery store.*

PINEAPPLE ORANGE CHEESECAKE

Fresh pineapple and orange marmalade transform a purchased cheesecake into an elegant after-dinner treat.
—**TASTE OF HOME TEST KITCHEN**

START TO FINISH: 15 MIN. • **MAKES:** 6 SERVINGS

- 2 cups cubed fresh pineapple
- 2 tablespoons brown sugar
- 2 tablespoons butter
- ⅓ cup orange marmalade
- 1 package (30 ounces) frozen New York-style cheesecake, thawed
  Whipped topping, optional

In a large skillet, saute pineapple and brown sugar in butter for 8 minutes. Spread orange marmalade over cheesecake; top with pineapple mixture. Garnish with whipped topping if desired.

ROCKY ROAD FREEZER PIE

Whip up this simple chocolaty pie the day before a party and take time to relax before guests arrive!
—**ADDRENNE ROTH** DONNA, TX

PREP: 15 MIN. + FREEZING • **MAKES:** 16 SERVINGS

- 1½ cups half-and-half cream
- 1 package (3.9 ounces) instant chocolate pudding mix
- 1 carton (8 ounces) frozen whipped topping, thawed
- ⅓ cup semisweet chocolate chips
- ⅓ cup miniature marshmallows
- ⅓ cup chopped pecans
- 1 graham cracker crust (9 inches)

In a large bowl, whisk cream and pudding mix for 2 minutes. Fold in whipped topping. Stir in the chocolate chips, marshmallows and pecans. Transfer to pie crust. Freeze until firm, about 6 hours. Remove from the freezer 10 minutes before serving.

DARK CHOCOLATE CARROT CAKE

Carrot cake has a dark side—and it's delicious! Cream cheese and shredded carrots in the batter keep this cake so moist, while toasted nuts, cinnamon and chocolate boost the flavor.

—DARLENE BRENDEN SALEM, OR

PREP: 20 MIN. • **BAKE:** 25 MIN. + COOLING • **MAKES:** 16 SERVINGS

- 1 package dark chocolate cake mix (regular size)
- 4 ounces cream cheese, softened
- 1 package (3.9 ounces) instant chocolate pudding mix
- 1 cup 2% milk
- 3 eggs
- 1 teaspoon ground cinnamon
- 3 cups shredded carrots
- 1 cup chopped walnuts, toasted, divided
- 2 cans (16 ounces each) cream cheese frosting

1. In a large bowl, combine the cake mix, cream cheese, pudding mix, milk, eggs and cinnamon; beat on low speed for 30 seconds. Beat on medium for 2 minutes. Stir in carrots and ½ cup walnuts. Pour into three greased and floured 8-in. round baking pans.

2. Bake at 350° for 25-30 minutes or until a toothpick inserted near the center comes out clean. Cool for 10 minutes before removing from pans to wire racks to cool completely.

3. Spread frosting between layers and over top and sides of cake. Sprinkle top with remaining walnuts. Store in the refrigerator.

◀ BLUSHING GRAPEFRUIT SORBET

You can make this citrus dessert year-round, though I especially enjoy it as a light summer refresher.

—MARY MARLOWE LEVERETTE COLUMBIA, SC

PREP: 35 MIN. + FREEZING • **MAKES:** 1 QUART

- 3 cups water
- 1 cup sugar
- ½ cup honey
- 1 tablespoon grated grapefruit peel
- 1 tablespoon minced fresh gingerroot
- 2 whole star anise
- 2 whole cloves
- 1 bay leaf
- 2 cups ruby red grapefruit juice, chilled
- 3 tablespoons lemon juice

1. In a large saucepan, combine the first eight ingredients. Bring to a boil; cook until liquid is reduced by half, about 20 minutes. Strain and set aside to cool.

2. In a large bowl, combine the grapefruit and lemon juices and sugar syrup. Fill cylinder of ice cream freezer; freeze according to manufacturer's directions. Transfer to a freezer container and freeze for 4 hours or until firm.

CRUNCHY AMARETTO PEACH COBBLER

All your guests will find room for this rich peachy dessert. It's irresistible!

—DEBRA KEIL OWASSO, OK

PREP: 10 MIN. • **BAKE:** 30 MIN. • **MAKES:** 12 SERVINGS

- 2 cans (21 ounces each) peach pie filling
- ½ cup amaretto
- 1 package (17½ ounces) sugar cookie mix
- 1 cup sliced almonds
- ½ cup butter, cubed

1. Spread pie filling into an ungreased 13-in. x 9-in. baking dish; drizzle with amaretto. Sprinkle cookie mix and almonds over top; dot with butter.

2. Bake at 350° for 30-35 minutes or until filling is bubbly and topping is golden brown. Serve warm.

CAKE WITH LEMON SAUCE

You only need cream cheese, milk and pudding mix to create a scrumptious sauce to drizzle over pound cake for the perfect mealtime finale. You could also top the cake with your favorite berries. And the best part? You can bring it all to the table in just 10 minutes.

—CLAIRE DION CANTERBURY, CT

START TO FINISH: 10 MIN. • **MAKES:** 4 SERVINGS

- 1 package (3 ounces) cream cheese, softened
- 1¾ cups cold milk
- 1 package (3.4 ounces) instant lemon pudding mix
- 4 slices pound cake or angel food cake
  Fresh raspberries, optional

In a small bowl, beat the cream cheese until smooth. Add milk and pudding mix; beat for 2 minutes or until smooth and thickened. Serve with cake. Garnish with raspberries if desired.

REAL DEAL APPLE PIE

Everyone should know how to make a classic apple pie, and this recipe shows why it's become such an American icon. The pie gets its stunning height from a full 3 pounds of apples.

—**MARGO FERRICK** WESTFORD, MA

PREP: 35 MIN. • **BAKE:** 1¼ HOURS + COOLING • **MAKES:** 8 SERVINGS

- 2¼ cups all-purpose flour
- 2 teaspoons sugar
- ¾ teaspoon kosher salt
- 1 cup cold unsalted butter, cubed
- 6 to 8 tablespoons ice water

FILLING

- 5 medium Braeburn apples (about 1½ pounds), peeled and cut into ¼-in. slices
- 4 medium Granny Smith apples (about 1½ pounds), peeled and cut into ¼-in. slices
- ½ cup sugar
- 3 tablespoons lemon juice
- 2 tablespoons all-purpose flour
- ½ teaspoon kosher salt
- ¾ teaspoon ground cinnamon
  Dash ground nutmeg
- 3 tablespoons unsalted butter, cut into pieces
- 1 egg, lightly beaten
- 1 to 2 tablespoons superfine sugar

1. In a large bowl, mix flour, sugar and salt; cut in butter until crumbly. Gradually add water, tossing with a fork until dough holds together when pressed. Divide dough in two portions so that one is slightly larger than the other; wrap each in plastic wrap. Refrigerate for 1 hour or until easy to handle.

2. Preheat oven to 425°. In a large bowl, combine apples, sugar, lemon juice, flour, salt, cinnamon and nutmeg.

3. On a lightly floured surface, roll out larger portion of dough to ⅛-in.-thick circle. Transfer to a 9-in. pie plate, trimming

even with edge. Fill with apple mixture, mounding in the center. Dot apples with butter. Lightly brush rim of pastry with some of the beaten egg.

4. Roll out the remaining dough to fit top of pie; place over filling. Trim, seal and flute edges. Cut slits in pastry. Brush top with egg; sprinkle with superfine sugar. Place on a foil-lined 15-in. x 10-in. x 1-in. baking pan.

5. Bake 20 minutes. Reduce heat to 375°. Bake 50-60 minutes or until crust is golden brown and filling is bubbly. Cool on a wire rack for 2 hours before serving.

CHOCOLATE BUTTERSCOTCH TARTLETS

Tartlets are like cake pops—tiny, tasty and a tempting way to experiment with different fillings.

—**JENNIFER NIEMI** TUCSON, AZ

PREP: 40 MIN. + CHILLING • **MAKES:** 3¾ DOZEN

- 1 cup (6 ounces) semisweet chocolate chips
- ½ cup butterscotch chips
- 1½ cups heavy whipping cream, divided
- 1½ teaspoons apricot brandy
- 4½ teaspoons confectioners' sugar
- ¼ teaspoon vanilla extract
- 3 packages (1.9 ounces each) frozen miniature phyllo tart shells
  Grated orange peel

1. Place chocolate and butterscotch chips in a small bowl. In a small saucepan, bring 1 cup cream just to a boil. Pour over chips; whisk until smooth. Stir in brandy. Cool to room temperature, stirring occasionally. Refrigerate until chilled.

2. In a large bowl, beat remaining cream until it begins to thicken. Add confectioners' sugar and vanilla; beat until stiff peaks form. Spoon the chocolate mixture into tart shells; top with whipped cream and garnish with orange peel. Refrigerate until serving.

STRAWBERRY CHEESECAKE CUPCAKES

The petite graham cracker "crust," chopped fresh berries and cream cheese frosting offer all the goodness of cheesecake in these bite-sized portions.

—JILL DRURY MILWAUKEE, WI

PREP: 30 MIN. • **BAKE:** 20 MIN. + COOLING • **MAKES:** 2 DOZEN

- 1½ cups graham cracker crumbs
- 2 tablespoons sugar
- ⅓ cup unsalted butter, softened

BATTER

- 4 egg whites
- ¾ cup unsalted butter, softened
- 1 cup plus 2 tablespoons sugar
- 1 teaspoon vanilla extract
- 1½ cups all-purpose flour
- 1 teaspoon baking powder
- ½ teaspoon salt
- ½ cup sour cream
- 2 cups coarsely chopped fresh strawberries

FROSTING

- 2 packages (8 ounces each) cream cheese, softened
- 1 cup unsalted butter, softened
- 3¾ cups confectioners' sugar
- 1 teaspoon vanilla extract
  Fresh strawberries and graham cracker crumbs

1. Line 24 muffin tins with paper liners; set aside.

2. Place the cracker crumbs, sugar and butter in a food processor; cover and process until fine crumbs form. Press tablespoonfuls onto bottoms of liners. Bake at 350° for 3-5 minutes or until lightly browned. Set aside to cool.

3. Place egg whites in a large bowl; let stand at room temperature for 30 minutes. In another large bowl, cream the butter, sugar and vanilla until light and fluffy. In another bowl, combine the flour, baking powder and salt; add to the creamed mixture alternately with the sour cream, beating well after each addition.

4. Beat egg whites with clean beaters until stiff peaks form. Fold a third of the egg whites into batter. Fold in remaining egg whites and strawberries.

5. Fill muffin cups three-fourths full. Bake at 350° for 18-22 minutes or until a toothpick inserted near the center comes out clean. Cool for 10 minutes before removing from pans to wire racks to cool completely.

6. In a large bowl, beat cream cheese and butter until fluffy. Add confectioners' sugar and vanilla; beat until smooth. Frost tops. Garnish with strawberries and cracker crumbs. Store in the refrigerator.

OVER-THE-TOP BLUEBERRY BREAD PUDDING

Good warm or at room temperature, this dessert is out of this world! For a change, top it with fresh mint and sweetened whipped cream.

—MARILYN HAYNES SYLACAUGA, AL

PREP: 15 MIN. + STANDING • **BAKE:** 50 MIN. • **MAKES:** 12 SERVINGS

- 3 eggs
- 4 cups heavy whipping cream
- 2 cups sugar
- 3 teaspoons vanilla extract
- 2 cups fresh or frozen blueberries
- 1 package (10 to 12 ounces) white baking chips
- 1 loaf (1 pound) French bread, cut into 1-inch cubes

SAUCE

- 1 package (10 to 12 ounces) white baking chips
- 1 cup heavy whipping cream

1. Preheat oven to 350°. In a large bowl, combine eggs, cream, sugar and vanilla. Stir in blueberries and baking chips. Stir in bread cubes; let stand 15 minutes or until bread is softened.

2. Transfer to a greased 13-in. x 9-in. baking dish. Bake, uncovered, 50-60 minutes or until a knife inserted near the center comes out clean. Let stand 5 minutes before serving.

3. For sauce, place baking chips in a small bowl. In a small saucepan, bring cream just to a boil. Pour over baking chips; whisk until smooth. Serve with bread pudding.

BANANA SPLIT ICEBOX CAKE

Salute Ohio's annual banana split festival with this version that turns graham crackers and toppings into an icebox cake!

—**SHELLY FLYE** ALBION, ME

PREP: 30 MIN. + CHILLING • **MAKES:** 10 SERVINGS

 1 **carton (16 ounces) frozen whipped topping, thawed**
 1 **cup (8 ounces) sour cream**
 1 **package (3.4 ounces) instant vanilla pudding mix**
 1 **can (8 ounces) crushed pineapple, drained**
24 **whole graham crackers**
 2 **medium bananas, sliced**

Toppings: chocolate syrup, halved fresh strawberries and additional banana slices

1. In a large bowl, mix the whipped topping, sour cream and pudding mix until blended; fold in pineapple. Cut a small hole in the corner of a pastry or plastic bag; fill with pudding mixture.
2. On a flat serving plate, arrange four crackers in a rectangle. Pipe about 1 cup pudding mixture over crackers; top with about ¼ cup banana slices. Repeat layers five times. Cover and refrigerate overnight.
3. Before serving, top with chocolate syrup, strawberries and banana slices.

RED RASPBERRY CREME BRULEE

An enticing twist on traditional creme brulee, my rich and creamy dessert makes a lovely ending to any special-occasion meal.
—**BARBARA HAHN** PARK HILLS, MO

PREP: 30 MIN. • **BAKE:** 30 MIN. + CHILLING • **MAKES:** 6 SERVINGS

- 1 can (21 ounces) raspberry pie filling, divided
- 1½ cups heavy whipping cream
- 6 egg yolks
- 6 tablespoons sugar
- ¼ cup coarse sugar

1. Preheat oven to 325°. Coat six 6-oz. ramekins or custard cups with cooking spray. Spoon a scant 3 tablespoons pie filling into the bottom of each ramekin; set aside.

2. In a small saucepan, heat cream until bubbles form around sides of pan. In a small bowl, whisk egg yolks and sugar. Remove cream from heat; stir a small amount of hot cream into egg mixture. Return all to pan, stirring constantly.

3. Pour into prepared ramekins. Place in a baking pan; add 1 in. of boiling water to pan. Bake, uncovered, 30-35 minutes or until centers are just set (mixture will jiggle). Remove ramekins from water bath; cool 10 minutes. Spoon remaining pie filling over tops. Cover and refrigerate at least 4 hours.

4. If using a creme brulee torch, sprinkle custards with coarse sugar. Heat sugar with the torch until caramelized. Serve immediately.

5. If broiling the custards, place ramekins on a baking sheet; let stand at room temperature 15 minutes. Sprinkle custards with coarse sugar. Broil 8 in. from heat for 4-7 minutes or until sugar is caramelized. Refrigerate 1-2 hours or until firm. Garnish as desired.

HAZELNUT CHOCOLATE MOUSSE

I love this treat, and it's so easy to make that I can surprise my family with it often. It's also good with chocolate-flavored whipped topping—depending on how much you like chocolate!
—**KARLA KROHN** MADISON, WI

START TO FINISH: 10 MIN. • **MAKES:** 6 SERVINGS

- 1¾ cups cold 2% milk
- 1 package (3.9 ounces) instant chocolate pudding mix
- ½ cup Nutella
- 1¾ cups whipped topping
  Additional whipped topping

1. Whisk milk and pudding mix in a large bowl for 2 minutes. Let stand for 2 minutes or until soft set. Whisk in Nutella until smooth. Fold in whipped topping.

2. Spoon into six dessert dishes. Chill until serving. Garnish servings with additional whipped topping.

FROZEN LIME CAKE

This is just the thing for block parties, cookouts or anytime you need a cool, frosty dessert. The crust is a snap, and the ice cream and sherbet layers tempt your taste buds.
—**KATHY GILLOGLY** SUN CITY, CA

PREP: 15 MIN. + FREEZING • **MAKES:** 9 SERVINGS

- 1½ cups ground almonds
- ¾ cup crushed gingersnap cookies (about 15 cookies)
- ⅓ cup butter, melted
- 2 pints pineapple coconut or vanilla ice cream, softened
- 4 cups lime sherbet, softened
  Whipped topping, optional

1. In a bowl, combine the almonds, cookies and butter. Press onto the bottom of a 9-in. square pan. Freeze for 15 minutes.

2. Spread ice cream over crust. Cover and freeze for 30 minutes. Top with sherbet. Cover and freeze for 4 hours or overnight.

3. Remove from the freezer 10 minutes before serving. Garnish servings with whipped topping if desired.

PISTACHIO CARDAMOM CHEESECAKE

Cardamom has a sweet and warm taste that makes you think of clove, allspice and pepper all at once. Mix it with pistachios and add to cheesecake for an exotic and sophisticated dessert.

—**CAROLYN HARKONNEN** LOOMIS, CA

PREP: 30 MIN. • **BAKE:** 35 MIN. + CHILLING • **MAKES:** 12 SERVINGS

1¼ cups finely crushed animal crackers
3 tablespoons packed brown sugar
¼ cup butter, melted

FILLING
2 packages (8 ounces each) cream cheese, softened
1 can (14 ounces) sweetened condensed milk
1 tablespoon lemon juice
1½ teaspoons ground cardamom
1 drop green food coloring, optional
3 eggs, lightly beaten
½ cup pistachios, finely chopped
    Sweetened whipped cream, optional
    Additional chopped pistachios and animal cracker crumbs, optional

1. Place a greased 9-in. springform pan on a double thickness of heavy-duty foil (about 18 in. square). Securely wrap foil around pan.

2. In a small bowl, combine the cracker crumbs and brown sugar; stir in butter. Press onto the bottom of prepared pan. Place pan on a baking sheet. Bake at 325° for 15 minutes. Cool on a wire rack.

3. In a large bowl, beat cream cheese until smooth. Beat in the milk, lemon juice, cardamom and, if desired, food coloring. Add eggs; beat on low speed just until combined. Fold in pistachios. Pour over crust. Place springform pan in a large baking pan; add 1 in. of boiling water to larger pan.

4. Bake at 325° for 35-40 minutes or until center is just set and top appears dull. Remove springform pan from water bath; remove foil. Cool cheesecake on a wire rack for 10 minutes; loosen edges from pan with a knife. Cool 1 hour longer. Refrigerate overnight.

5. Remove rim from pan. Top cheesecake with whipped cream and sprinkle with pistachios and cracker crumbs if desired.

NOTE *To toast nuts, spread in a 15-in. x 10-in. x 1-in. baking pan. Bake at 350° for 5-10 minutes or until lightly browned, stirring occasionally. Or, spread in a dry nonstick skillet and heat over low heat until lightly browned, stirring occasionally.*

TWO LAYER BAKED ALASKA

Once I mastered this recipe, it quickly became a favorite among my family members.

—**LORRAINE CALAND** SHUNIAH, ON

PREP: 45 MIN. + FREEZING • **BAKE:** 5 MIN. • **MAKES:** 8 SERVINGS

3 ounces semisweet chocolate
⅓ cup shortening
1 cup graham cracker crumbs
¾ cup finely chopped pecans
¼ cup packed dark brown sugar

FILLING
2 cups chocolate ice cream, softened
2 cups strawberry ice cream, softened

CHOCOLATE SAUCE
¼ cup sugar
¼ cup water
2 tablespoons butter
4 ounces semisweet chocolate

MERINGUE
4 egg whites
½ cup sugar
½ teaspoon cream of tartar

1. In a microwave, melt chocolate and shortening; stir until smooth. Stir in the cracker crumbs, pecans and brown sugar. Press onto the bottom and up the sides of a greased 9-in. pie plate. Refrigerate for 30 minutes.

2. Spread chocolate ice cream into crust. Layer with the strawberry ice cream. Cover and freeze 1-2 hours or until firm.

3. In a small saucepan, bring the sugar, water and butter to a boil; stirring constantly. Remove from the heat. Add the chocolate; stir until smooth. Cool to room temperature. Drizzle ½ cup over ice cream. Freeze until firm.

4. In a small heavy saucepan, combine the egg whites, sugar and cream of tartar. With a hand mixer, beat on low speed for 1 minute. Continue beating over low heat until egg mixture reaches 160°, about 4 minutes.

5. Transfer to a bowl; beat 5-7 minutes or until stiff glossy peaks form and sugar is dissolved. Immediately spread over frozen pie. Heat with a creme brulee torch for 3-4 minutes or until meringue is lightly browned. Serve immediately with remaining chocolate sauce.

COCONUT-FILLED CHOCOLATE CUPCAKES

If you are nuts about chocolate and coconut, this is definitely the cupcake for you. You might have to stop yourself from eating the chocolate ganache beforehand!
—LUANN KLINK FROSTBURG, MD

PREP: 45 MIN. + STANDING • **BAKE:** 20 MIN. + COOLING
MAKES: 26 CUPCAKES

- 1 **egg white**
  Dash salt
- 1 **cup flaked coconut**
- 1 **tablespoon all-purpose flour**
- 2 **tablespoons sugar**

BATTER
- ⅔ **cup shortening**
- 1½ **cups sugar**
- 2 **eggs**
- 1 **teaspoon vanilla extract**
- 2½ **cups all-purpose flour**
- ½ **cup baking cocoa**
- 1 **teaspoon salt**
- ¾ **teaspoon baking soda**
- 1 **cup buttermilk**
- ½ **cup water**

GLAZE
- 2 **cups sugar**
- ½ **cup milk**
- ½ **cup shortening**
- 1 **cup (6 ounces) semisweet chocolate chips**
  Toasted coconut and chocolate curls

1. For filling, place egg white and salt in a small bowl; let stand at room temperature for 30 minutes. Combine coconut and flour; set aside. Beat egg white on medium speed until soft peaks form. Gradually add sugar, beating on high until glossy peaks form and sugar is dissolved. Gradually fold in coconut mixture, about ¼ cup at a time; set aside.

2. In a large bowl, cream shortening and sugar until light and fluffy. Add eggs and vanilla; mix well. Combine the flour, cocoa, salt and baking soda; add to creamed mixture alternately with buttermilk and water. Fill paper-lined muffin cups half full. Drop filling by teaspoonfuls into center of each cupcake. Cover with 2 tablespoons batter.

3. Bake at 350° for 18-22 minutes or until a toothpick inserted in the cake portion comes out clean. Cool for 10 minutes before removing from pans to wire racks to cool completely.

4. For glaze, in a small saucepan, combine the sugar and milk. Bring to a boil, stirring constantly. Remove from the heat; stir in shortening and chocolate chips until melted. Beat until thickened. Spread over cupcakes and garnish with toasted coconut and chocolate curls.

STRAWBERRY CHEESECAKE POPS

Yum! These homemade cheesecake pops are sure to hit the spot on those sticky, hot, dog days of summer.
—EMILY PAULY HEWITT, TX

PREP: 15 MIN. + FREEZING • **MAKES:** 9 POPS

- 2 **cups 2% milk**
- ½ **cup heavy whipping cream**
- 1 **package (3.4 ounces) instant cheesecake or vanilla pudding mix**
- 2 **tablespoons strawberry drink mix**
- 1 **cup chopped fresh strawberries**
  Fresh mint leaves and quartered fresh strawberries
- 9 **Popsicle sticks**

1. Place the milk, cream, pudding mix and drink mix in a blender; cover and process until blended. Let stand for 5 minutes or until soft-set; stir in strawberries.

2. Place foil-lined muffin cups in a muffin pan; fill each liner with ⅓ cup strawberry mixture. Garnish with mint leaves and strawberries. Cover pan with foil and insert sticks in the middle of each cup; freeze. Peel off liners to serve.

NOTE *This recipe was tested with Nesquik brand drink mix.*

BERRY BASICS

When buying berries, keep the following in mind:
- Find a batch of berries that looks brightly colored and plump. Once home, throw out any that look soft, shriveled or moldy.
- Don't wash berries until you're ready to use them in a recipe or eat them.
- Strawberries, raspberries and blackberries will stay fresh in the refrigerator for up to 2 days. Blueberries will last for up to 5 days.
- Berries can be frozen for up to 1 year. Wash, blot dry and arrange on a single layer on a pan. Freeze until firm, then transfer berries to a freezer bag.

Substitutions & Equivalents

EQUIVALENT MEASURES

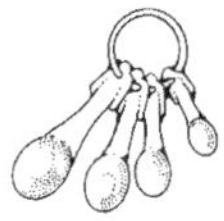

3 teaspoons	= 1 tablespoon	16 tablespoons	= 1 cup
4 tablespoons	= ¼ cup	2 cups	= 1 pint
5⅓ tablespoons	= ⅓ cup	4 cups	= 1 quart
8 tablespoons	= ½ cup	4 quarts	= 1 gallon

FOOD EQUIVALENTS

GRAINS

Macaroni	1 cup (3½ ounces) uncooked	= 2½ cups cooked
Noodles, Medium	3 cups (4 ounces) uncooked	= 4 cups cooked
Popcorn	⅓ to ½ cup unpopped	= 8 cups popped
Rice, Long Grain	1 cup uncooked	= 3 cups cooked
Rice, Quick-Cooking	1 cup uncooked	= 2 cups cooked
Spaghetti	8 ounces uncooked	= 4 cups cooked

CRUMBS

Bread	1 slice	= ¾ cup soft crumbs, ¼ cup fine dry crumbs
Graham Crackers	7 squares	= ½ cup finely crushed
Buttery Round Crackers	12 crackers	= ½ cup finely crushed
Saltine Crackers	14 crackers	= ½ cup finely crushed

FRUITS

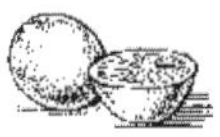

Bananas	1 medium	= ⅓ cup mashed
Lemons	1 medium	= 3 tablespoons juice, 2 teaspoons grated peel
Limes	1 medium	= 2 tablespoons juice, 1½ teaspoons grated peel
Oranges	1 medium	= ¼ to ⅓ cup juice, 4 teaspoons grated peel

VEGETABLES

Cabbage	1 head	= 5 cups shredded	Green Pepper	1 large	= 1 cup chopped
Carrots	1 pound	= 3 cups shredded	Mushrooms	½ pound	= 3 cups sliced
Celery	1 rib	= ½ cup chopped	Onions	1 medium	= ½ cup chopped
Corn	1 ear fresh	= ⅔ cup kernels	Potatoes	3 medium	= 2 cups cubed

NUTS

Almonds	1 pound	= 3 cups chopped	Pecan Halves	1 pound	= 4½ cups chopped
Ground Nuts	3¾ ounces	= 1 cup	Walnuts	1 pound	= 3¾ cups chopped

EASY SUBSTITUTIONS

When you need...		Use...
Baking Powder	1 teaspoon	½ teaspoon cream of tartar + ¼ teaspoon baking soda
Buttermilk	1 cup	1 tablespoon lemon juice or vinegar + enough milk to measure 1 cup (let stand 5 minutes before using)
Cornstarch	1 tablespoon	2 tablespoons all-purpose flour
Honey	1 cup	1¼ cups sugar + ¼ cup water
Half-and-Half Cream	1 cup	1 tablespoon melted butter + enough whole milk to measure 1 cup
Onion	1 small, chopped (⅓ cup)	1 teaspoon onion powder or 1 tablespoon dried minced onion
Tomato Juice	1 cup	½ cup tomato sauce + ½ cup water
Tomato Sauce	2 cups	¾ cup tomato paste + 1 cup water
Unsweetened Chocolate	1 square (1 ounce)	3 tablespoons baking cocoa + 1 tablespoon shortening or oil
Whole Milk	1 cup	½ cup evaporated milk + ½ cup water

COOKING TERMS

Here's a quick reference for some of the most common cooking terms used in recipes:

BASTE To moisten food with melted butter, pan drippings, marinades or other liquid to add more flavor and juiciness.

BEAT A rapid movement to combine ingredients using a fork, spoon, wire whisk or electric mixer.

BLEND To combine ingredients until *just* mixed.

BOIL To heat liquids until bubbles form that cannot be "stirred down." In the case of water, the temperature will reach 212°.

BONE To remove all meat from the bone before cooking.

CREAM To beat ingredients together to a smooth consistency, usually in the case of butter and sugar for baking.

DASH A small amount of seasoning, less than ⅛ teaspoon. If using a shaker, a dash would comprise a quick flip of the container.

DREDGE To coat foods with flour or other dry ingredients. Most often done with pot roasts and stew meat before browning.

FOLD To incorporate several ingredients by careful and gentle turning with a spatula. Used generally with beaten egg whites or whipped cream when mixing into the rest of the ingredients to keep the batter light.

JULIENNE To cut foods into long thin strips much like matchsticks. Used most often for salads and stir-fry dishes.

MINCE To cut into very fine pieces. Used often for garlic or fresh herbs.

PARBOIL To cook partially, usually used in the case of chicken, sausages and vegetables.

PARTIALLY SET Describes the consistency of gelatin after it has been chilled for a short amount of time. Mixture should resemble the consistency of egg whites.

PUREE To process foods to a smooth mixture. Can be prepared in an electric blender, food processor, food mill or sieve.

SAUTE To fry quickly in a small amount of fat, stirring almost constantly. Most often done with onions, mushrooms and other chopped vegetables.

SCORE To cut slits partway through the outer surface of foods. Often used with ham or flank steak.

STIR-FRY To cook meats and/or vegetables with a constant stirring motion in a small amount of oil in a wok or skillet over high heat.

GENERAL RECIPE INDEX

GROUND BEEF (continued)

Chipotle Mac & Cheese, 65
Family-Favorite Spaghetti Sauce, 92
Farmhouse Barbecue Muffins, 109
Italian-Style Salisbury Steaks, 87
Old-World Pizza Meat Loaf, 67
Sloppy Joe Veggie Casserole, 66
Spicy Cajun Salsa Burgers, 44
Taco Shepherd's Pie, 68

HAM & PROSCIUTTO

Cheese & Ham Filled Sandwiches, 61
Ham and Avocado Scramble, 76
Ham & Noodles with Veggies, 124
Lemon Beans with Prosciutto, 26
Potluck Ham and Pasta, 84
Scalloped Potatoes & Ham, 91
Spiral Stromboli, 56
Stacked Chicken Cordon Bleu, 69

HERBS

(also see Mint)

Basil Polenta with Ratatouille, 68
Bella Basil Raspberry Tea, 13
Chicken with Rosemary Butter Sauce
   for 2, 136
Chili-Basil Tomato Soup, 55
Chimichurri Monkey Bread, 117
Citrus-Herb Pork Roast, 99
Classic Pesto Sauce, 25
Crunchy-Herbed Chicken Breasts, 87
Golden Roasted Turkey, 74
Herb & Sun-Dried Tomato
   Muffins, 114
Herb-Roasted Mushrooms, 27
Herbed Blue Cheese Steaks, 72
Italian Pesto Pizzas, 125
Land of Enchantment Posole, 58
Lemon & Sage Roasted Chicken, 82
Mandarin Watermelon Salad, 51
Pasta & Sun-Dried Tomato Salad, 49
Rosemary Walnuts, 10
Seafood Cakes with Herb Sauce, 15
Shallot & Basil Green Beans, 139
Strawberry Cheesecake Pops, 179
Sweet Corn with Parmesan and
   Cilantro, 142
Turkey-Tarragon Noodle Soup, 61
Winter Herb Tea Mix, 12

HONEY

Apricot-Honey Chicken, 131
Desert Oasis Chicken, 66
Honey Mustard Coleslaw, 38
Seeded Honey Wheat Bread, 113

Sweet Potato Biscuits with Honey
   Butter, 109

ICE CREAM

Caramel-Mocha Ice Cream
   Dessert, 167
Chocolate Chip Ice Cream Pie, 145
Cinnamon Apple Shakes, 18
Frozen Lime Cake, 177
Pistachio Meringue Sundaes, 166
Praline Ice Cream Cake, 166
Raspberry-Swirled Lemon Milk
   Shakes, 8
Rhubarb Sundaes, 144
Two Layer Baked Alaska, 178
Warm Pineapple Sundaes with Rum
   Sauce, 142

LEMON & LIME

Cake with Lemon Sauce, 173
Citrus-Marmalade Vinaigrette, 26
Frozen Key Lime Delight, 168
Frozen Lime Cake, 177
Lemon & Sage Roasted Chicken, 82
Lemon Beans with Prosciutto, 26
Lemon Date Couscous, 24
Lemon Mint Spritzer, 7
Raspberry-Swirled Lemon Milk
   Shakes, 8
Tilapia & Lemon Sauce, 71
White Grape Punch, 17

MARSHMALLOWS

Backwoods Bonfire Bark, 149
Chocolate Mallow Pie, 169
Mocha Mint Coffee, 93
Peanut Butter Swirled Fudge, 148
Rocky Road Freezer Pie, 171
Salted Peanut Squares, 151
Sweet & Salty Marshmallow Popcorn
   Treats, 7
Whoopie Cookies, 148

MINT

Blueberry & Ginger Tart, 161
Lemon Mint Spritzer, 7
Mint Papaya Sorbet, 168
Mocha Mint Coffee, 93
Strawberry Cheesecake Pops, 179

MUSHROOMS

Asian Spaghetti, 140
Bacon-Wrapped Filets with Scotched
   Mushrooms, 141
Country Chuck Roast with
   Mushroom Gravy, 85
Crab Imperial Casserole, 79

Green Bean Casserole Stuffed
   Mushrooms, 37
Herb-Roasted Mushrooms, 27
Homemade Cream of Mushroom
   Soup, 60
Mom's Turkey Tetrazzini, 72
Mushroom Salad, 52
Mushroom Steak, 92
Old-World Pizza Meat Loaf, 67
Sausage Florentine Potpie, 80
Sausage Stuffed Mushrooms, 18
Shiitake & Butternut Risotto, 138
Vegetable Trio, 36

NUTS & PEANUT BUTTER

APPETIZERS & SNACKS

Almond Coffee Walnuts, 19
Beef & Onion Cheese Ball, 18
Peanut Chicken Wings, 6
Rosemary Walnuts, 10
Sweet & Salty Marshmallow Popcorn
   Treats, 7

BREADS

Grandma's Pumpkin Bread, 106
Praline Sweet Potato Bread, 105

BREAKFAST

Brunch Cinnamon Rolls, 111
Cherry-Pecan Streusel Rolls, 116
Coconut-Pecan Coffee Cake, 111
Slow-Cooked Fruited Oatmeal with
   Nuts, 101

CANDIES

Backwoods Bonfire Bark, 149
Candy-Licious Fudge, 153
Caramel Nut Logs, 156
Nutter Butter Truffles, 148
Peanut Butter Swirled Fudge, 148

COOKIES & BARS

Drizzled Nanaimo Bars, 153
Giant Monster Cookies, 156
Hazelnut-Mocha Bonbon Cookies, 152
Macadamia-Coffee Bean Cookies, 150
Million Dollar Pecan Bars, 154
Raspberry Linzer Bars, 154
Salted Peanut Squares, 151
Triple-Layer Pretzel Brownies, 151

DESSERTS

Apple-Cranberry Tart, 160
Bourbon Chocolate-Pecan Pie, 163
Caramel-Mocha Ice Cream
   Dessert, 167
Crunchy Amaretto Peach Cobbler, 173
Dark Chocolate Carrot Cake, 172
Frozen Key Lime Delight, 168
Frozen Lime Cake, 177

ALPHABETICAL RECIPE INDEX